Ideas for the Animated Short, Second Edition

Ideas for the Animated Short
Finding and Building Stories

Second Edition

Karen Sullivan, Kate Alexander, Aubry Mintz and Ellen Besen

Focal Press
Taylor & Francis Group

NEW YORK AND LONDON

First published 2013
by Focal Press
70 Blanchard Road, Suite 402, Burlington, MA 01803

Simultaneously published in the UK
by Focal Press
2 Park Square, Milton Park, Abingdon, Oxon OX14 4RN

Focal Press is an imprint of the Taylor & Francis Group, an informa business

Library of Congress Cataloging in Publication Data
Sullivan, Karen, 1958-
   Ideas for the animated short : finding and building stories / Karen Sullivan,
Kate Alexander, Aubry Mintz, Ellen Besen. – Second edition.
      pages cm
   ISBN 978-0-240-81872-6 (Paper Back)
   1. Animated films–Authorship. 2. Short films–Authorship. 3. Animators–
United States–Interviews. I. Alexander, Kate. II. Mintz, Aubry. III. Besen,
Ellen, 1953– IV. Title.
   PN1997.5.S85 2013
   808.2'3–dc23   2012039668

ISBN: 9780240818726 (pbk)
ISBN: 9780240818825 (ebk)

Typeset in Futura by
Keystroke, Station Road, Codsall, Wolverhampton

Printed in the United States of America by Courier, Kendallville, Indiana

Contents

Foreword

MEMO
To: Animated Short Film Directors

From: John Tarnoff, former Head of Show Development, DreamWorks Animation; Adjunct Professor and Head of Industry Relations for Carnegie Mellon University's Masters of Entertainment Industry Management graduate program; Strategic Advisor to the ACME Network.

Short films aren't so different from feature films. The rules of storytelling still apply. But the beauty of short films is their ability to distill, in just a few minutes, the essence of an idea, and concentrate that essence in such a way that the audience is moved and stimulated in as strong a fashion as if it had just sat through a full-length feature film.

Animated short films provide even more opportunity to engage the viewer. Animated films are distinguished by the uniqueness of their artwork, and this completely invented and imagined aspect is what sets animated shorts so resolutely apart from live-action shorts. This is your challenge and your opportunity in the realm of animation—a realm where it takes both a graphical, painterly talent (and skill), in addition to a photographic, cinematic, and narrative inspiration. Because an animated film has so many more visual possibilities than a live-action film, the bar is significantly raised for the animation filmmaker to attempt something truly integral and affecting.

What makes for a good idea for a short animated film?

To fulfill their inspiration, the filmmakers have many options to express the one idea. Just as mash-up videos show how it is possible to create different stories, genres, and styles out of existing material, at the concept stage in developing a short, the filmmakers need to balance their inspiration with a format that, to their mind, best expresses the impact they want to make with their film.

This can mean that the film is narrative or non-narrative (poetic), that it draws from a particular artistic style, uses a particular style of animation, mixes up styles and genres to create something unique . . . the possibilities are endless.

While there are rules of good artistic composition, good storytelling, good character development, good visual design, and of all the large and small elements that go into the creation of a film, filmmakers must not get bogged down by too many conventions that can be creatively stifling.

Animated films are *films* first and foremost. Films exist in five dimensions: the two dimensions of line, tone and color, the third dimension of space, the fourth dimension of time, and the fifth dimension of content. It is this fifth dimension that unites and binds the other four and, if successful, touches an audience and resonates with it in a mental, physical, emotional and artistic (some might say "spiritual") way.

How should fledgling filmmakers proceed? Assuming they have learned the basics, and spent time cultivating their eye, their techniques, their tools and most of all, their own creative voice, there are a few guidelines before jumping in. For me, a good film is always an exercise in contrasts and in the unexpected: a conventional story with unconventional characters or situations, or, conversely, an unconventional story with a conventional character. It can be a conventional story with a surprising punch line, or maybe an unconventional, nonlinear story that concludes in a familiar way. The point is to create a particular, definitive and definable dynamic. Perhaps the film displays a specific, evolving color palette as it unfolds, and that palette reflects the precise evolution of the story or characters as they transform over the course of the narrative.

It is the dynamic (or dynamics) that supports the execution of the film and makes it intriguing beyond merely one's inspiration that it "seems like a good idea."

For the two-dimensional elements, there are centuries of artistic references, and a whole world of physical references for artists to create the look of their film. Care should be taken to draw from multiple sources in synthesizing a single vision, and to weigh those sources in comparison with one another. The filmmaker uses references to build the look of their film, and can create sketches or workbooks of ideas based on these references. This visual development phase is key, no matter what the size of the film is, as it must co-exist with the story in a highly compatible way for the film to work. Various design elements assist the filmmaker in creating a visual script for the ultimate look of the film. Set designs, whether in rough line sketches or fully rendered paintings, establish the locations or environments where the film will take place. Color and lighting keys establish the flow of visual elements over the course of the film. Character designs and turnarounds establish the look of the characters, and their visual relationships to one another. While a short animated film is arguably less complex than a full-length feature, because it is short, it is subject to perhaps increased scrutiny or attention as all of its design elements will be so much more important in proportion to the length of the overall film. People will look more closely at a short film, and expect more from it, merely because it is expected or hoped to be a gem.

The third dimension is where animation has branched off into a new realm over the last 20 years, and the medium has never been the same. Whether one is creating a 2D film by hand-drawing, or in the computer in Flash, or creating a 3D CG film, the visualization possibilities of working in 3D have irrevocably changed the way animation is made. Audiences are now so much more attuned to seeing animation in virtual three-dimensional space that their expectations have been altered significantly from a time when everything was basically flat. Even Disney's Multiplane system from the 1950s, where layers of animation elements were photographed in real depth, one behind the other, still created an essentially "proscenium" experience, where the audience was looking at a stage-like environment and action was taking place largely in a horizontal, right-to-left-to-right space. In addition to allowing shapes to have a greater sense of weight and dimensionality, 3D animation allows the camera to explore and to light these objects and their environments with a much greater degree of variation and movement.

The fourth dimension is the truly cinematic dimension, the dimension of time. No other art form has worked in the fourth dimension in the same way as cinema. From the early revolving zoetropes to today's high frame-rate digital projectors, the element of time, of beginning, middle and end, is the hallmark of this medium. The editor is the high priest of the filmmaking process, taking the raw elements of shots and scenes, and piecing them together so as to create rhythm, pace, and narrative coherency. Indeed, the juxtaposition of images, as the early master directors like D.W. Griffith and Sergei Eisenstein discovered, is the highest expression of this art form. This juxtaposition of image, and juxtaposition over time, creates emotions, from joy to sadness to suspense and fear. The addition of sound, both music and sound effects, further dimensionalizes the timeline, making the pace seem longer or slower, punctuating the visuals and improving the flow.

The fifth dimension, content, what the film is about and how it unfolds, is the keystone that brings the other dimensions together and gives them life. Without a compelling visual or dramatic narrative, the graphical elements are static, the 3D elements are distracting, and the timeline is boring or frenetic.

Every film really needs some form of beginning, middle and end, whether it is a short tone poem or a character-driven narrative.

Key images, "movie moments," establish the tone or the essence of the film: a great opening shot, signature lighting, a musical theme. This tells us what the film is going to be about, about the world we are about to be immersed in. Remember that you are communicating with your audience. For you to touch them, you're going to have to make your expression understandable, whether this is through your use of visual language, choice of artistic style, cultural reference, or otherwise. So from the first frames, we the audience need to know where we are and feel like something is happening that is engaging. From there, the filmmaker has to stay "on point." Everything that follows must serve the purpose of the film. This process of choosing and editing what goes into the film is the most painstaking part of the process and will challenge you to really discover what it is you are actually saying in your film.

Having laid down these ground rules, it is now important to say: Break them! Trust your instincts, trust your experience. Don't get bogged down by anything that stands in the way of your vision. This is perhaps the most important lesson: Dare to fail, because in your failure is always the seed of your eventual success. Be open to the lessons and dare to try again.

Preface

Karen Sullivan

Many things have changed since we wrote the first edition of this book. Brick and mortar video stores have disappeared. Vimeo, YouTube and film festivals are the dominant distribution points for animated shorts. And the quality and quantity of animated shorts have proliferated and improved.

And as much as things change, they also remain the same. Many of the basics for planning and pre-production are the same. Images may be created traditionally or digitally, but the thought process behind them hasn't changed much. In fact, as we polled readers in preparation for the second edition, many implored us to keep much of the information from the first edition. So we did. We reviewed it and tweaked it to clarify the information and make it more specific to the short format. But there were also some things that were clearly missing.

Readers gave us great feedback. To round out the book, we needed more information on sound design. To this end, Perry La Marca provides an interview on creating music to support narrative; Ginny Kopf provides tips on voice and dialects for animators; and student director George Fleming and student composer Stavros Hoplaros describe their collaboration in creating sound for the in-progress short, *The Hoard*, in our web collection on Working in Collaboration.

In addition, more case studies were requested. Aubry Mintz discusses the preproduction of his in-progress short, *Countin' on Sheep*; Karen Sullivan discusses the preproduction process of *A Good Deed, Indeed*; and Brandon Oldenburg and Adam Volker of Moonbot Studios generously discuss the making of the Academy Award winning short, *The Fantastic Flying Books of Mr. Morris Lessmore*.

To supplement this, Steve Hickner and Nilah Magruder provide detailed analysis of staging choices.

And finally, more emphasis is placed both on linear and nonlinear structure. The chapter on Building Story is completely revised and additional discussion on nonlinear narrative and nonlinear narrative structure has been provided by Ellen Besen.

The most useful change has been the addition of an accompanying website (www.ideasfortheanimated short.com). On the website we have been able to expand our Case Studies. New films have been added. These are featured in a section called Designing for a Skill Set, where examples are given to focus your planning to result in productions that emphasize different jobs in animation and the need to work collaboratively. Here you will find examples and interviews from new graduates who are now working in their desired fields, as well as an interview with Terry Moews from the Disney Associates Program and Bert Poole from DreamWorks on lighting. Kate Alexander has provided a new series of Acting Workshops. And finally, we also were able to archive all of the films and interviews from the first edition.

The goal of the book remains the same: To provide a guide to help you make good stories for the animated short. It is not a "how to book" that will provide a step-by-step process for a successful story. There is no magic formula for story. This book covers the things you need to think about and consider so you will be able to recognize a good idea, make a good story, produce good designs, make functional story-boards, and productively plan your animated short.

The animated short is one of the most enjoyable forms of entertainment. It doesn't take too long, but it can be as poignant, humorous, and moving as any other form of storytelling. Doing it well constructs meaning and creates memories.

Acknowledgments

We would like to acknowledge the following people for their help, support and contributions to the book:

Family:

Larry and Mack Sullivan; Milton and Helen Alexander; Dallas Mintz, Ron and Ricky Mintz; Stephen Barr, Tamar Lipsey and the rest of my family

Editors:

David Bevans, Taylor & Francis

Editorial Assistant:

Lauren Mattos, Taylor & Francis

Proposal Reviewers:

Mark T. Byrne, Craig Caldwell, David Maas, Joseph Guilland, Alan Choi

Technical Reviewers:

Larry Sullivan, Ron Mintz, Christianne Greiert, Craig Caldwell, Sharon Cavanaugh, Sharon Katz

Colleagues:

Jim McCampbell, Computer Animation Faculty and students at Ringling College of Art and Design; Richard Hopkins and Florida Studio Theatre; Steve Woloshen and the other, always helpful, members of the non-narrative animation community

Contributing Students:

Casey Robin from Studio Arts Center, International; Kristin Lepore from Maryland Institute College of Art; Robert Showalter, Avner Geller and Stevie Lewis; Meghan Stockham, Chelsea Bartlett, Meng Vue, Eric Drobile, Gwynne Olson-Wheeler, Nick Pitera, Chris Nabholtz, Thelvin Cabezas, Fernanda Santiago, Kevin Andrus and Maria Clapis; Kevin Passmore, Nicole Gutzman and Alex Bernard; Yahira Milagros Hernandez Vazquez and Javier Aparicio Lorente from Ringling College of Art and Design; Parrish Ley from Sheridan College; Mark Shirra and Alejandra Perez from Vancouver Film School; Chris Perry from University of Massachusetts at Amherst; Sven Martin, Moritz Mayerhofer, Jan Locher, Hannes Appell, Holger Wenzl, and Jan Thuring from Filmakademie Baden-Wuerttemberg, Germany; Alex Cannon from Brigham Young University

Contributing Studios and Independent Professional Producers:

Bill Kroyer, head of the Digital Arts Department at the Lawrence and Kristina Dodge College of Film and Media Arts at Chapman University; Jeff Fowler, Sean McNally and Chuck Wojtkiewicz, Blur Studios; Sande Scoredos, Sony Pictures Imageworks; Sylvain Chomet, Django Films; *Countin' on Sheep* crew: Director/Producer Aubry Mintz, Co-producer/Key Clean-up Dori Littell-Herrick, Art Director Doug Post, Artists Lennie Graves, George Fleming, Kristen Houser, Jarvis Taylor, Frank Lima, Ryan Richards, Dallas Worthy, Jennie Cotterill, Cuyler Smith, Melissa Devine, Robin Richesson, Erik Caines, Kevin White, Alina Chau, Mona Kozlowski, Cindy Cheng, David Coyne, Lynn Barzola, Jesse McClurg, Jennifer But, Jamie Ludovise, Music Charley Sandage and Harmony Mary and Robert Gillihan and Dave Smith; Contributors to *A Good Deed, Indeed*: Original Story Gary Schumer, Script Karen Sullivan, Storyboards and Animatics Nilah Magruder, Steve Hickner, Visual Development Gary Schumer, Jon DeVenti, Special Thanks to Ed Gavin, Michael Gabe Marynell, Julia Bacak, Keith Osborn, Billy Merritt, Heather Thomson, Chris Torres, Sandor Felipe

Foreword:

John Tarnoff, former Head of Show Development, DreamWorks Animation

Interviews:

Brandon Oldenburg and Adam Volker, Moonbot Studios; Bill and Sue Kroyer, Kroyer Films; Ginny Kopf, voice coach; Perry La Marca, Assistant Professor CSULB; Steve Hickner, DreamWorks Animation; Bert Poole, DreamWorks Feature Animation; Mike Cachuela, Laika Studios; Jeff Fowler, Blur Studios; Andrew Jimenez, Pixar Animation Studios; Kendal Cronkhite, DreamWorks Feature Animation; Kathy Altieri, DreamWorks Feature Animation; Tom Bancroft, Funnypages Productions, LLC; Chris Renaud, Blue Sky Studios; Mike Thurmeier, Blue Sky Studios; Sande Scoredos, Sony Pictures Imageworks; Nathan Greno, Walt Disney Feature Animation; Barry Cook, Story Artist and Director; Steve Gordon, Professional Story Artist; Jim Story, Instructor of Story at University of Central Florida; Paul Briggs, Walt Disney Feature Animation; Frank Gladstone, Independent Animation Consultant; Casey Robin, Kristin Lepore, Meghan Stockham, Chelsea Bartlett, Robert Showalter, Avner Geller and Stevie Lewis; Jack Canfora, playwright; Jason O'Connell, actor and Billy Merritt, animator and instructor at Ringling College of Art and Design; Deanna Morse, Grand Valley State University

Video Taping:

Andrew Burhoe, Brad Battersby, Sena Kwasi Amenor

Video Editing:

Andrew Burhoe

Scriptwriters:

Nick Pierce and Christianne Greiert, Karen Sullivan

Stories:

Jamie DeRuyter

Actors:

Katherine Michelle Tanner, Adam Ratner, Christianne Greiert, Brooke Wagstaff, Porter Anderson, Christine Alexander

Illustrators and Photographers:

Mike Peters, Adam D. Martens, Gary Schumer, Jon DeVenti, Karen Sullivan

Additional Chapters:

Special thanks to Gary Schumer for allowing us to continue to publish his wonderful chapters in this edition of the book!

Other Great People Who Helped Us Connect with Other People:

Patricia Galvis-Assmus, University of Massachusetts at Amherst; Brent Adams, Brigham Young University; Larry Bafia, Vancouver Film School; Thomas Haegele and Tina Ohnmacht, Filmakademie Baden-Wuerttemberg, Germany; Marilyn Friedman, Olivier Mouroux, Fumi Kitahara, DreamWorks Feature Animation; Steven Argula, Pixar Animation Studios; Christina Witoshkin, Blue Sky Studios; Samantha Brown, Sony Pictures Imageworks; Mark Shapiro, Laika Studios; Margaret Adamic and Dawn Rivera-Ernster at Disney; Billy Merritt, Ringling College of Art and Design; Jamie DeRuyter, Ringling College of Art and Design; and all of our friends who were of constant encouragement.

Bee Sting

Demetri Martin

Maureen

I was in the park, having a picnic with some friends. All of a sudden, a bee started to circle around my head. Then the bee attacked me. I calmly attempted to shoo it away, but it would not leave me alone. Then it became even more aggressive. I then tried to move away, but the agitated bee followed me. Hoping to stop its assault, I attempted to gently swat it away with a magazine. I missed, and, sure enough, the bee stung me. I'd never been stung by a bee before. It hurt, but I did my best to grin and bear it. I put some ointment on the bee sting, and after that I felt fine.

Brenda (Maureen's Friend)

I was on the phone when Maureen got stung by the bee. I felt bad for her. But I think she overreacted a little bit if you ask me, especially when she started to scream and wildly swing her arms around. It was really pretty embarrassing.

Bee

I was in the middle of another busy workday, flying my usual route. I was on my way back to the hive, minding my own business, when an enormous, fleshy monster began to scream, and then it spastically lunged at me. At first I thought I might have flown into the middle of a medical emergency or some sort of tribal dance that the monster was performing. But then it quickly became clear that the monster was trying to kill me. I turned around and started to fly away. But the monster became even more enraged and began to chase me. I could not escape it. I flew faster, but the wailing beast pursued me and kept swinging its rolled-up paper weapon at me. As much as I didn't want to, I had no choice but to sting the monster. It was the only thing I could do to stop it from following me home and threatening the wellbeing of the hive or worse, the safety of my family. I hoped that if I stung the monster I could thwart its assault enough to save my kids. I knew that I would die soon after administering the sting, but I really had no other option. What a tragedy it is to be forced by a senseless, hysterical beast to take one's own life.

Magazine

I'm not sure what happened. I was being held and slowly read by some woman when all of a sudden she rolled me up and started to choke me and violently whip me around. After having my face smashed into the arm of a lawn chair a couple times and then into the surface of a picnic table, I was tossed to the ground. It was a terrible and demeaning experience that I'll never forget.

Lawn Chair

I don't know what his problem was, but the magazine I was hanging out with abruptly got up and smacked me twice for no reason.

Brenda's Phone

Brenda was talking into me when the incident happened. I didn't get to see or hear anything because Brenda is such a loud and obnoxious phone talker. Whenever she uses me it's like I'm cut off from the world. If I had enough power in my lithium battery to electrocute her face, I would. Seriously, I would do it. She is that annoying.

Lithium Battery

I second that.

Ointment

I am effective at temporarily relieving pain and itching associated with insect bites, minor burns, sunburn, minor skin irritations, scrapes, and rashes due to poison ivy, poison oak, and poison sumac.

Squirrel in Nearby Tree

I am still too upset to talk about what happened. I was good friends with Chris. I can't believe what that woman did to him. He was a hardworking, God-fearing bee, who had a family and a good job. What that woman had against him, I'll never know. To tell you the truth I don't even think she knew him. What a bitch. I'm going to find out where she lives, go to her yard, and act crazy on her fence.

Tree

No comment.

God

Forcing a bee to commit suicide is one of my biggest pet peeves. This is not good for this Maureen person.

From *This is a Book* by Demetri Martin. Copyright 2011 by Demetri Martin. By permission of Grand Central Publishing. All rights reserved.

Why Do We Tell Stories?

The purpose of Demetri Martin's *Bee Sting* is **to entertain**. It takes the simple act of swatting a bee away and escalates that action into a situation where nothing less than life, death and eternal salvation are at stake.

In this story Maureen **relates** what would be the **ordinary situation** for most of us. But then the other characters are allowed to **share their experiences**. We get to **see the situation through their eyes.** We learn that Maureen's friend Brenda is not really such a good friend. And because of this we **create sympathy** for Maureen. The bee's experience explains to us that a bee only stings as a last resort—to save his family—to preserve his species. It **tells us things we didn't know**. The ointment **delivers facts**. The squirrel expresses the loss of the bee and helps us to **process the problem**. And God's perspective helps us to **understand the consequences of** Maureen's actions. The next time we are tempted to swat a bee, we might pause and not even do it. If this happens then we have **learned something** about the act of killing bees. And if enough people read this story and learn the same thing we could create **a tradition** of celebrating the bee. Stories become a map for living.

There are many reasons to tell stories, but all of them have one purpose: to show us something about ourselves. Stories are about people.

Chapter 1

Story Background and Theory

We live in story all of the time. We all have stories to tell every day. But telling our personal stories to each other and constructing a story from scratch are two very different things. Usually when we tell stories on a daily basis, we are relating events to one or two other people. When constructing story, we are trying to communicate with a mass audience. When we tell stories to a friend it is because it is important to us or to them. When we construct story, we are moving not just an individual, but an audience. The goal then becomes to make the personal universal.

Before we can begin, we need to understand the background of story and how that background lays the foundation for what we want to make: a story for an animated short film.

WHAT IS A STORY?

Screenwriter Karl Iglesias has a very simple definition of story: "A story has someone who wants something badly and is having trouble getting it."[1]

This definition determines the three base elements necessary for a story: character, character goal, and conflict. Without these elements, story cannot exist.

1. *Character.* This is whom the story is about and through whose eyes the story is told.
2. *Goal.* This is what the character wants to obtain: the princess, the treasure, the recognition, and so on.
3. *Conflict.* Conflict is what is between the character and his goal. There are three forms of conflict:
   ○ Character vs. Character
   ○ Character vs. Environment
   ○ Character vs. Self

Conflicts create problems, obstacles, and dilemmas that place the character in some form of jeopardy, either physically, mentally, or spiritually. This means that there will be something at stake for the character if they do not overcome the conflict.

The other elements of story include:

- *Location.* This is the place, time period, or atmosphere that supports the story.
- *Inciting Moment.* In every story, the world of the character is normal until something unexpected happens to start the story.
- *Story Question.* The inciting moment will set up questions in the mind of the audience that must be answered by the end of the story.
- *Theme.* Themes are life lessons. Stories have meanings. A theme is the deeper meaning that a

story communicates. Common themes include: be true to yourself; never leave a friend behind; man prevails against nature; and love conquers all.

- *Need.* In story there will be what a character *wants*—his goal. Then there will be what the character needs to learn or discover to achieve his goal.

- *Arc.* When a character learns there will be what is called an emotional arc or change in the character as the character moves from what he wants to what he needs.

- *Ending/Resolution.* The ending is what must be given to the viewer to bring emotional relief and answer all of the questions of the story. The ending must transform the audience or the character.

WHY DO ALL STORIES SEEM THE SAME?

With so many different story elements and seemingly infinite ways to combine them, why do all stories seem familiar? Nearly every story told follows the same structure and formula with similar characters, themes, and conflicts.

The Universal Story

From the turn of the nineteenth century on, there are documented discussions between writers and theorists who noticed that the similarities in story went beyond specific regions, cultures and time periods.[2] Some of them theorized that this was because mankind had similar natural phenomena that needed to be explained. This might be the reason for similarities in theme, but didn't explain the similarities in story and plot.

All of these stories followed a three-act structure that Aristotle, nearly 2,300 years ago, called plot. Plot is the sequence of events and the emotions necessary to move the audience through the story. In the first act, pity and empathy must be established for the hero so that the audience cares about him and will engage in his pursuit. The second act is the scene of suffering and challenge, creating fear and tension surrounding the hero and his challenges. In the final act, fear and tension are released by catharsis, the emotional release that allows for closure to end the story.[3]

In the twentieth century, Joseph Campbell, an American mythology professor, writer and orator, found that there were universal images and characters in *one* story shared by all cultures over time. Because this story occurred again and again, he called it the monomyth—the one story, the universal story.

The monomyth is appropriately called the *Hero's Journey.* Campbell's theory has many stages, but they can be summarized as follows:[4]

- *Introduce the Hero.* The hero is the character through whom the story is told. The hero is having an ordinary day.

- *The Hero has a Flaw.* The audience needs to empathize with the hero and engage in his pursuit of success. So the hero is not perfect. He suffers from pride or passion, or an error or impediment that will eventually lead to his downfall or success.

- *Unexpected Event.* Something happens to change the hero's ordinary world.

- *Call to Adventure.* The hero needs to accomplish a goal (save a princess, retrieve a treasure, and so forth). Often the hero is reluctant to answer the call. It is here that he meets with mentors, friends, and allies who encourage him.

- *The Quest.* The hero leaves his world in pursuit of the goal. He faces tests, trials, temptations, enemies, and challenges until he achieves his goal.

- *The Return.* The hero returns expecting rewards.

- *The Crisis.* Something is wrong. The hero is at his lowest moment.

- *The Showdown.* The hero must face one last challenge, usually of life and death against his greatest foe. He must use all that he has learned on his quest to succeed.

- *The Resolution.* In movies this is usually a happy ending. The hero succeeds and we all celebrate.

Example:

Table 1.1   Feature Film Plots Against the Hero's Journey

	Shrek	**Mulan**	**The Incredibles**	**Howl's Moving Castle**	**Rango**
Introduce the Hero	Shrek is an ogre who lives in a swamp and just wants to be left alone.	Mulan is the only child of the honored Chinese family, Fa.	Former Superhero, Mr. Incredible—now Bob Parr—is stuck in a dead-end job where he tries to help people, be a good dad and fit into "normal" society.	Sophie is a girl who lives in a magical land. At a parade she is accosted by soldiers and saved by a wizard. Her friend warns, "Wizards steal the hearts of beautiful girls."	A chameleon lives in an aquarium. He has a large imagination, loves theater and is the hero in his own imaginary life.
Hero has a Weakness	Shrek is an ogre.	She's a girl. She is smart, headstrong and loud. This is not a good combination for an honorable Chinese female.	Bob wants to fight crime—and lies about it to do so. Bigger problem: He likes to work alone.	Sophie doesn't see herself as beautiful. There are esteem issues.	He has no real identity.
Unexpected Event	Shrek's swamp is invaded by fairy tale characters displaced by Lord Farquaad. Shrek wants his swamp back. Donkey knows where Farquaad lives. Shrek is forced to go with Donkey.	Mulan's weakened father, Fa-Zhou, is called to join the army and fight the Huns.	Mr. Incredible gets a secret message calling for his services to defeat a government robot gone haywire.	The Witch of the Waste visits Sophie's hat shop after hours. When Sophie won't help her, she turns Sophie into an old hag.	The aquarium is in the back of the family car. The brakes are hit and he flies out onto the pavement and into real life. Uh oh.
Call to Adventure	Farquaad gives Shrek a choice: Rescue the princess or die. Well, OK. Shrek goes to rescue the princess, but only after Farquaad promises to give him his swamp back if he does.	Knowing her father would never survive, Mulan disguises herself as a man and joins the army.	Bob takes the bait. Come on, Bob—her name is MIRAGE. He answers the call, defeats the robot, and accepts a new job—all while deceiving his family.	Unable to tell anyone she is cursed, Sophie leaves to find a way to remove it. She meets a scarecrow who gets her a job in Howl's moving castle. There she cuts a deal with a cursed fire: I'll free you if you free me.	He ends up in a town called Dirt, proclaims himself to be a gunslinger, Rango, kills a hawk. Mayor makes him sheriff and he loses the water supply to gophers.

Table 1.1 *Continued*

	Shrek	**Mulan**	**The Incredibles**	**Howl's Moving Castle**	**Rango**
The Quest	Ogres are like onions. Shrek makes friends with Donkey, crosses rickety bridges above lava, fights a fire-breathing dragon, and rescues the princess.	With the help of a dragon and a lucky cricket, Mulan learns skills to fight the Huns under the leadership of Shang, her captain.	Fighting robots is a trap set by his rejected wanna-be side-kick Syndrome. Mr. Incredible's family finds out and sets out to retrieve him.	Sophie learns Howl is a mess because he has no heart, using his powers for selfish reasons that will destroy him. He keeps turning into a bird and flying away. And there is a war going on that depends on Howl.	If you control the water, you control everything. Rango forms a posse, promises the town that he will bring back the water.
The Return	Shrek has to persuade the princess to go to Duloc, fight Robin Hood, play with spider web balloons, and find a place to sleep because the difficult princess insists and fall in love over grilled rat.	The Huns attack. Mulan starts an avalanche, defeats the Huns, saves Shang, but gets wounded. Mulan is discovered to be a girl.	Syndrome sends a robot that only he can control to the city, defeats it and becomes the greatest superhero of all. He must be stopped.	Howl's hair is a different color. Can't go on if he's not beautiful. Sophie screams she's never been beautiful. Everyone's ugly and they get weaker and uglier.	Rango and the posse return with nothing. Rango accuses the Mayor of taking the water but a rattlesnake, Jake, reveals that Rango is a fake.
The Crisis	Fiona, the princess, is about to marry Farquaad. Shrek has his swamp back, but is miserable. Donkey tells him to go tell Fiona he loves her before it is too late.	She is outcast. On the way home she discovers the Huns are going to attack the Emperor's city. She hurries but no one will believe her.	But, Mr. Incredible is captured. Believes his family is dead. City is in jeopardy.	Howl flies away from the castle (again). It falls apart. Howl is dying. Sophie is desperate.	Rango leaves the town in shame. He believes he is nothing and tries to kill himself crossing the road but no man can walk out on his own story.
The Showdown	Shrek rides the dragon to Duloc, stops the wedding, confronts Farquaad, and tells Fiona he loves her.	Huns kidnap the Emperor. Mulan defeats the Huns. Emperor offers her honor and a job. She just wants to go home. Shang still won't have anything to do with her.	Family isn't dead. They save him. Follow Syndrome to the city. Mr. Incredible wants to take on Syndrome alone. Learns he needs his family. He can't work alone.	The Witch of the Waste has Howl's heart. Sophie asks her for it. She gives it up. Sophie puts Howl's heart back.	Rango finds the source of the water and returns to town. Rango calls out Jake and brings back the water—but the Mayor has Beans.

	Shrek	Mulan	The Incredibles	Howl's Moving Castle	Rango
Happy Ending	Fiona loves Shrek too. She turns into an ogre, Shrek gets his swamp back, Farquaad is eaten by the dragon, the dragon and Donkey fall in love. We all celebrate.	Emperor gives Shang a good talking to. He goes after Mulan. Mulan's father is proud. She has honor and she gets the guy. We celebrate.	They save the city but Syndrome has Jack-Jack, their son. Jack-Jack can hold his own. Syndrome is defeated and the family is a happy unit.	Howl is fine. Loves Sophie. Sophie thinks she's beautiful. The fire is free, but chooses to stay. The scarecrow is a prince who can end the war. True love transforms everything.	With one shot— Rango saves himself and Beans. The Mayor is washed away. Jake and Rango become legends. Rango gets the girl. Water is restored. The town celebrates.

Disney films have driven home the opportunity of the individual to succeed, and above all, it is personal success that we celebrate. In Disney films there is a clear hero who fights a clear villain. Nearly all of the classic Disney movies are excellent case studies of the hero's Journey.

On the other hand, Pixar films follow every aspect of the structure except that of the hero. If we define a hero simply as the eyes through which the story is told, then Pixar, too, more or less fits the formula. If we define the hero as the one who succeeds and whose success we celebrate then this changes the dynamics when we look at a Pixar film.

In Pixar films, from *A Bug's Life* on, the role of hero is more often played as if it were a baton passed among characters.[5] For example, in *Finding Nemo*, it is Marlin's quest to find Nemo. But Marlin fails. He begins to return home without his son. It is Nemo who brings himself home and it is Dory's role to reunite Nemo with his dad. At different times, Gill is the hero and Dory is the hero.

Miyazaki also orders the events in a classic structure. However, in most of his stories, the identification of good and evil is not clear. For Miyazaki and Studio Ghibli, evil, if it can be called that, is that which dwells within us. His stories have conflict that is often more internalized. Success comes through personal resurrection. Through the character's personal transformation, the peace in society is restored.

Character Archetypes

In movies there are definite character roles that appear repeatedly in all of the stories. These roles come from character archetypes. An archetype is a pervasive idea or image that serves as an original model from which copies are made. For our purposes, this means that there are baseline character traits that any surface or costuming can be placed upon. The hero is a baseline that can be an obvious superhero (Mr. Incredible); or a more subtle hero (an ogre, Shrek; a girl, Mulan; a woolly mammoth, Manfred); or a character that grows into a hero (an iron giant; a boy, Hiccup; a lizard, Rango, and so on).

The term first comes from Carl Jung, a twentieth-century psychoanalyst who studied dreams and the unconscious. Jung found that there were recurring images and themes running through the dreams of his patients that were so similar that they could not come from individual conflicts. He believed that these images originated in the collective unconscious of all men. And he called these images *archetypes*.

Jung's four archetypes, attributes common in everyone, are: the female, the great mother; the male, the eternal child; the self, a hero, wise old man; and the shadow, which might be a trickster, and so forth. They were the different ways in which the individual would see themselves. And these formed the basis for the stories that his patients would tell.

In the stories of feature films we find the same thing. There are archetypes that form the basis of nearly all characters we watch. Chris Vogler, in his book *The Writer's Journey*, identifies seven archetypal characters found in most feature films:

1) The Hero—the character through which the story is told.

2) The Mentor—the ally that helps the hero.

3) The Herald—this character announces the "Call to Adventure" and delivers other important information. This role sometimes shifts from character to character.

4) The Shadow—this is the villain or major protagonist. Sometimes, as in Miyazaki's films, the shadow resides in the character himself.

5) The Threshold Guardian—this is a character, passageway or guardian that the hero must get past to proceed on the quest, or to retrieve the object of the quest.

6) The Trickster—this character is usually the comic relief. He sometimes leads the hero off track or away from the goal.

7) The Shapeshifter—this character is not who he appears or who he presents himself to be.[6]

Archetype Silhouettes by Gary Schumer, Ringling College of Art and Design

In Table 1.2 we can see how these characters manifest themselves in selected movies. Sometimes more than one role is fulfilled by the same character.

Table 1.2 Character Archetypes in Feature Films

	Shrek	**Mulan**	**The Incredibles**	**Howl's Moving Castle**	**Rango**
The Hero	Shrek	Mulan	Bob Parr, Mr. Incredible	Sophie	Rango
The Mentor/ Friend	Donkey	Mushu	Elastigirl	The Boy, Markl Calcifer	Beans
The Herald	Farquaad's soldier, the mirror on the wall, Gingerbread Man	The Ancestors	Mirage	The Scarecrow	The Owl, Mariachi Band, The Armadillo, Roadkill, The Spirit of the West
The Shadow	Farquaad	The Huns	Syndrome	Howl	Mayor
The Threshold Guardian	Dragon	Shang	Robot	Witch of the Waste	The Highway
The Trickster	Donkey	Army buddies, Mushu	Kids: Dash, Violet, Jack-Jack	Calcifer Madam Suliman	The town
The Shapeshifter	Fiona	Mulan	This is a story about superheroes—everyone changes form!	Sophie, Howl, the Scarecrow	Rango

It is important to note that an archetype is not a stereotype. A stereotype is a simplified generalization about a specific group. For example: All elderly people are forgetful; all Asians have high IQs; all French are romantic; all African-Americans can dance; etc.

An archetype, on the other hand, is a character attribute that can manifest itself in any human (or in animation, nonhuman) body and that is a recognizable icon by the audience. For example, in *Iron Giant*, the giant is the child that has to be taught. In *Ice Age*, Manfred becomes the great mother—of both the Indian child and the "herd."

Universal Conflicts

Conflict is the situation or problem in the way of the character's goal. It is a dilemma that creates tension for the character. It is something that puts the character in jeopardy.

With all the infinite problems and predicaments that face mankind, you would think that the expressions of conflict would be infinite. But again, we find recurring motifs of conflict. In fact, these motifs occur so often that instead of recognizing these as forms of conflict, we categorize them into types of stories:

- *Brains vs. Brawn.* Pitting intelligence against strength.

- *Rags to Riches.* Personal struggle for achievement.

- *Good vs. Evil.* Equal forces against each other.

- *Role Reversals.* Allow us to see through the eyes of the "other" and experience how others live.

- *Courage and Survival.* This conflict is usually environmental. There is a disaster or disease that must be overcome.

- *Peacemakers.* Underdog stories where the "good" are those who protect the weak or stand up for what is right.

- *Tempting Fate.* The conflict arises when the hero goes against the established order (the law, God, nature), sometimes for the greater good, but more often for personal gain.

- *Fish Out of Water.* A character/characters are transported to a different time or place where they must learn how to survive.

- *Ship of Fools.* Several well-defined, but different characters must navigate an adventure together.

- *Buddy Stories.* Focus on the strengths and contrasts of the characters to overcome adversity and become friends.

- *Love Stories.* Study of romantic relationships that focuses on the trials that bring two people together or tear them apart.

- *Quests and Journeys.* In these stories, a hero traverses space and/or time to retrieve an object or person only to find themselves changed.[7]

Often, in feature films, there will be one conflict motif that is the main conflict or problem. Then there may be secondary motifs that emerge in the subplots.

Universal Themes

Conflicts are not themes. Stories have meanings. They are not just a series of events. They communicate something to us that is larger than the story itself. The meaning or dominant idea of the story is called the *theme*.

For example, DreamWorks's *How to Train Your Dragon* is a story about Hiccup, the scrawny but brainy son of Stoick, a strong but not brainy Viking chief. Hiccup ends a 300-year-old feud with fire-breathing dragons, taking on assumptions about dragons and what it means to be a Viking. It is basically a David and Goliath/Brains vs. Brawn/Underdog story, but these are the conflicts, not the themes. Throughout the film, Hiccup's father references Hiccup's lack of Viking qualities and Hiccup says, "You just gestured to *all* of me." The Vikings are in battle with dragons, considering them pests until Hiccup discovers that a Night Fury—the most mysterious and powerful dragon of all—is as afraid of him as he is of it.

Hiccup learns that real strength is on the inside and "all of this" is enough. These are themes. Themes are life lessons.

Because themes are life lessons, they are often based on human needs. These needs fall into three categories:

1. Physical needs

2. Mental needs

3. Spiritual needs.

Within these three categories we find basic needs:

- Food
- Shelter
- Security
- Acceptance
- Stimulus
- Love
- Order.

This limited number of needs forms nearly all of the themes of our stories.

At the end of *Mulan*, the Chinese Emperor admonishes Mulan: "I have heard a great deal about you, Fa Mulan. You stole your father's armor, ran away from home, impersonated a soldier, deceived your commanding officer, dishonored the Chinese army, *destroyed my palace!* . . . and you have saved us all." As Mulan heads home, the Emperor tells Shang (Mulan's commanding officer and love interest), "A flower that blooms in adversity is the rarest and most beautiful of all."

In Pixar's *UP*, Carl is an elderly gentleman adjusting to life without his wife, Ellie. He is lamenting that "life" got in the way of fulfilling Ellie's dream of adventure, when Russell, a young wilderness scout, tells him about getting ice cream and counting cars with his father. He says, "The boring stuff is what we remember most." And Carl finds that in Ellie's adventure book about the stuff she was going to do in her life turns out to be about the life they had together.

For other movies, theme is not so obvious. Sometimes, if you look at what the main character wants and what he needs to learn it often points you to the theme. It is not the objective of a movie to have the audience leave the theater spouting themes. It is the job of the film to move them unconsciously toward the theme through their emotions. As a creator of films, however, it is necessary to know what you are trying to say in your film.

Brian McDonald, in his book *Invisible Ink*, makes a distinction between plot and theme. He compares the movies *E.T.* and *Iron Giant*. Both are timeless stories of friendship that seem to have similar plots. In both there is a lonely boy who befriends a being from outer space. As the boy bonds with the being, it learns to speak English and the boy in turn tries to teach it what it means to be human. The government wants to capture the potential threat and that pursuit results in life and death possibilities for both the boy and the being. So what is the difference?

In the beginning of *E.T.*, Elliott says something hurtful to his mom and his brother declares, "When are you going to grow up and learn how other people feel for a change?" This is the story question and theme of the movie. The entire film is about Elliott learning to empathize with others. When Elliott finds E.T., he declares "I'm keeping him," without any regard to the feelings or needs of the alien. But as the movie progresses, he feels what E.T. is feeling until eventually he is able to send E.T. home.[8]

In *Iron Giant*, however, Brad Bird raised the question, "What if a gun had a conscious and didn't want to be a gun anymore?" We learn that "You are what you choose to be." This is what Dean, the scrap-metal artist, tells Hogarth Hughes as he rants about his classmates. Hogarth then teaches it to the Giant who repeats it to himself. At the climax of the film, the Giant has transformed into a very large, defensive weapon when Hogarth reminds him that he doesn't have to be a weapon. The Giant chooses to be a hero—like Superman.

The two stories are amazingly similar in plot, but what we learn from the theme is distinctly different.

Likewise, movies can be very different in plot but teach us the same lessons.

Rango is similar in theme to *Iron Giant*. Rango is a chameleon who has no identity. He lives a solitary life in an aquarium where he has an active imagination and is the hero of his own life. One day he is propelled into the real world and wanders into a desert Western town with a water problem. He is asked repeatedly, "Who are you?" to which he responds, "I could be anybody." Then he takes on a persona of a hero until he is discovered to be a fake to which he responds, "I am nobody." He rallies at the end, deciding to return and help the town declaring, "I'm going back because this is who I am." You are who you choose to be. He finds his true path.

A theme is what your audience learns from watching your film.

ORIGINALITY IN STORY

If there are limited themes, conflicts, structures, and character types, what makes each story unique?

Robert McKee states that story is about form, not formula.[9] While the themes, conflict, structures and archetypes may be the same, what is unique is a compelling character and emotionally driven sequence of events. Each character will react to events in a different way. Observing how someone else reacts is compelling. It is why we watch.

The other thing that makes a unique story is character *desire*. In theme, we talked about basic character needs. But often what we want or desire is not what we need. Therefore, conflict in story can be about desire vs. need. Desire is often unrealistic. It is complicated by greed, pride, ambition, fear, laziness, apathy, and so forth. To be successful, characters must overcome desire and learn what they need.

Example: Shrek wants (desire) to be left alone, but what he needs to learn is that not only does he need others, but he deserves others. Manfred just wants to be left alone, but he finds he needs a herd. Mr. Incredible works alone, but learns he needs his family and friends.

What makes a story interesting for an audience is the ability to engage with a character and either vicariously, voyeuristically or viscerally, watch the unique ways that that character reacts to the problems and obstacles they confront.

MAKING THE LONG STORY SHORT: THE DIFFERENCE BETWEEN FEATURES AND SHORTS

Beyond the obvious differences in running time, scope, complexity, and resources, the animated short requires a directness, clarity, simplicity, and economy of plot and assets not found in feature films.

Initial ideas for a short are often too big, too complicated and cover too much territory because most of our references are based on the Hero's Journey.

In the Hero's Journey, the characters (many of them) meet with conflict (several events in several locations), until they reach a crisis (of monumental spiritual or physical proportions) where they learn a lesson (the many themes and subtexts converge), make a decision (which calls for more action) and succeed (usually in celebration with the many other characters).

For the individual filmmaker, the short should have one theme, concept or idea that the piece communicates and one conflict that intensifies or gets worse. It should have one or two characters, one or two locations, and only the props necessary to populate the scene appropriately or drive the story.

The inciting moment, the moment when something unexpected happens for the character, usually occurs within the first 10 to 15 seconds. In *A Great Big Robot from Outer Space Ate My Homework*, we enter the film after the alien has eaten the homework and when the boy is rushing to tell his teacher.

A Great Big Robot from Outer Space Ate My Homework, by Mark Shirra, Vancouver Film School

In the short, the character will *arc*, which means he will change emotionally from the beginning to the end. But he doesn't always learn, make big decisions or even succeed. Sometimes it is enough to retrieve an object, understand an environment, solve a problem, reveal a secret, or discover something. Shorts can be as small as a one-liner or a single event as in *Caps*.

Caps, **directed by Moritz Mayerhofer and Jan Locher, Filmakademie Baden-Wuerttemberg, Germany**

In *Caps*, four hooded and colored figures have offerings for an Altar. There is a green one who is clearly behind. He has a different character and tempo. Red, Blue and Yellow all offer their gifts to the Altar, but when Green arrives he has drunk most of his offering. Yet he can pull out a scooter and color the world.

Remember our most basic definition of a story: a character who wants something badly and is having trouble getting it. When you are looking for ideas, this is still the basis of what you are looking for, only smaller.

Let's work this definition a little bit further: The short story has ONE character that wants something badly and is having trouble getting it. That "trouble" is, at most, ONE other character or environment that causes conflict. The resolution to the conflict communicates ONE specific theme.

This will translate into the following structure:

- It is an ordinary day
- Something happens that moves the character to *action*
- A *character wants* something badly
- He meets with *conflict*
- The conflict intensifies until
- He makes a *discovery*, learns a *lesson*, or makes a *choice*
- In order to *succeed*

That sounds a lot like the Hero's Journey. The difference is in the singularity of the conflict.

The Disney short *Chalk* is a great example of this.

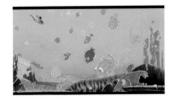

©Disney

© Disney. For Training Purposes Only—Property of WDAS 2010 Talent Development

First, viewers are dropped into a girl's 3D "real" life. Her street is a line of monochromatic row houses. It is hot outside. That is the first major conflict. It is here that she is creating her fantasy world of color, and more importantly, a place where she can get some relief from the heat. She draws a kiddie pool with sidewalk chalk, and slips into a daydream as she visits a place that is cool.

In this 2D fantasy water world, a youngster's imagination can run wild, and she interacts with colorful fish, far from her other world where there were no other living things.

Then she meets a whale, a potential threat and the second major conflict, which surprises her by singing, "Din-ner!" This shocks her into returning to the real world and the realization that what she heard was her mother.

Stories need rising conflict. In this piece, the drama builds gradually toward the supreme conflict, without the audience really seeing what is happening. First, she has a surprising encounter with a jellyfish, and then she is spun around by a whoosh of a school of fish, and then the slow looming arrival of a very large whale.

More importantly, the encounter with this huge mammal is the intellectual pivot point of the piece. The whale's size, stealthy movement and teeth combine to give the audience some sinister clues about its relationship to the girl, and when it says, "Din-ner," the worst is feared. But there are contradictory clues. The whale's voice is high and feminine, some teeth are missing, its mouth hangs open lazily. Not what you would expect from a killer whale.

In the end she heads back to her real world having taken us along to her fantasy world.

So let's look at this in terms of our structure:

- A little girl is playing outside
- The sun glares on her and she *wants to get out of the heat,* so she *draws a pool and slips inside*
- She swims with fishes until a jellyfish bounces on her stomach
- She gets knocked around by a school of fish
- A huge whale arrives that seems to want to eat her for dinner
- She discovers it is her mother calling her
- And she runs home leaving a colorful world of chalk friends behind.

When reading the following chapters, keep this kind of simplicity in mind. One good, simple idea is the key to making a solid short. The simpler the better because you don't have much time to say what you want to say, but more importantly, the viewer does not have much time to grasp what you are trying to say.

Summary

Why do we tell stories?

- To entertain
- To teach
- To compare our existence to others
- To communicate with others
- To see the world through the eyes of others
- To learn how to be human.

Many stories seem to be the same as other stories because:

- There is an archetypal story structure
- There are a limited number of archetypal characters
- There are a limited number of conflicts
- There are a limited number of themes.

Original stories are created through the audience's engagement with unique characters and the way that they react to and solve the conflicts they encounter.

As filmmakers, we deliver emotion. It is through emotional engagement that we move an audience.

When making the animated short, the story needs to have limited characters, limited locations, one conflict, and one theme.

Additional Resources: www.ideasfortheanimatedshort.com

- Working in Collaboration: *The Disney Summer Associates Program: An Interview with Terry Moews*
- Industry Interview: *Story and Humor: An Interview with Chris Renaud and Mike Thurmeier, Blue Sky Animation Studios*

Recommended Reading

1. Joseph Campbell, *Hero with a Thousand Faces*
2. Chris Vogel, *A Writer's Journey*

Notes

[1] Karl Iglesias, *Writing for Emotional Impact*, WingSpan Press, Livermore, CA.

[2] Christopher Booker, *The Seven Basic Plots*, Continuum, New York, NY, 2004, pp. 8–10.

[3] http://classics.mit.edu/Aristotle/poetics.1.1.html. In addition to Plot, Aristotle defined four other elements of story. These are 2) Thought, which is dialogue; 3) Diction, the way the dialogue is said; 4) Sound, the soundtrack; and 5) Spectacle which is the equivalent to special effects. Of these elements Spectacle was the least important. It seems that even Aristotle realized that effects are only good if the audience is not distracted by them.

[4] This is a modified version of the Hero's Journey as defined by Chris Vogler in his book, *The Writer's Journey*. In his book is an excellent chart that compares Vogler's Map of the Hero's Journey and Campbell's. See Chris Vogler, *The Writer's Journey*, Michael Wiese Productions, Studio City, CA, 1992, p. 16.

[5] Ed Hooks, *Newsletter*, Acting Notes, CA.

[6] Chris Vogler, *The Writer's Journey*.

[7] John Douglas, Glenn P. Harnden, *The Art of Technique; An Aesthetic Approach to Film and Video Production*, Allyn and Bacon, A Simon & Schuster Company, Needham, MA, 1996, pp. 16–20.

[8] Brian McDonald, *Invisible Ink*, Libertary Editions, Seattle, WA, 2003–2005, p. 22.

[9] The original quote is: "Story is about eternal, universal forms, not formulas." Robert McKee, *Story: Substance, Structure, Style, and the Principles of Screenwriting*, Regan Books, 1997, p. 3.

Making the Animated Short: An Interview with Andrew Jimenez, Pixar Animation Studios

Andrew Jimenez went to San Diego State University. His first big break was on *Iron Giant* after which he moved to Sony Pictures to work on the first Spider-Man movie as a story reel editor and storyboard artist. That job led to a move to Pixar with Brad Bird to be a co-director of photography on *The Incredibles*. Most recently, Andrew worked on the animated short, *One Man Band*.

***One Man Band*, directed by Andrew Jimenez and Mark Andrews, Pixar Animation Studios**

Q: How do you recognize a good idea for an animated short?

Andrew: Feature films and shorts are two completely different types of stories. When Mark Andrews and I were trying to come up with the idea for *One Man Band*, even when we were considering very un-fleshed-out ideas, it was clear that, OK, this idea belongs in a feature film and then this idea belongs in a short film.

It's a strange analogy to make, but a good short film is like a good joke. It has a great setup, gets to the point, and pays off right away. And it doesn't demand too much in terms of where the story has to go. It gets to the idea right away. You get it. Even if it takes you somewhere different than what you expected, it gets *there* right away too. It's just very simple. And it's about one idea. It can have multiple characters, but it has to be very clear, because in three or five minutes you don't have time to really develop all these side stories and other plot lines.

To use the "joke" analogy again, if my timing isn't perfect and I go on a little bit too long, I can ruin it. I also think it's almost a little bit harder to tell a short film story because you don't have the luxury to develop anything deeply, but yet it should be as meaningful.

It's funny because so many short films aren't short anymore. I think the biggest pitfall is that they are always the first act of a feature film, or they seem to be used as a vehicle for: "I'm just making this part of my bigger idea, but I'm using this to sell it." I'm always disappointed when I find out a short film has done that, because it ignores what is so wonderful about making short films.

Q: When you're building the story, how do you stay focused on one idea?

Andrew: One of the most important parts is the pitch. When your students or any new storyteller tells somebody else the idea, whoever is listening and/or the person pitching should really pay attention to how they are pitching.

I'll use *One Man Band* as an example:

There's a guy on a corner, and he's playing music. He's pretty good, but not really that good, and there is another musician that he is going to battle. That's the story. That's it. The second I start pitching and telling, or describing events to the story that sort of breaks out of that little quad that this movie takes place in, that's the point where I start to get a little worried. The entire pitch should never break from that initial setup.

I think you should be able to pitch your idea in really 15 seconds. Even in *One Man Band* the film never really breaks out away from what's presented in the first 15 seconds of the movie.

And it gets back to the joke analogy, which is a silly analogy, but I think it really makes the point well.

If I'm telling a joke, every beat of the story has to be right on the spot. In the feature film I can wander a little bit, lose you a little bit, I have time to get you back, but in the short film, if I lose you, there is no time to get you back. In the short film, if I go one beat too long, I can ruin it.

For example, if I start setting up giving too much background and explaining too much, then you, as an audience, start getting bored, and by the time I get to the punch line, it's like, uh, OK, that wasn't funny, because you gave me way too much information.

I keep using the analogy of telling a joke. That is not to say a good short film has to be funny. It's just a way of illustrating how important timing is in the short film format.

Q: Is it hard to be funny?

Andrew: Yes, absolutely. I know if I'm trying to be funny, then I should stop right there. Stories are just like people. The funniest people never really try to be funny, they're just really funny. And in story, the funniest stories come out of the situations.

The only thing with *One Man Band* that we started with before we created the story was that we knew we wanted to tell a story about music. There was a theme about what people do with talent and how people view other people that may have more talent than they do. Humor came out of story development but we never tried to *do humor* before we even knew what our characters were doing in the story. It is what the characters do—the acting—that makes it funny. Of course their designs played a big part of that too.

Everything comes out of story. Whether you try to be depressing or sad, or funny, humorous, or make a statement, I think the second you try to do that without arriving at that through your story, then it's kind of like telling your punch line before your joke.

Q: What was the hardest part of making *One Man Band*?

Andrew: For *One Man Band* the hardest thing—it's true for the features, too—was that after Mark and I got the green light just to come up with ideas (and we were so ecstatic about that) was to actually come up with the ideas.

There's no science to coming up with a story. You can't say, "All right, go—come up with a story." So, Mark and I started having lunch every day. We started talking about things we had in common, things we liked, things we didn't like in other movies.

I had this book I called "The Idea Book," and I wrote down all the ideas we came up with, about 50. One of the common themes in all these little ideas was music—and competition. I have been an avid film score collector since I was a child and have always wanted to tell a story where music was our characters' voices.

So we started developing and working around that theme. That time was the hardest part of the entire production of *One Man Band*—really getting that theme through the progression of the story. Because if you don't have that locked down and perfect, no matter how good the CG is or the acting is, you're never going to save it.

Don't worry about your perfectly rendered sunset, and shading and modeling of the set. It's the characters and their story. People will forgive so much if they really believe and love your characters and your story. When *André and Wally B.* was shown at SIGGRAPH for the first time many years ago, most people in the audience didn't realize it wasn't finished because they were so involved with the characters.

Q: What advice do you give to an animator making their first short?

Andrew: My advice would be: don't overcomplicate it. Just find one idea that you want to tell, stick with that and trust it. If it's not working ask yourself why. Don't think you have to pile a bunch of other stuff on top of it to make it work and make it longer. Students, especially, will pack so much stuff into the film to try to show what they can do and to make *the* amazing film. I know I learned so much more by making several shorter films in the span of a year instead of making only one gigantic opus.

I know at Pixar, when we look at other short films, the thing we respond to the most is a short simple idea that grabs us, that we get to react to, and then it lets us go.

Chapter 2
Finding Ideas

Eureka!, **by Parrish Ley, Sheridan College**

For every project, whether it is a 15-second exercise or a feature film, you will need a good idea. And if it is a good idea, is it good for the animated short?

DEFINING THE ANIMATED SHORT

The short film is defined as 24 minutes or fewer. In animation, commercial shorts usually run 6 to 11 minutes and are created by teams with big budgets and resources. We are defining the short as what is feasible for the individual, beginning animator. This is a running time of approximately one to three minutes, about the length of one scene in a feature film.

The story ultimately determines the size of the short. It depends on whether you are working alone or in a group, the time you have and the amount of time you are willing to spend on the project. It depends on your resources. And it depends on how much information and complexity you can handle, both conceptually and technically, and still move an audience emotionally.

BEFORE YOU START

Before you start, it is good to know a few rules of the playground.

The Rules of the Playground

Rule #1: Story is King

Story will infuse all the work that you do. As a shorts producer, you may wear all the hats of production: writer, director, concept artist, storyboard artist, modeler, rigger, animator, lighting and texturing artist, sound director and editor. What ties all these positions together is the story. Without a story, all you have is technique.

Technique and skill are crucial, but there are times when an audience (not an employer) will forgive poor technique. However, it will never forgive a poor story.

Rule #2: Keep It Simple

A good idea for a short is simple. It isn't too complicated and it isn't too big. It has a set up, makes a point and ends.

Remember: one theme, one conflict, two characters, two locations and only the props necessary to tell the story. If you can't define how something in the story supports the theme, get rid of it.

What types of ideas work for the short?

- Simple, single situations
  - Someone wants a bite of your food
- One conflict that intensifies
  - I give him one bite. Now he wants more. I give him all but one bite—which I eat. Now he wants me . . . uh oh.
- A single, memorable moment
  - Ed Hooks, author of *Acting for Animators*, calls a memorable moment an adrenaline moment.[1] Something that happens to the character that is of such great emotional significance that he will remember it when he is 90. I remember the day a bull chased me for an apple.
- Slices of life
  - I once shared an apple with a bull by a pond.
- Demonstrations of personality
  - Let me show you what a bull looks like when he's mad.
- Jokes
  - Did you hear the one about a bull and a bee? I tried to rescue it—but it rescued me!

Fantasia Taurina by Alejandra Perez, Vancouver Film School

Of these, the hardest is a slice of life because the conflict is usually inherent. For instance, in Chelsea Bartlett's *Treasure*, the conflict is that a woman lives in a junk yard. We watch her go through her day, wondering why she selects certain objects and discards others—when we discover she is making the junk yard a beautiful place.

***Treasure* by Chelsea Bartlett, Ringling College of Art and Design**

What types of stories don't work for the short?

- Hero's Journeys
- Epic Tales
- Uncharted Territories or Complicated Concepts
  - You will spend all your time explaining where we are or how it works.
- Little-Known Facts
  - You may know that penguins use oil from a gland to make their feathers waterproof, but if your story is that a penguin is out of oil, most people won't get it.

Rule #3: Know the Theme

Remember that stories have meaning and themes are life lessons. The theme is not the premise or the plot. For any theme, there could be many narratives that communicate it.

For the short, there should be one theme and you should be able to state it in one sentence. Keep it simple, clear and direct. It should have a viewpoint. There is little time to present an unbiased and balanced commentary.

Fantasia Taurina

Concept: Sharing is better than selfishness

Premise: A bull is angry when a young child steals its apples, but is soon in need of her help.

The theme is the one non-negotiable element of your story. Everything else is swappable—characters, locations, plots. But what you want to say, your theme, is the backbone of your story. When you're not sure what is necessary in your film, put it against your theme.

Rule #4: Avoid Cliché

A cliché is a concept, character, symbol or plot device that has been so overused that it has lost its originality.

Cliché Concepts:

- Love conquers all
- Technology is bad
- Nature is good.

Characters:

- Robots
- Aliens
- Mimes
- Ninjas
- Fairies
- Dragons
- Pirates
- Superheroes
- Big-breasted women with guns.

Symbols:

- Butterflies
- Open windows
- Chess boards
- Sunsets
- Gravestones.

Plots:

- It was all a dream.
- Country mouse (or woodland animals) in the city or vice versa.
- Child's imagination (usually with monsters or imaginary friends) takes him on an adventure.
- Little kid learns something that makes them grow up.
- A lonely kid makes a robot friend.
- A character must choose between two pathways or doorways.

In an effort to be clear, it is easy to default to cliché. If you have heard it before, stop and rethink it. If you choose to use something that is cliché, you have to find a way to make it fresh and original.

Example:

Nilah Magruder uses zombies (which are a cliché) in her animatic, *Teddy*, about a young girl running from them in a destroyed suburb. When a zombie girl surprises her, she drops her teddy bear, they struggle, and she pulls off the zombie's arm. The zombie girl grabs her arm back, sits and cries. Key point: Who knew zombies had feelings? The girl offers her the bear, and in turn, the zombie girl offers her the arm—which although dismembered is still alive and gives the girl a hug. The story does not work because of the zombies—it works because it is about empathy and understanding someone different.

Preproduction Animatic: *Teddy* by Nilah Magruder, Ringling College of Art and Design

When you are working with a cliché, go to the theme, the life lesson, to make it fresh.

Rule # 5: Create a Memorable Character

Shrek, Hogarth, Nemo, Woody, Howl, Rango, Hiccup—we remember them all. Why?

A memorable character is ordinary enough for the audience to relate to with flaws that make them unique and accessible.

There is "something" (extraordinary) about their design and personality that makes us empathize with their plight.

The test of a good character is that he cannot be replaced with someone or something else. Replaceable characters are flat. You can swap them out (a boy for a girl for a squirrel for a squid) and it doesn't affect the story. But when you find the right character, it is difficult to remove them from the story because it is *their* story. And through their story, they teach us something.

***Poor Bogo* by Thelvin Cabezas, Ringling College of Art and Design**

Rule #6: Emotion Drives Action

A story is defined by the character. More specifically, it is defined by how the character *reacts* to a situation.

Action never just happens. Action is the *result* of thought and emotion.

Too often the beginning storyteller will create the events—what the character does, the action he takes—instead of looking at the emotional changes in the character as he meets the rising conflicts. If story is king, emotion is ruler of the universe. It is how the character feels and then how he reacts to how he feels that retains your audience.

"My Tomato!" *Gopher Broke* **crow, Illustration by Sean McNally, Blur Studios**

Rule #7: Show Don't Tell

This is the golden rule of film. "Telling" means the use of exposition or description without engaging the emotional or sensory experiences of the character or the audience. Usually this involves bad dialogue that hits you over the head, explanatory narration or the use of signs (not symbols and semiotics here, but actual written signs like "This Way to the Death Chamber").

Showing means to make clearly evident, by the appearance, behavior, action or reaction, the character's emotional experience too. It is the epitome of the adage, "Actions speak louder than words." Through gesture or props, showing creates a visual that communicates the theme, feeling or content. Showing involves communicating the emotional and visceral experience of the content.

In the animated short, where there is little or no dialogue, the question of what we see becomes critical.

You need to consider, from the initial idea, what we are going to see. It is never too soon to begin to make your piece visual. It is often the visual that sells the idea. And in animation, it is not only what a character does, but how he does it that makes it poignant or entertaining.

Rule #8: Create Conflict

This may seem obvious given our base definition of story. However, an initial pitch will often include wonderful characters moving through events, but it is all exposition. There is no conflict and consequently, there is no ending because there is nothing to resolve.

In *Respire, Mon Ami* there is a lonely boy, but this conflict is resolved in the inciting moment when he finds a severed head at a guillotine. From that moment until the boy believes his friend has "died" we have nothing but exposition as we build the relationship. If the head did not expire, we would never have a conflict.

Respire, Mon Ami by Chris Nabholz, Ringling College of Art and Design

Conflict = drama.

Remember that there are three, and only three, kinds of conflict:

1. *Character vs. Character*: Characters need opposing goals. If both characters want the same thing, there is either: a) no conflict or b) you can tell the story with one character.

2. *Character vs. Environment*: The character struggles against the environment. "Environment" can be an interior, or exterior.

3. *Character vs. Self*: This is the hardest to animate because the conflict is internal. *Eureka!* does a good job of making an internal conflict (the need to think of an idea, to solve a problem) externalized in the light bulb above the professor's head. When the normal process or pathway to creativity is broken, the professor flails wildly in frustration, unaware the source of his ideas is still there. Order is restored only when a new pathway found.

When discussing conflict, it is also necessary to discuss what conflict is not. Conflict is not a sword fight, war, car chase or competition. These are the *results* of the character in opposition.

Rule #9: Know Your Ending

You can't really tell your story until you know the ending. Sometimes the idea you find will be the ending—the punch line or the payoff. Endings must transform the character, the audience, or both.

Rule #10: Entertain Your Audience

Audiences are entertained when they are visually, intellectually and emotionally engaged.

When audiences watch a film, they are looking for an experience. They will suspend disbelief and travel with you as long as you maintain the rules of your world and keep the story truthful and the characters believable.

The best shorts are the ones that have some adventure, sorrow and laughter. They are the ones that hold a few surprises and the ones you continue to think about after you see them. How will your audience feel, and what will they remember from yours?

Rule #11: Make Me Laugh

Most people, when they think of humor and animation, think of Tex Avery, Chuck Jones, sight gags and visual puns. Humor can also be parody, satire or pathos.

The best humor in a short is the type that grows out of the situation, reinforces the conflict or emotion of the characters or subtly reveals more about the character. It is sometimes funny, sometimes nervous, and sometimes empathetic.

In *Respire, Mon Ami*, the young boy tries to revive his friend with mouth-to-mouth resuscitation. The humor comes from three sources: 1) from the fact the head is dead and cannot be revived, 2) from the gross factor of the act itself, and 3) from the breath of the boy escaping out the neck to rustle the leaves on the ground.

Respire, Mon Ami by Chris Nabholz, Ringling College of Art and Design

Humor can come from empathy and failure as we watch a character attempt to fly a kite.

Kite **by Glynn Olson-Wheeler, Ringling College of Art and Design**

It can come from the burp of a Cap who has drunk the magic potion. Burps, farts and body jokes are popular forms of humor. We can point to numerous feature films that include them. However, if you analyze these carefully, these kinds of jokes are usually secondary humor. They are not the primary content that drives the scene. If they are, they are related to the situation in which they occur and what is poignant is not the burp or fart, but the *reaction* to it. Note the reaction of the green Cap's friends. And note the result of him drinking the potion.

Caps, directed by Moritz Mayerhofer and Jan Locher, Filmakademie Baden-Wuerttemberg, Germany

Rule #12: Answer the Question: Why Animation?

How are you going to employ the unique characteristics of animation? When someone asks you why you are using animation to create a film there needs to be a good reason. There needs to be something in the design and the storyline of your piece that *requires* animation.

This could be exaggeration, caricature, or process. Sometimes animation is a better medium to use because of your proposed content. Using anthropomorphic animals allows us to look at our human characteristics, our failings and shortcomings that otherwise would be difficult to watch.

Why? Much of this has to do with time and cost. If it is a piece that you could produce easier, cheaper, faster and *better* in live action, why are you doing it with animated media?

The Cardinal Rule: DO SOMETHING YOU LIKE

If you don't like what you are doing, it will show in the work and no one else will like it. Choose something that you like, that can sustain you for the months it will take to produce it.

Finally, for every rule, there is an exception to the rule. Learn the rules, and then break them.

GETTING IDEAS

Now that we know the rules of the playground, where do good ideas come from?

Kevin Andrus, Ringling College of Art and Design

The Ideal

The most linear path for getting and developing ideas comes from first knowing your theme. If you know what your piece is about, it is easy to determine early on which elements you need to tell your story: the situation that will *best* convey your message; the characters that will be in conflict; your genre; time period; lighting, costuming; etc.

This is the most straightforward approach because your theme is what drives everything else. It is the sounding board against which you place your possibilities and if your possibilities do not support your concept, you eliminate them.

Chris Perry's piece *Catch* is an example of a piece that started with a concept:

Catch by Chris Perry, University of Massachusetts at Amherst

Catch really grew out of a statistic I heard a while back. I think it was something like "50 percent of all middle school girls are on a diet." This came up in the context of a conversation about how advertising succeeds at making people, especially girls, feel unhappy with themselves. At the time, my wife and I were expecting a girl and I pictured her wandering through fields of giant billboards which were coming to life, reaching down and trying to snare her. But she was trying to chase this ball as it rolled underneath the billboards, and she was so small they couldn't grab her.

The simplicity of *Catch* is deliberate: I wanted the advertisement image to stand out as striking and unusual because such images don't stand out in our everyday existence (and they should). The models used in advertisements represent the smallest sample of what women's bodies really look like, and the money spent to craft the perfect image defies the final result's impromptu, casual appearance.

The story was basically intact from the storyboard phase on, though I did have her try to throw the ball up at the tree while lying on her back (something I used to do). But that was hard to stage clearly so I switched it for the throwing game. The little gag about the sagging breast was an exception: it came up between storyboarding and animation when I was acting out that key moment of the film and trying to figure out how to visually show that this new breast wasn't doing anything for her. It was also always part of the film that gaining the adult-like chest required the removal of the ball game (putting those two desires completely against each other, so she couldn't have both).

The primary theme of *Catch* to me is about being yourself. If the film works, it works because when she is standing still with a big chest and doing nothing, it is a complete and absurd contrast to her activeness and creativity at the start of the film. "Is this what being like that person in the picture is like? How dull!"

The Real

More often than not, we start with a seed or inspiration from somewhere or something else. It could be a character design we have drawn, a location we have seen or a situation we have experienced. All of these are harder, but more visual places to start. It just takes a little more work to find the essence of your piece.

When starting with a character, you will need to figure out who that character is and then fabricate a situation that will put him in conflict.

When starting with a location, you need to discover why you are attracted to it and what potential it has for story. Populate it with characters. Who would be in that space? What do they do? What would disrupt what they usually do? If the location is generally familiar, what has changed or what is out of place that creates implications or questions in your audience's mind? What is the atmosphere of the place and what does that mean?

In *Triplets of Belleville*, three great cities—New York, Montreal, and Paris—were combined to create a place that felt familiar and communicated wealth, materialism and scale, in contrast to the poverty of Mme. Souza and her dog.

Evgeni Tomov, art director on *Belleville*, explains:

The direction Sylvain Chomet gave me, he told me it should be a very interesting city, where there is an abundance cult for consumerism and food is a typical thing. And that's why you see so many obese people—and the characters in Belleville—you can see it for yourself—they represent this over consumerism.[2]

The Triplets of Belleville, directed by Sylvain Chomet

Sometimes, the location can tell the whole story. Ray Bradbury wrote the short story, "There Will Come Soft Rains," that follows the functions of a "smart house" long after the residents have died. Through the house itself, the lives of the people who lived there are revealed and the purpose of the house to protect them is jeopardized.[3] There are a lot of mechanical devices and effects to watch that could make this good for animation.

When starting with a situation, you have to create conflict. Two people at a table having a conversation is a situation. Two people at a table fighting over the check is a conflict. To make this stronger, there has to be something at stake. What does it mean to each of these characters if they do not pay the bill? What could make this better for animation than live action? What are the extremes that the characters go to in order to win the conflict? What other situations are similar that could tell the story better?

When You Have Nothing . . .

1. Start with Yourself.

There is no better source of story than you: likes, dislikes, what you know. Story is driven by emotion, so start with that. What makes you happy, mad, sad, frustrated, surprised, or hopeful? What makes you laugh? What is the one thing you would like to change about the world? What's your perfect day? What is your biggest ambition? What is something you've always wanted to do but haven't? Be your own character.

2. Ask Why?

Look at the assumptions in your life. Why are things the way they are? Turn them over. Look at them from another viewpoint. Monsters have hidden under children's beds and in children's closets forever. Everyone knows they are there to scare children. But no one until Pixar, with *Monsters, Inc.*, asked why. What's in it for the monster? It's their job. But what is the payoff for doing this? Ah . . . it is their source of power. Brilliant.

3. Go into the World and Watch.

Observation is one of an animator's greatest tools. The world is full of people in conflict—from the simple choice of paper or plastic, to climbing Mount Everest. And people do the craziest things for the silliest reasons. The human race is full of emotions, logic, faults, quirks, fallacies which all make great fodder for animation. They have great movements, expressions, walks and weight shifts. Sometimes something as simple as an interesting walk can reveal a character and launch a story.

Educator and Animator Jamie DeRuyter tells this story:

> I was in a bar. The bartender is telling a story to a couple of guys sitting at the bar. He begins to wash some glasses while he's yappin'. He picks up two glasses, plunges them into the swirling washer in the sink, splashes them into the rinse sink #1, then rinse sink #2 (the one with the sanitizer that is required by law), then sets them down to dry. I'm not sure how many people have tended bar or sat at a lot of bars, but that is a standard bar glass wash: scrub, rinse, sanitize, stack.
>
> So, he's getting further along in his story, washing glasses (lots of them), when I notice he skipped the second rinse (sanitize) on one set of glasses. He's really getting into telling this story. The dudes he's telling it to are totally on the edge of their seats waiting to hear how this comes out. They can't see the wash sinks and what he's doing under the bar in front of them. As the bartender continues to wash and talk, he skips the sanitize a couple more times. Then, on one set of glasses he skipped *both* rinses. *Hahahaha*, the story is really getting funny now. All three of the guys are laughing out loud. Then he grabs four glasses, gestures with them once or twice as he lays down the climax of his tale, waves them *past* all three sinks . . .

Then the guys order another round for the bar and he fills the glasses . . . *those* glasses . . . my glass has lipstick. I'm sure my reactions were priceless. Uh, bartender, check please?

4. Create Some Innocent Trouble.

When we are in negotiation, we are emotionally involved and rarely have the opportunity to observe the reactions and emotions of ourselves and other people. At the grocery store, when the cashier asks if you want paper or plastic, reply "Both." And then be specific about which items you want in paper and which you want in plastic. Watch how they react. See if they will do it. Be careful not to push too far. You are doing a study, not getting in trouble.[4]

My student, Ryan, went to McDonalds. He ordered a Big Mac but asked that everything be wrapped in a separate piece of paper or put in a separate container—the beef patty, special sauce, lettuce, cheese, pickles, onions and sesame seed bun. They did it. Then he sat at the table closest to the cashier, put it back together, and ate it. The reactions were perfect for animation.

5. Read the News.

The news is full of stories. Sometimes you just get handed one that would make a good film.

Look at this headline: "Thief Makes Getaway on Pedal Go-cart." Apparently a thief was caught while loading his car with stolen merchandise. Taking off on foot, he lost a shoe and sock in the mud. Thinking it would be a faster getaway, he jumped into a pedal go-cart that he later abandoned for faster transportation—a bicycle. Dumping the bicycle he ran through a cemetery where the police were able to track his one-shoed footprints to where he was hiding behind a tombstone.[5]

The only thing that would make this better is if he had stolen a pair of shoes.

6. Look at Art.

What attracts you? Why? Is it color, composition, light, subject matter? Cezanne told story through light. Brancusi created flight out of stone. Each piece of art tells a story. If you lay that story over time, what is it?

Meghan Stockham's animation, *Beware of Monster*, was inspired by a piece of art that illustrated a little girl blowing bubbles on a dock. Below her in the water was a creature. Meghan asked, what if the monster really wanted the bubbles? The bubbles were eventually swapped out for flowers.

7. Make an Adaptation of Another Story.

You don't want to illustrate another story, but use it as inspiration or reference. What is the essence or concept of the story? What are parallel situations and conflicts? How can you translate it into your own form? What if you tell the same story from another viewpoint? Tell "Little Red Riding Hood" as the wolf or the basket or the path. Don't be afraid to steal the essence of another story. Remember that there are a limited number of stories recreated in new forms. Without "Cinderella" we wouldn't have *Pretty Woman*. The advantage of revising a known story is that instead of spending time telling a new story, you can reinvent it or up the visuals to make us see it in a new way.

8. Parody a Current Story or Event.

A parody is a humorous imitation that makes fun of or mocks someone, or something. It plays in the world of irony, sarcasm and sometimes ridicule. Politics, current events, songs and popular culture are frequently the subject of parody and satire. Think of *South Park*, *Family Guy* or old Warner cartoons like *Bugs Bunny*.

9. Create a Competition, Play with Status.

In conflict, we talked about characters that have opposing goals. Sometimes, in stories of competition, characters have the same goal and are pitted against each other. These stories often use status relationships (who has power) and status often transfers from character to character as they meet with conflict. In *Kung Fu Panda*, Po competes with Master Shifu for a dumpling. Dueling chopsticks and kung fu moves bring Po to the level of kung fu master—and he can eat.

10. Combine Unlike Things Together.

What if you had enough balloons to lift a house? What if food rained from the sky? What if fish had hands? What if's and unusual combinations can result in unique ideas. In *Toy Story*, think of all Sid's combined toys. They each have a weird little story. Or in *Coraline*, think about the transformation of the "other mother" into a spider.

> "There's no use trying," [Alice] said. "One *can't* believe impossible things."
>
> "I daresay you haven't much practice," said the Queen. "When I was your age, I always did it for half-an-hour a day. Why, sometimes I've believed as many as six impossible things before breakfast."
>
> —Lewis Carroll, *Through the Looking Glass*

Getting ideas takes practice. Can you get six ideas today?

PURSUING IDEAS

> Trust yourself. If it moves you, give it a chance. Don't hold back. *Monty Python* had a great working principle. They went with any idea one of them had, even if others didn't like it. They gave anything a chance to live on. Sometimes this resulted in a failed skit, but other times the results were completely unexpected and fantastic. If they had held back during early conceptualizing, they wouldn't have reached the unusual peaks they reached.
>
> —Larry Weinberg[6]

In the short, you are searching for the *best* way to tell your story. Planning your animation takes as much time, rigor and engagement (fun and frustration) as it will take to animate it. Try to defer judgment until you play out your ideas.

Because we are people, and stories are about people, we draw from our own experiences, dreams, and observations. Frequently our first ideas have characters that are people and situations that initially are better for live action than animation. You have to play with these ideas and find exaggeration, metaphor and analogies that push the idea outside the boundaries of live action or communicate what you want to say in another form.

There are some tools we use to do this: Research, Brainstorming, Condensation and Displacement. These are not isolated tools, but you move back and forth between them as you develop a story.

Research

There are three forms of research that you can employ to learn more about the content you need.

1. Factual Research.

Once you have your characters, conflict and location, there will be a lot of things that you don't know. What do you know about medieval dragons or being lost at sea? This kind of research includes the mechanics of how something works, the architecture, costuming or products of a particular era (what did a Coke bottle look like in 1962?); cultural influences on your character or even what film, photography, advertising and art look like in the time period of your film. When Brad Bird made *Iron Giant* he filmed it in Cinemascope because that was the film ratio that was used in the 1950s, the time period of the story. He believed that using a film ratio from the time period of the story helped support the story itself.[7] Factual research can be an incredibly inspiring tool that can lead you to all types of potential for conflict and change. Change may lead to more research. Understanding the parameters of your content is important because in your audience, someone knows your topic better than you. And if you pass this off as "just animation" you will break the suspension of disbelief for someone in your audience.

***Ritterschlag* directed by Sven Martin, Filmakademie Baden-Wuerttemberg, Germany**

2. Observational Research.

We have already covered the fact that observation is one of an animator's greatest tools. You can learn a lot by watching. If you need to animate a lizard, get one. Time the pacing of its movements. Record how it shifts weight when it walks, climbs, or twitches its tail. What else can you learn about it? How does it eat, sleep and socialize? Observation can help you discover the essence of your character, location or situation.

3. Experiential Research.

This type of research is the most fun because you get to *do* things. When Pixar was making *Finding Nemo*, John Lasseter had the animators go scuba diving. He thought they could not accurately animate an underwater movie unless they had experienced it. It is an entirely different thing to feel the resistance of the water, see the diffusion of the light, and swim with fish than to read about them or look at pictures.[8]

Experiential research is also where you act out what your character has to do. It is not enough to think about or observe an action. You need to get on your feet and *do* that action. Feel the force, weight and pacing of the movement. Sometimes you will have to animate a character or creature who moves very

***Flight of Fancy* by Casey Robin, Video Reference and Drawn Frame from Animatic**

differently than you do, that has a very different weight, force and attitude than yours. A great exercise is to follow someone with a very different build and attitude from your own. Try to walk in their shoes—literally. Mirror their gait, the tilt of their head, the angle of their shoulders, the turn of their feet, the swing of their arms, and the angle of their hips. You will learn a lot about them from how they move as opposed to how *you* move.

Brainstorming

Most creativity texts will direct you to be uninhibited when you brainstorm. Anything goes. Play "what if" extensively. To some degree, this is true. But when developing story, you may get there faster if you work within parameters:

- Define the time period and genre of your piece. Is it a horror, mystery, comedy, action-adventure, Western, sci-fi, film noir, etc. and when does it take place?

- Cast and recast your characters until you find the right personality.

- List the attributes of your character, what they do and where they do it. Attributes are all of the details you need to include your visuals. Look at this sentence: "The owner chased his dog through the crowded street." Clear enough. Until you draw it. What does the owner look like? How does exactly does he "chase"? Does he run, hobble, limp? What is the breed of dog? And who or what is around the street? Is it a parade? Marketplace? Wall Street traders?

- Finding metaphors. A metaphor is something that takes the place of something else. A child at play becomes a monkey. A methodical engineer becomes a robot. And they become something else because that "something" is closer to the actual essence of the character than the default package (human) in which you find it.

Brainstorm and share your ideas with others. Your piece will make sense to you because you made it. That doesn't mean it makes sense to others—and remember, stories are meant to be told to other people. Kick around your ideas. More minds make for more ideas.

Condensation

What if your idea has too many characters, events or locations? Do you automatically abandon it? No. It may be that when you understand the essence of the story, it is possible to condense armies into a single soldier, or a journey around the world into a walk around the block.

Let's play what if and condense one of our bigger stories, *Noggin*. Let's say that this was your idea but you either didn't have, or didn't want to work with anyone else. Could you tell this story with two characters?

First, we need to determine what *Noggin* is about. What is the concept of the piece?

Possible concepts that are within a standard deviation might be:

- Mutations save the species.

- Sometimes your differences are your strongest asset.

- Survival of the fittest.

Premise: Noggin, a caveman, lives in conflict with the Bellyfaces who don't appreciate how his differences complicate their lives. Noggin's differences are what save him.

Without the introduction, we assume that Noggin is the first man, a mutation, living with Bellyfaces who ostracize him for being different—a head on the shoulders. He scares prey because his head sticks above their hiding place, and his head smothers fire, which they worship, when he bows before it. The Bellyfaces decide his head must go. But it is storming. And when a great flood comes, Noggin is the only creature who has his head above the water.

***Noggin*, directed by Alex Cannon, Brigham Young University**

The Bellyfaces are essentially all the same, so we could condense them into one character. Then populate the environment with symbols or images of the Bellyfaces, so your audience knows that Bellyfaces dominate the region. And we could probably do it all in and around the camp.

***Noggin*, directed by Alex Cannon, Brigham Young University**

So we have two characters and one location. But in this piece, we still have a long traditional intro, a quadruped deer and a flood. Cut the intro. The flood, the way it is staged and handled, is OK. The deer is a problem. You have to model, rig and animate a deer for just a few seconds of movement. Maybe it could be a gopher that pops his head out of a hole. Simpler, better. The "prey" is swappable for feasibility without hurting the idea or action.

Displacement

Displacement means to change or displace to another viewpoint or context of a piece while maintaining the same story. When beginning to work ideas, look at all of the characters and toys at your disposal. Try telling the story through each of them individually and see what happens.

Poor Bogo is a story about a conflict between a father and his small daughter. The father wants his daughter to go to sleep and she wants to continue telling a favorite bedtime story. Initially, this is an idea that would *seem* better for live action. You could caricature the players and stylize the room, and exaggerate the antics of the child and the sheer exhaustion of the father and this might suffice. But Thelvin Cabezas did a brilliant thing. He displaced the story to the object that was between the father and the child—the bedtime story.

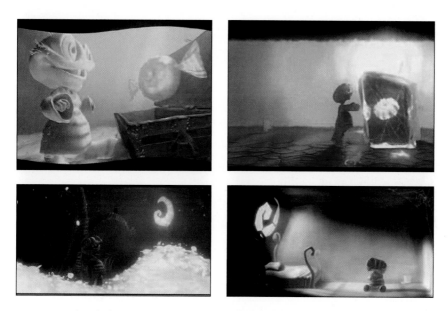

Poor Bogo, by Thelvin Cabezas, Ringling College of Art and Design

This makes *Poor Bogo* more complex. The conflict is character against character. The child wants to stay awake and expand on the story of *Bogo*. This conflict is negotiated as the audience watches the child's imagination and the continuing story of *Bogo*. We have a story within a story.

Bogo, the hero of the child's story, pursues candy. His conflict is twofold. He is in conflict with his environment, which poses physical obstacles to the candy: treasure chests, ice cubes and falling stars. He is also in conflict with the father, who uses logic to dispel the obstacles, just before Bogo can get the candy. And when the obstacles disappear, so does the candy. This has an emotional effect on Bogo and he relies on the child to infuse his goal with situations and hope.

By displacing the conflict between the father and child to the imaginary story, the artist allows the audience an insight into the much richer world of the child. Each time the father dispels the illusion with logic, Bogo is disappointed and we, too, are afraid that the story is over.

The main characters, father and child, do not have an arc, learn or experience an adrenaline moment. However, Bogo does. Remember the time I found a treasure chest? Remember the time there was an ice cube in the desert and when candy fell from the sky? Remember that there won't be any more adventures until another night (and remember I never got to eat my candy!). Poor Bogo.

Swappables

There will be times when you have an idea but you need to make dramatic changes to make it appealing, entertaining or executable in animation. So many short ideas start in a contemporary time period and setting with characters. This is because stories are about us—and we have been repeatedly told to write (or draw) what we know. Often this results in a story that stems from personal experience but not in a form that is entertaining. Remember: one of the challenges of constructing a story is that we are trying to communicate with a mass audience. When working on your idea, you want to make sure it is the most entertaining way to reach them.

Example:

Theme: Some of us grow faster than others, but it is going to happen to everyone.

Premise: On a playground, Sarah Jenkins, a blossoming adolescent, is taunted by her slightly younger friends.

This premise has some problems:

- It has multiple human characters—Sarah and her peers.
- The location, a playground, has multiple props to model.
- The conflict—taunting—seems to require using dialogue.
- The basis for the story is blossoming adolescence or puberty. This is a time of life that is hard to talk about as you are going through it and after you've been through it—you never want to go there again. It includes the visual attributes of pimples, greasy hair and budding bodies. Yuck. How do you make the physicality of adolescence appealing?

However, it has a strong life lesson for both Sarah and her peers and since this is a premise you want to develop, and you're passionate about it, the question becomes, how do we improve it?

Stories have *essentials* that must be kept. In this story the essentials include Sarah, something that develops, taunting and Sarah's desire to belong. Everything else is "swappable." Swappables are things we can "trade out" to try to find better toys with which to tell the story.

Swappables include:

- *The character's physicality.* What is something more palatable and interesting that develops, transforms or mutates? What about a caterpillar, Spider-Man or a transformer?
- *Genre.* Right now this is a coming of age story, but what if you change the genre? What if it is a sci-fi story, an action adventure or a Western? What if Sarah is just a stranger in town that needs to learn who she really is?
- *Time and place.* What if the story takes place during prehistoric time and Sarah becomes Noggin, taunted by Bellyfaces because she has a head?
- *Point of view.* Whose story is it? Right now it is Sarah's. Would it be a better story, or would we learn a better lesson, if it were told through the eyes of the friend?

Early Bloomer, directed by Sande Scoredos, Sony Pictures Imageworks

Early Bloomer

There are many stories that, if you look close enough, are the same story.

Sony Pictures Imageworks told this story through the eyes of a tadpole that begins its transformation just ahead of its peers. It works well because:

- It displaces a common and overused theme to something fresh and new.
- It is told from the *point of view* of a tadpole.
- It takes us to a new *place*, underwater, where we are not sure exactly what we will find.
- Tadpole metamorphosis follows a visual pattern over a relatively short time. The development involves the growth of feet and arms. Hands and feet are something we don't mind watching develop. The feet and arms can "pop" from the body adding surprise and entertainment.
- All tadpoles look the same to us so, aside from color, all the models are the same. There is still a lot to animate but suddenly we have something feasible for the individual animator.
- Underwater is a hard place to be for an animator, but thinking carefully about style choices often make this feasible as well.
- It allows us to look at a time that was awkward for many of us with empathy and humor. It turns teenage angst into a *comedy*.
- It maintains the essentials of the premise while adding appeal and entertainment value.
- It works as an animation because the characters are stylized and the medium provides imaginative possibilities.

New premise: A green tadpole is taunted by her slightly smaller friends as she begins her transformation into a frog.

Theme or concept: Some of us grow faster than others, but it is going to happen to everyone.

Bottle

Another piece where swappables turn something mundane into an extraordinary film is Kirsten Lepore's *Bottle*. The initial concept is pretty boring. This piece is about penpals who decide to meet. It isn't very interesting to watch people write to each other. But Kirsten did an amazing job of incorporating swappables that make this piece an award winner. Penpals become a sandman and a snowman—polar opposites environmentally. What separates them is an ocean. And how they communicate is through a message in a bottle (using objects not words) . . . something that holds intrigue for us as they discover more about each other and finally decide to meet. And to meet they must venture into the ocean . . .

Bottle **by Kirsten Lepore**

Summary

Before you start looking for ideas, know the rules of the animation playground:

- Story is King
- Keep It Simple
- Know Your Concept or Theme
- Avoid Cliché
- Create a Memorable Character
- Emotion Drives Action
- Show Don't Tell
- Create Conflict
- Know Your Ending

- Entertain Your Audience
- Make Me Laugh
- Answer the Question "Why Animation?"
- Do Something You Like
- There Are No Rules.

Getting ideas takes practice and hard work. Ideas come from:

- Everywhere
- Concepts
- Characters
- Location
- Situation
- Experience
- Questions
- Observation
- Negotiation
- Newspapers
- Art
- Other Stories
- Competition
- Combination
- Thinking Impossible Things.

Giving ideas form involves thinking through the possibilities. Tools for pursuing ideas include:

- Research
- Brainstorming
- Condensation
- Displacement
- Swappables.

Additional Resources: www.ideasfortheanimatedshort.com

- Industry Interviews: *The Ideas Behind* Gopher Broke*: An Interview with Jeff Fowler, Blur Studios*
- All the films are located on the web in one of the following three places:
  - Case Studies
    - *The Fantastic Flying Books of Mr. Morris Lessmore:* An Interview with Brandon Oldenburg and Adam Volker. Find out where the idea for this film came from.
    - *A Good Deed, Indeed* documents a initial brainstorming session on the beginning of a film.
  - Designing for a Skill Set

- Make sure to check out Robert Showalter's interview in Designing for a Lighting Project. It has a wonderful story on how his idea developed.
  ○ More Films

Recommended Reading

1. Don Hahn, *Dancing Corndogs in the Night*
2. Ollie Johnston and Frank Thomas, *Too Funny for Words: Disney's Greatest Sight Gags*
3. Michael Rabiger, *Developing Story Ideas*
4. James L. Adams, *Conceptual Blockbusting*
5. Jack Ricchiuto, *Collaborative Creativity*

Notes

[1] Ed Hooks, *Acting For Animators*, Heinemann Press, Portsmouth, N.H., 2003, p. 116.

[2] Sylvain Chomet, *The Triplets of Belleville DVD: The Cartoon According to Director Sylvain Chomet featurette*, by Michel Robin, Beatrice Bonifassi, Jean-Claude Donda and Mari-Lou Gauthier, released by Sony Pictures, 2004.

[3] Ray Bradbury, *The Martian Chronicles: There Will Come Soft Rains*, Spectra; Grand Master edition, 1984, p. 166.

[4] Katherine Tanner, Florida Studio Theatre, Acting Workshops for Animators Homework Assignment.

[5] http://www.spiegel.de/international/zeitgeist/0,1518,543275,00.html

[6] Angie Jones and Jamie Oliff, *Thinking Animation: Bridging the Gap between 2D and CG*, Course Technology PTR; 1 edition, 2006, p. 116.

[7] Salon.com, *Arts and Entertainment Column: Iron without Irony*, August 1999. http://www.salon.com/ent/col/srag/1999/08/05/bird/index.html

[8] Eric Bana, Nicholas Bird (II), Albert Brooks, and Willem Dafoe, *Finding Nemo DVD, Collector's Edition: Making Nemo*, Pixar Animation Studios, released by Walt Disney Pictures, 2003.

The Ideas Behind *Technological Threat*: An Interview with Bill and Sue Kroyer

William "Bill" Kroyer has been an award-winning director of animation, commercials, short films, movie titles and theatrical films for over 30 years. He was one of the main animators for the CGI sequences in *Tron*, and worked on Disney's *The Black Cauldron*. He was Senior Animation Director at Rhythm and Hues on *Garfield*, *Scooby Doo*, and *Cats & Dogs*. Bill is currently the head of the Digital Arts Department at the Lawrence and Kristina Dodge College of Film and Media Arts at Chapman University.

Sue Kroyer is an animator and producer who has worked in the animation industry for over 30 years. She has worked for Disney, Warner Brothers, Brad Bird, *The Simpsons*, Richard Williams and Bob Kurtz.

Bill and Sue Kroyer also owned their own studio, Kroyer Films, where they produced the feature film *FernGully: The Last Rainforest*. Their studio also produced numerous theatrical film titles such as *Honey, I Shrunk the Kids* and National Lampoon's *Christmas Vacation*. Their short film, *Technological Threat*, was nominated for an Academy Award.

Technological Threat is a five-minute animated film made in 1988. It was the first example of early computer animation, integrated with traditional animation. It is a story about robots that are taking over humans (in this case they are dogs) in the workplace. The robots and backgrounds were a combination of drawings and computer-generated 3D models, while the dogs were drawn by hand. The film is an allegory for the threat that computer animation represented to traditional animators at the time.

Image from *Technological Threat*, courtesy of Bill and Sue Kroyer, all rights reserved

Q: What advice would you give to a student on how to make a short film?

Bill: Have a good idea and have something to say. An image or gag is not enough. It's difficult to create something totally original. As long as you don't directly copy something that has been done, it doesn't mean you can't be influenced. At the end of the day you want to try and make something that's wholly your statement. If you do that it will be unique and hopefully it will be something that people respond to. You also want to try and pick something that's within your skill sets so that you can do a good job and get it done. Hopefully it will represent you from a skill point of view as well as being a strong film in itself. You should also keep it short enough so that you can do a good job.

Q: If a student came to you and said "I want to start my own business" what would you tell them?

Sue: I would tell them "GO FOR IT! Go down to the state board and take out a business license." It is incredibly easy to start a business and you should. The hardest part is finding people to pay you for your work but it allows you to be unique when you have your own thing going.

I would also tell them that the industry is changing all the time. You should never look at the prevailing reality. Your "now" is the creative vision you have within you. Although I try to avoid saying "you are the future," . . . you really are the future. Pay no attention to the man behind the curtain. I really believe that.

Q: What was it like for you coming from Disney and transitioning to your own studio?

Sue: When I was at Disney, some of the Nine Old Men were still working there. They were incredibly friendly and welcoming. They loved the new artists coming in and were always supportive.

But, then there was the political structure at Disney at the time, which was not as supportive. Many people that went through that studio were laid off or fired because of that political structure. I saw a lot of people who were laid off from Disney at the time just because they had strong ideas. So many people came and went that they used to call Disney a "clearinghouse for talent." It's like this quote I once read, "Reasonable men expect to adjust to the world, unreasonable men expect the world to adjust to them, therefore all progress is made by unreasonable men." Every one of those people that left or got fired created the "new reality" because it was impossible for them to do so in the studio system.

Q: So you were two people who left and started your own studio where you made *Technological Threat*. How did *Technological Threat* come about?

Bill: I'll never forget the day. We had just paid for this software to develop a TV show called *Ultracross* when it got cancelled. All of a sudden this show—that was supposed to be paying all of our bills—was gone.

Steven J. Campbell Productions was generous enough to let us use the offices for a few months. Since no one had ever combined 2D and 3D animation before we figured we should at least create a demo since we had the equipment.

So we decided to do a short film. We had three employees and we quickly boarded an idea. Brad Bird (director of *The Incredibles*) came in and gave us really great notes. So we revised the boards and we started cranking out this movie. We had a lot of friends in the business and we asked them all to animate a scene. Most of them worked for free.

With a loan from Sue's father, we were able to buy our very first computer. This computer had 4 MB of RAM, a 700 MB hard drive and it cost $57K. This ONE computer was going to do the entire short. It was the only computer at the time that could do this kind of work.

Then we bought these HP machines called "plotters" that would model an image on the computer, turn it into a line drawing and then print it out on paper. Then we could seamlessly combine these with hand-drawn animation.

Q: Did you have a sense that this film was groundbreaking?

Bill: Well, we would bring people in to look at the plotter. And I remember it was like they were looking into the abyss. It was like they were seeing their own death. The computer was drawing pictures and we couldn't draw as fast as it could.

Q: And this was the analogy of your film?

Bill: Well that's the irony of it. That's where I got the idea. People that saw the plotter starting thinking, "wait a minute, I'm going to be replaced!" I said, "If all of our friends are worried about being replaced by the plotter why don't we do a film about hand-drawn characters being replaced by computer characters. And we will create the hand-drawn characters by doing hand-drawn animation and computer characters by computer animation."

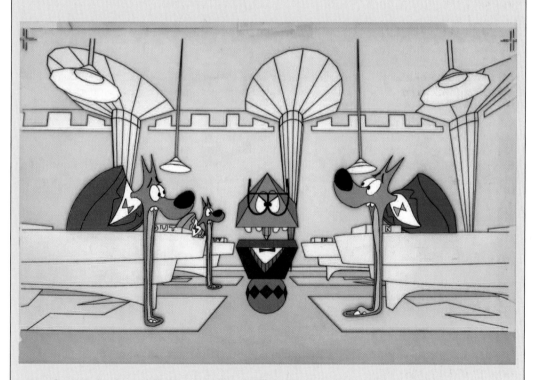

Image from *Technological Threat*, courtesy of Bill and Sue Kroyer, all rights reserved

Q: There was obviously a Tex Avery influence in *Tech Threat*?

Sue: Yes definitely. Rich Moore designed the wolves and Eric Pigors designed the robot. It was our philosophy that if you have great design that is everything. You can have wonderful animation but if the design is not great it won't work.

Bill: The Tex Avery/Warner Bros. influence was to depict the quintessential hand-drawn animation. What could be more symbolically organic than Tex Avery's wolves vs. the Computer Animation—which was stiff and generic like the Robots.

I wanted to model the environment after Frank Lloyd Wright's Johnson Wax Building in Wisconsin (where Sue was from). It had a cool design with a big open office space with desks. I saw it and I said, "That's the scene in our movie." Since this was a movie about workers being replaced by robots it fit well.

Q: How did your traditional animation training help?

Bill: Since we were trained as Disney animators, we understood the sensitivity of the 2D world. Our traditional training helped with timing and motion. The computer tools were very primitive and difficult to use. Since I had the ability to visualize the motion, I had the patience to comprehend how to use these tools to get the end result I wanted.

When we finished, Terry Thoren asked to use the film in an animation compilation called "The Tournée of Animation." Then *Technological Threat* started winning at film festivals (Monte Carlo, Annecy). Based on those wins we were able to submit for the Oscar. I remember Terry called me up and said, "I think you're going to get a nomination," and I said "Are you serious?" Sure enough, our very first film gets an Oscar nomination.

Q: So, in retrospect . . . was the threat of tech good or bad? What do you think of the impact of computers on animation? Has it been a good thing or a bad thing or just something different?

Bill: Technology is totally a good thing because it has given rise to a totally new art form. Animation has been pushed into a world where it's never been before. Technology is never a bad thing; it's how you use it that makes it good or bad. In the hands of good artists it can do wonders.

Q: *Technological Threat* is about computers taking over pencils. If you did *Tech Threat* today what would it be about?

Bill: It would probably be about Stereoscopic. I was actually thinking of doing a sequel called *Stereoscopical Threat*.

We will be looking for the sequel.

The Ideas Behind *Moongirl*: An Interview with Mike Cachuela

Mike Cachuela is a director and artist who has contributed visual design and story development to some of the best-loved animated films of the last twenty years. His credits include *Coraline, Toy Story, The Incredibles, Ratatouille, FernGully: The Last Rainforest* and *The Life Aquatic with Steve Zissou*. Mike was also part of the effects team nominated for an Academy Award for *The Nightmare Before Christmas*. He joined Laika in 2005 as a Director of Story for features. In collaboration with Henry Selick, he served as Head of Story on the award-winning short *Moongirl*. Mike has made several short films for the festival circuit and he is currently developing a feature film based on his own original idea.

Q: What is the basic premise for *Moongirl*?

Mike: *Moongirl* is a story that answers the question, why does the moon light up? How does that work? And it's not what you think. It's not scientific. It's just a kid with fireflies . . . and candles.

Q: What was the inspiration for the story?

Mike: When Henry Selick and I came to the studio there was a young animator, Mike Berger, who had come up with the basic concept about a girl who lives on the moon. I believe that the studio had already completed an iteration of the idea in storyboards. In the original version the little girl fished for stars.

Q: So when you came on board, was the story written?

Mike: The inspiration was there, but Henry re-imagined it. Henry had the idea that the girl lived inside the moon and she regulated some kind of clock that lit the moon. And she had to battle creatures from the dark side of the moon. No one has ever seen the dark side of the moon so that gave us the opportunity to create some curiosity there. What lives there? What do they want? And Henry's idea was that there were these shadow creatures, the Gargaloons, who wanted to extinguish the light of the moon.

Q: So how do the fireflies come into the story?

Mike: Henry wanted this kid, Leon from the bayou, to bring fireflies to the moon. Fireflies are this magical source of light and they are the primary element needed to create moonlight.

Coincidently, I had never seen fireflies until about a year after we did the film. We don't have them on the West Coast. I was in Virginia when I saw them. At first I thought they were sparks in the air. I had no idea. I was blown away. The Virginians were just laughing at me.

So anyway, Leon likes to fish at night. He catches fireflies to use as bait. The fireflies catch the attention of this starry "delivery" catfish that brings Leon and his fireflies up to the moon where he discovers Moongirl and helps her fight the Gargaloons.

Q: How did you come up with the ending?

Mike: The ending of the story? Well, as we developed the story, we never really had an answer for what happens after the kids light the moon. How do they get along? Do they stay forever, happily ever after? What happens? I think it was during a brainstorming session that I came up with the "changing of the guard" idea where Moongirl's stint is done and Leon is left on the moon.

This could have been going on since the beginning of time. Select a kid with a light source and recruit them. This idea has a little bit of that fear element to it—which I think every good story should have—that you never know when it is your time to go to the moon. I don't think we thought about how distressing it would be for Leon's parents! I'm hoping he returned in good shape after a month or so.

Q: Either that, or all these kids across the Midwest are catching fireflies, just waiting to be taken to the moon.

Mike: Oh, yeah! You know after I saw *Close Encounters* I would sit out at night and flash flashlights at the stars to see if I could get aliens to come down and pick me up. It had to be better than elementary school on Earth. If the story has that effect on a kid, that is great.

Q: How much time was spent on the development of the story?

Mike: About six months.

Q: What was the preproduction pipeline like for this piece?

Mike: There was a small art department and they also ended up illustrating the book. There were two story artists, besides myself and we had a team that did the pre-viz, the sets, the test modeling and the rigging, once the character designs were finalized.

Q: How did you come up with the style for the piece?

Mike: Henry wanted the moon to be like a paper lantern, with a lighted carousel inside—like a lighthouse. He was obsessed with Fresnel lenses, which are these beautiful exquisitely crafted lenses that have all these facets and grooves. It is a bit of a nightmare for a lighting guy, but those objects dictated a lot of the look.

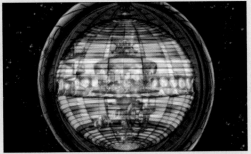

We also wanted the look to be illustrative. We looked at a lot of storybook illustrations to see if we could make it look like this, or look like that. It was one of the goals to make the film look a little more analog and less of what CG looked like at that point in time.

Q: What, if anything, changed in the story?

Mike: We tried a couple different approaches with the story. At one point, Moongirl was raising star babies in a star nursery inside the moon. Leon had to babysit. Both Henry and I had toddlers, and so we thought this would be funny, with it being very awkward for Leon, you know, for a young guy. But it skewed too juvenile and it became annoying with all these screaming star babies. So we went back to the drawing board.

You know a good story person will want to argue their point of view about a story. And those discussions can get pretty heated. I think a good director will listen to those opposing voices even if he doesn't like the idea. The discussion is sometimes an indication that something isn't working in the story. Most people don't realize that you're going to go through ten ideas to find the one good idea. And you're going to have to be willing to let those other nine go.

Q: How did this story get chosen for production at Laika? What was the value in producing a short for the studio?

Mike: The short was basically a move to see if Henry and the studio could work together on something short that wasn't too involved. And for me, I thought Portland was pretty awesome. The studio had all this stop-motion equipment and they were very eclectic with lots of really talented artists. I was curious what it would be like to work at this studio that had a little bit more artistic integrity than most.

And of course for the studio the short would be a calling card as well. They had done a lot of CG commercials at the time and wanted to set their sights a little higher, do something more theatrical and test their CG pipeline.

Q: What advice would you give someone who was planning their first film?

Mike: Test your story as many ways as you can to get it working. Use storyboards, pre-viz and just tell the story verbally. It will keep you and your team invested in the project.

Keep your ideas simple and the number of your locations and characters down to a minimum. You can always get bigger with your next effort!

The film Moongirl *can be viewed on the Laika website at www.laika.com.*

Chapter 3

Acting: Exploring the Human Condition

The Songs of Jacques Brel, Photo Courtesy of Florida Studio Theatre

The Kite by Gwynne Olson-Wheeler

Animators are actors. They create every nuance of a performance and breathe life into each character that they animate. The very essence of their art embodies the root of the word animation—*anima*, which in Latin means breath of life. Kathy Altieri, Production Designer at DreamWorks Feature Animation, explains it this way:

> When you're an artist, you have to feel and experience what you're trying to draw.
>
> For example, if I'm drawing a figure, I need to feel the weight of her hip on the chair. I need to feel the pull of her waist as she twists. It has nothing to do with the external shape, it has to do with sympathy for what the model is doing and feeling, and how that affects the line that comes out of my hand. In animation, it's all about getting the audience to feel a certain way. We do this

in every department, through music, lighting, color and line. The animator has us in his powerful grip. If he can *feel* what his character is feeling, he will communicate that through even the smallest movements his character performs. He quite literally becomes the actor portraying the role. The more fluent he becomes at acting himself, the better his character will communicate to us, the audience, and the more we will feel what we are supposed to feel at any given moment in the film.

Acting is truth. This is an adage in the acting world. It means that every moment in your story must be imbued with the emotional intensity of life itself. Whether you are creating a man, a child, a teapot or a lion, character is created by the pulse of true emotion. Like Geppetto breathing life into Pinocchio, you must bring the vividness of authentic emotion into your work. In this chapter you will learn how to create this truth in your work. You will learn a simple acting technique that will teach you:

- **How to develop a character's *inner* life:**
  - How thought creates emotion
  - How emotion creates gesture.
- **How to develop a character's *outer* life:**
  - How a character is further defined in the scene by specifically identifying the Objectives, Intentions, and Tactics.

Additionally, by studying the art of acting you will learn to:

- Use the tools of *Emotional Recall* and *The Magic If* to "get inside" your character and avoid creating cliché expressions and gestures

- Understand and create characters that are different from you, the animator.

Ultimately, by learning and using an acting technique during the animation process, you will be able to create believable characters that will capture and move your audience during every moment of your film.

ACTING I: TECHNIQUE

***Prelude to a Kiss*, Photo Courtesy of Florida Studio Theatre**

***The Dancing Thief*, by Meng Vue**

Building a Character

At the turn of the twentieth century, Russian actor Constantin Stanislavski—the father of modern acting—discovered how an actor could access human emotion and express it onstage to an audience. He found that when preparing to build a character one must first develop the *inner life*—the emotions, thoughts, and gestures—that makes that specific character become alive and real to the audience. Therefore, Stanislavski developed a method, called the *Theory of Psycho-Physical Action*, through which an actor could create the inner life, or emotional core, of any character by employing two elements:

- *The Psychological Mind*: The images in our brains that create emotion
- *The Physical Body*: The gestures and movements that reflect the images in the psychological mind.

By utilizing these two elements you will be able to think, feel, and move like your character; and eventually, you will be able to make stronger, emotionally active choices that reveal the character's development in your story.

We will begin the actor training process with exercises that focus on each element separately. We will then put the two elements—Psychological Mind and Physical Body—together, for then you will see why and how both must be present to create authentic characters.

Element 1: Exploring the Psychological Process

Fox Cry, by Gary Schumer

Proof, Photo Courtesy of Florida Studio Theatre

An actor must learn to create authentic emotion. The internal emotions are the underground current in the psyche that informs all the body's physical action. For example, when you feel good or happy, your body is open, loose, jaunty. You walk with a swing in your step and your voice has more music in it. When you are sad, every movement is heavier, slower and ponderous. You are burdened with your inner life. Psychology and movement are one. They are reflections of each other. A good actor learns how to create authentic emotion.

To create emotion, an actor can use the following techniques:

- *Emotional Recall*: recalling memories or past experiences
- *The Magic If*: imagining yourself in the given circumstances.

In this section you will learn which psychological technique you're comfortable with. Let's begin.

Images in the mind create emotion. Imagine that at any moment of the day there is a film in your mind that continuously runs and creates pictures. These pictures, in turn, create emotion.

Example #1: You broke up with your girlfriend or boyfriend. You're at a café having coffee with friends, but the whole time you're daydreaming about the past—when you first met, a gift they gave you, a special song you share. You begin to miss your ex terribly and can only sit there twirling your coffee spoon. In fact the whole day or week is spent recalling your relationship, the moments you shared with friends, the fear you feel telling people about the break up, the desire to call. Every moment of your life is imbued with these memories moving like a deep current under every action. The simple tasks you do, drinking coffee, doing homework, eating lunch seem to be burdened by the sadness of your inner conflict. This "current" of emotion created by the images of what we are thinking is called our inner life. Every character, every person has this inner life. It is the replaying of these memories, or the reel of film, in your mind that creates the flow of emotion.

The Magic If: imagining yourself in circumstances. The process of imagining an unknown experience is what Stanislavski called *The Magic If*. What would I do "if" I were in this circumstance? Like Emotional Recall, mental pictures or thoughts bring about the opportunity to explore The Magic If and empathetically experience the character's situation.

Example #2: Your character is a superhero and is frightened because he must jump off a building to rescue someone for the first time. You personally have never experienced a situation like this; however, you have experienced the emotion of fear. You must imagine everything you would see in this situation and how it would feel. *If* you stepped to the edge of a ledge and saw the street racing below, would your heart begin to race and your knees go weak? *If* you leaned forward and saw the great height from which you could fall would you begin to sweat or feel a sense of desperation?

Theater artists use and remember every moment of their lives whether it's the pride of a friend's graduation or the fear they have experienced walking down an unknown street at night. They remember every funny look someone gave them at a party, every surprised reaction in their life. They think, "I must remember this and use it!" They also spend time imagining what it's like to "walk in someone else's shoes."

A fantastic illustration of using one's personal life as the flesh and substance of art can be found in the true experience often humorously relayed in the classroom of Billy Merritt, a Pixar Animator from 1996 to 2006 and current faculty member at Ringling College of Art & Design.

I recall a day earlier in my career, while working on the film *Finding Nemo*, when I walked into a fellow animator's office to say hello and something strange struck me. Everywhere I looked, in all directions, there was a picture of his very recent ex-girlfriend. You couldn't turn your head without seeing her sublime face in a close up or the two of them together in happier times. I cautiously asked how he was, making small talk but the vibe was palpable. I nonchalantly backed out and ran over to another office saying, "Whoa, I think he's cracking up, we gotta get him outta there or something, there's pictures everywhere, it's not good."

My friend said not to worry, that he was working on that heavy scene when Marlin believes Nemo is dead and he's walking away from Dory, essentially breaking up their relationship. The scene for Marlon is about solitary grief and for Dory it's about parting ways and the loss of a person who makes you feel more complete. It's a truly beautiful scene inspired by honest emotion.

Similarly, actors continuously observe life around them. While in the park, they look at an elderly person sitting on a bench or a child at play and ask, "What would it be like to be them?" Even mischievous squirrels racing through the trees hold a particular fascination for the actor. For an actor, using images derived from Emotional Recall or The Magic If will unlock what a character is feeling in a specific situation.

The Actor's Toolbox: Generating Emotion

In the next few exercises you will explore both techniques: Emotional Recall and The Magic If. The exercises will help you learn how to generate authentic emotion. Sometimes Emotional Recall will serve you best to express a character. Sometimes it might be a better choice to use The Magic If or empathy. Sometimes both work. Now it's your turn to explore. You will need a chair and a quiet room. Afterwards, you can record your observations.

(*Special Note: view the companion website to see an example of these exercises in action.)

Exercise A: Generating the Emotion of Love. Sit in a chair and make yourself comfortable. Close your eyes and imagine someone you love. Pick an image of that person. You may use:

- *Emotional Recall*: the memory of a loved one
- *The Magic If*: an imagined future love.

Think of them specifically: the color of their hair, the way their lip curves, something they have said to you, and when you last saw them. Let the images get deeper within you. Let them flow. The images should create a flood of feelings for this person that you love. Observe these feelings.

Observe:

- How do these feelings move through your body?
- How does your heart feel?
- Does your pulse quicken?
- How does your face change? (the curve of your mouth, the muscles in your cheeks)
- How does this feeling affect your hands? Your feet?

Sample:

Feeling	Image	Sensations
Love	Grandmother	Flood of warmth; heart muscles relaxed

Record your impressions.

Feeling	Image	Sensations
Love		

Repeat this exercise focusing on the love of a different person—a grandfather, a child, a sister.

How do the feelings change or intensify within your body?

Exercise B: Generating the Emotion of Anger. Sit in a chair and make yourself comfortable. Close your eyes and imagine someone you have a conflict with. Just as in Exercise A, think of them specifically until you have a flood of feelings. Notice whether it's easier for you to use Emotional Recall, or The Magic If.

Observe:

- How do these feelings move through your body?
- How does your heart feel? (hurt or tight)
- Does your pulse quicken?
- How does your face change? (furrowed brow, muscle tension)
- How does this feeling affect your hands? Your feet?
- Do these feelings make you feel constricted? How do they affect your body?

Record your impressions.

Feeling	Image	Sensations
Anger		

Trying Out Other Emotions. Experiment with different feelings. There are many kinds of loneliness, many kinds of joy. Emotions, like the colors you choose on an artist's palette, have different shades. In addition, some artists have difficulty "naming" feelings and pinpointing individual emotions that translate to their Psycho-Physical work. For example, someone may say "I'm feeling bummed out" or "I feel low." But this general feeling has many *specific* expressions including loneliness, sorrow, or frustration. The good actor, the good artist, is very specific in her choices. Like an accomplished violinist or a painter, she can play an infinite amount of notes or combine an array of colors to achieve a fresh, authentic interpretation. By utilizing this exercise, you will learn to incorporate authentic emotion in your work and also name emotions that might be challenging for you to reach.

Record your impressions and remember to be specific with your images.

ACTING NOTEBOOK FOR ANIMATORS		
Feeling	**Image**	**Sensations**
Love		
Anger		
Loneliness		
Jealousy		
Embarrassment		
Fear		

The Actor Trap #1: Avoid Cliché!

Cliché Sad, Emotionally Filled Sad, with actress Christianne Greiert, Photos by Maria Lyle

New artists will sometimes show cliché emotions. For example, when asked to portray an emotion, they will smile widely to show happy, or they will frown deeply to show sad. Using oversimplified external expressions that are crudely portrayed will not convey emotion. The result? A generic and empty character who will not impact your audience. Always infuse your character with authentic emotion.

Building a Character: Applying the Psychological Process

Grimmy **by Mike Peters**

You now know how to access an authentic feeling using Emotional Recall or The Magic If. Now, apply it to a character that you are developing. Whether the character is a vengeful chair, a rambunctious bull, or even Hamlet:

- Find the moment you want to express
- Use your acting technique to feel the corresponding emotion
- Observe how the emotion affects you
- Transpose this emotion to the character.

For example, an actor is studying Hamlet. He knows that Hamlet is consumed by revenge due to the wrongful death of his father. However, the actor has never experienced the death of his own father. How does he emotionally connect to Hamlet? Instead of playing the amateur idea of Hamlet as a crazy mad-man, the actor looks at each moment in the play and identifies what Hamlet is feeling. Then, by using Emotional Recall and The Magic If, he chooses images from his own life so that he can relate to the character's specific emotional moments. Thus, he can begin to fathom the depth of Hamlet's pain.

Remember—be *specific* to the moment that you want to express.

- Amateurs—project generalized feelings that do not correspond to the moment
- Trained Professionals—convey feelings specific to the moment.

Element 2: Exploring the Physical Gesture

Ethel Waters: His Eye is on the Sparrow,
Photo Courtesy of Florida Studio Theatre

A Great Big Robot from Outer Space Ate
My Homework, by Mark Shira

The body is the counterpart of the mind. Whether we are gently combing our hair or slamming a door, every physical gesture we express *reflects* our emotional state. For example, a first-time offender on trial who is trying to appear calm but nervously taps his pencil reveals the truth of how worried and anxious he is, whereas the physical expression of a hardened criminal who methodically taps his pencil, perhaps biding time as he awaits his expected sentence, reveals a different emotional state. In turn, a first-time father who is trying to appear calm while nervously tapping his pencil in a hospital waiting room, is also anxious, but in a completely different way. Yet in all instances, the physical gesture of tapping the pencil is colored by the emotional state of the character. The great Charlie Chaplin knew and embodied this principle whether he was holding out a flower for his love or stepping out of the way from being run over by a car. Emotion and physicality are intertwined. One cannot exist without the other.

Emotion, like a current of electricity, informs every gesture—every movement of the body. Using what we have learned in Element 1, you will now carry out exercises designed to explore how emotion *influences* the body. You will need a chair and a book.

The Actor's Toolbox: Exploring Physicality

Exercise A: Exploring the Physicality of Love. Sit in a chair and make yourself comfortable. Hold the book. Using Emotional Recall or empathy, select an image of someone you love. Again, think of them specifically: the color of their hair, the way their lip curves, something they have said to you, and when you last saw them. Let the images get deeper within you. Let them flow. The images should create a flood of feelings for this person. Observe these feelings.

(*Special Note: view the companion website to see an example of these exercises in action.)

Observe yourself while sitting in the chair. How does your body feel in that chair? (languid, relaxed, comfortable).

Pick a gesture:

- Curl your hair.
- Tap your foot.
- Twist a necklace.

Explore the tension in your muscles. Observe the tempo of your tapping.

Now, *rise and walk across the room*, carrying the book with you.

Explore how these feelings inform how you carry the book. Is the book held closely? Gingerly?

Observe your walk. How do you walk? Long strides or short? Dreamy or slow?

Observe how relaxed or excited you are.

Sample:

Feeling	Image	Sensations	Physical Gestures
Love	Grandmother	I feel a flood of warmth; heart muscles are relaxed.	I hold the book tenderly. The curve of my hand is relaxed. I slowly leaf through the pages.

Record your impressions.

Feeling	Image	Sensations	Physical Gestures
Love			

Exercise B: Exploring the Physicality of Anger. Sit in a chair and make yourself comfortable. Hold the book. Using Emotional Recall or empathy, think of an image that makes you angry. When you have a flood of feelings, begin to observe your physicality.

Observe yourself while sitting in the chair. How tense is your body?

Pick a gesture:

- Curl your hair.
- Tap your foot.
- Read a book.

Explore the tension in your muscles. Observe the tempo of the tapping.

How does it differ from love? Does the tap change into a stomp?

Observe how you hold the book. Do you grip it? What do your fingers feel like?

Now, *rise and walk across the room with the book.* Observe how the feelings of anger inform how you carry the book. Is the book held closely? Do you throw the book down?

Observe your walk. How do you walk? Long strides or short? What is the tempo?

Observe your posture. Is it tense? Slumped?

Record your impressions.

Feeling	Image	Sensations	Physical Gestures
Anger			

Trying Out Other Physicalities. Try out other movements and gestures. As we discussed, there are many kinds of feelings and each informs the body in a different way. Observe yourself in your daily life. Observe your mood and how it is reflected in your gestures at the checkout counter, walking to class, or taking a test. By incorporating this exercise you will learn to inform the physical characters you create with the specific emotional reality of their situation.

Try sitting at your desk and writing a letter to someone you are:

- Excited about
- Fearful about
- Hurt by
- Worried for.

Try pacing in the doctor's office waiting room while feeling:

- Bored
- Anxious
- Frustrated.

Record your impressions and remember to be specific with your images.

ACTING NOTEBOOK FOR ANIMATORS			
Feeling	**Image**	**Sensations**	**Physical Gestures**
Love			
Anger			
Loneliness			
Jealousy			
Embarrassment			
Fear			

Actor Trap #2: Only Using One Element Results in False Acting

Image without a Gesture, Gesture without an Image, Image and Gesture, with actress Christianne Greiert, Photos by Adam D. Martens

Often new actors will mistakenly use only one element, either psychological or physical, which will result in "false" acting. They will solely portray an emotion without any physicality, or only show a physical gesture without emotion. For example, if a director instructs a student to "act scared" and then he or she chooses to act "scared" by shaking their body nervously and bugging out their eyes, the performance will be a cliché of acting—an empty shell. (This should not be confused with comic caricature.) Again, bad actors *represent* emotion. Good actors know how to incorporate Stanislavski's Psycho-Physical technique, use both Elements, and *recreate authentic* characters using *emotion* and *gesture*.

A Note About Character

In Chapter 4 you will begin working intensively with *character*. The character design is a shell that must be informed by many elements including: education, culture, upbringing, personality, age, gender and more. Actors call this the *mask*. More importantly, remember that the emotional state is *filtered* through this shell (mask) of character. Therefore, how a character will react in a given situation is determined by their personal traits and emotions. For example, if a character is frightened, it will be expressed differently if the character is:

- A seventeenth-century French Countess who may have "learned emotions" and will not reveal anything that is not acceptable. Even her gestures are prescribed.

- A twentieth-century immigrant in Miami.

- A twenty-first-century teenager who tries to look "cool" and be aloof because she is afraid to show any real feelings.

Building a Character: Applying the Physical Process

***Grimmy* by Mike Peters**

You now know how to access an authentic physicality that is connected to your emotions. Now, apply it to a character that you are developing. Whether the character is a princess, a teapot, or even Ophelia:

- Find the moment you want to express

- Use your acting technique to feel the corresponding emotion

- Apply that emotion to your body

- Transpose the Psycho-Physical knowledge to the character.

For example, an actress is studying Ophelia. She knows that Ophelia is consumed by the deaths of her father and brother, Polonius and Laertes. However, the actress has never experienced death of this magnitude. In one particular scene Ophelia is throwing imaginary flowers on her father's grave. How does the actress emotionally connect to Ophelia doing this action? Instead of playing the amateur idea of Ophelia as a crazy young girl (running around wide-eyed), the actress looks at each moment in the play and identifies what Ophelia is feeling. In this specific moment, the actress discovers that Ophelia is sad as she remembers her father. She then explores how this specific emotion moves through her body and finds her movement to be languid and deliberate because she is reflecting on this loss. Thus, she throws the flowers slowly and deliberately onto the grave.

Whether your character is a chipmunk, a boy, or Buzz Lightyear, the emotions and physical manifestation of those emotions through the character's body must be true to capture the audience's attention. James McMullen, visual artist, grappled with just these challenges as he was developing the poster art for a new play, *Ten Unknowns* by Jon Robin Baitz. Using himself as the model to get to the emotion was not satisfying. He could not capture the essence of the play and character he intuitively knew he wanted.

To show how a visual artist moves beyond cliché, we only need to look at an excerpt from McMullan's biographical blog, *The Road to "Ten Unknowns,"* where he outlined his creative process. Unsatisfied with crude models and general conceptions, he went straight to the actor, whose presence exploded his imagination.

> I took the easel over to the theater and showed Sutherland my sketch. He said that he understood my idea and would give me a couple of variations. His variations were so full of a great actor's physical imagination and sense of what his face and body could project that I knew, watching his changes through my camera's viewfinder, that he was giving me the basis for a whole new kind of image. In place of the somewhat generalized melancholy of the figure in my sketch he was giving me a specific man, a heroic figure saddened by circumstance.

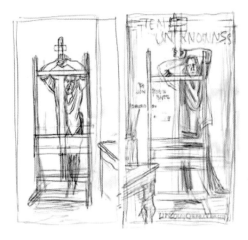 

Sketches and Final Publicity Poster of *Ten Unknowns* by James McMullen

ACTING II: TECHNIQUE

Exploring Scene Work

Metamorphosis, **Photo Courtesy of Florida Studio Theatre**   *Catch* **by Chris Perry**

Now that we have explored how to create emotion and gesture in a character, we will begin to place that character in a scene. *The essential elements of a scene in acting are as follows: Objectives, Intentions, and Tactics.*

- The *Objective/Goal* is what the character ultimately wants.
- The *Intentions* are the different ways the character tries to achieve the objective.
- The *Tactics* are the active choices the character uses in concert with the intentions.

We only need to look at life around us to understand scene work. As Shakespeare said, "All the world's a stage." Every day we live in dialogue and action. For example, suppose two sisters, Ashley and Christi, had an argument in their bedroom. Ashley storms out of the room while Christi remains sitting on the bed. Now, Ashley wants to end the argument and heal the relationship with her sister. That is her Objective. Ashley tentatively walks back into the room approaching Christi. Ashley's Intention is to make up. Her Tactics are the ways she attempts make up. Her first tactic is to stand at the door and look longingly at her sister, hoping for a response. Her second tactic will be to gently cross to her sister and put a hand on her shoulder. Finally, her third is to give Christi a hug and ask, "Will you forgive me?" Ashley has used physical action and language in concert with her intention, to make up. And if Christi turns around and hugs her, we've reached a resolution.

Similarly, we can find specific examples of these elements in scenes from animation. In *Up,* Carl's objective is to have control of his life and keep the memories of his wife intact. His Intention is to stay in his home, but when it is threatened the Tactic he uses to achieve his objective is to build a balloon.

The Actor Notebook for the scene with Ashley and Christi would read as follows:

Objective/Goal	To heal relationship
Intentions	To make up
Tactics	Entreat; move closer; ask
Actions	Enter the room; touch sister's shoulder; hug her sister

Keep in mind that the *tactics you choose are a reflection of the character*. For instance, the tactics in the previous scene change if:

- Ashley is a confident, headstrong 19-year-old girl
- Ashley is a quiet, shy, and needy person.

The use of these essential elements *gives your scene purpose and heightens the conflict*. Occasionally, characters are in accord and struggle for the same goal, just as when Woody and the toys band together to save Buzz. On the other hand, when the Queen seduced Snow White into eating the poisoned apple, each character was struggling for something different and were clearly at odds. Every film, play, or animated short uses scenes just like this to tell a story, and thereby builds the conflict to reach a dynamic conclusion—the resolution.

Developing Intentions and Objectives in the Dialogue and Action

The dialogue of the characters must be imbued with the character's Objectives and Intentions. As the great acting teacher Sonia Moore said, "The words are like toy boats on the water." Think of every important moment in your life. Did the words ever convey the depth of your feelings? Think of the final goodbye you said to a friend or your first break up. Underneath the words are the emotional currents— the intentions, needs, goals, and desires, as expressed through the silent actions of the characters. One of the delights of the animated short is the minimal use of language. Yet, while the dialogue of a scene is usually simple, it is important to remember that the words only become powerful when they are forged with authentic emotions.

The objective, intentions, and tactics give the language its meaning and context. To learn about how an intention clarifies the language, let's look at this sample scene with the assigned characters of A and B. You can view this work on the companion website titled *Acting: Exploring the Human Condition*, but first, read the scene without any inflection.

A. Hi.
B. Hi.
A. Are you okay?
B. Yeah.
A. Really?
B. Yeah.
A. Well, I'll call you later.
B. Bye.
A. Bye.

At first glance this is a "nonsense" scene. It doesn't really make sense, yet it feels slightly familiar because of the usage of common conversational words such as "Hi" and "Bye." However, we don't have any context for the scene so we don't really know what the characters are talking about.

Impose an objective/goal on the scene to create meaning. Let's say that Partner A's objective is to make up with Partner B. Partner A is in love with Partner B. They had a fight. Partner A wants to make up and Partner B does too. Now, using what you learned about emotional recall or empathy read the scene out loud or with a partner.

Objective #1: To make up

Result: You can probably feel how emotionally connected the two characters are. We have all felt this. The two characters are in agreement and a resolution is reached.

Write Down Your Result:

Read the scene again and change the objectives.

- Partner A will choose *to make up.*
- Partner B will choose *to reject.*

Notice how the change in Partner B's objective will affect the whole tenor of the script. Let's call this scene "The Break-Up."

Objective #2: Partner A's objective is to make up. Partner B's objective is to reject the offer.

Result: You will hear a completely different reading of the same scene as the objectives and intentions infuse the text with the emotional truth of the relationships. (See website.)

Write Down Your Result:

IMPROVISATION

Mark Shira and his character from *A Great Big Robot from Outer Space Ate My Homework*

I can't stress enough how acting out the scenes and filming myself on a web cam helped . . . it is so helpful in getting both the broad strokes as well as subtleties of performance.

—Mark Shira

The creation of something new is not accomplished by the intellect but by the play instinct.

—Carl Jung

Improvisation is unscripted, uninhibited play to discover something "new." When actors need to find the reality of a scene, explore a character's motivation, work out an ending, or even when they are stuck, they rely on Improvisation. Improvising a scene helps you get at its heart, for it can move you beyond the current limits of your imagination into new territory. Also, by freeing themselves from restrictions in the script and playing with the intentions and actions, the actor will discover unique gestures and movement choices that are particular to their character. Steve Smith, Director of the Big Apple Circus, author and lecturer says, "I use improvisation all the time. It gives adults permission to play; to get into the sandbox and discover and uncover the six-year-old inside of them—the innocence and naiveté that is the fountainhead of creativity. It is the truth."

- When Improvising, remember to use your Objectives, Intentions, and Actions.

- Let yourself be unedited as you explore the story. Kick. Stomp the floor. Giggle too loud. Cry. Experience rage. You can only discover something new if you move past your limits.

- Remember that self-consciousness is antithetical to the creative process. If you get embarrassed (like Mark Shira), stop for a moment and record that process as an emotional recall memory in your Actor Notebook.

THE ICONIC MOMENT

Fantasia Taurina by Alejandra Pérez Gonzalez

Study of Degas' Absinthe by Gary Schumer

The Iconic Moments are the important storytelling images in the scene. They are emotionally heightened because they are at once natural and familiar to the audience. They are moments that lift the audience out of the ordinary and say, "Life is important. Each moment is important. Look." We participate in these moments every day of our lives. We only have to look around us. It is:

- The mother brushing her child's hair
- A young son glancing back at his father before he leaves home for the first time
- Lovers parting and couples waving hello
- The greeting of long-lost brothers
- A mother carrying her dead child in war
- The teen behind the wheel of his first car.

We also see Iconic Moments in film, animation, and art. The opening moments of *Up* when Carl is looking through his photo albums is a powerful example because he is viewing the iconic moments of his life. Other familiar images include:

- A woman alone at a table in Degas' *Absinthe*
- Rafiki holding up a newborn babe
- Bambi screaming for his mother
- Shrek and Donkey sitting under the moon
- Rodin's sculpture *The Thinker.*

The *Iconic Moments* in the following scene can be viewed on the website, titled *Acting: Exploring the Human Condition*. The actors have improvised the scene that we called "The Break-Up." Look closely at the scene and find their iconic moments. We have chosen seven. They are as follows:

1. The Anticipation

2. Seeking Comfort

3. The Look

4. The Rejection

5. The Reach (Entreaty)

6. The Crisis

7. The Disconnect (Resolution) with actors Brooke Wagstaff and Adam Ratner

Choosing the Iconic Moments is important to your story because:

- You identify what is necessary and important to the scene
- You condense the story to a feasible time period
- You identify the *must-have* images for the audience.

Improvise your scene and choose your Iconic Moments. When you complete your scene concept, improvise it fully and freely many times over. Remember:

- Use Objectives/Goals, Tactics, and Actions that are forged with the emotional reality of the scene
- The scene will most likely be long and formless
- Step back and look at the scene as an observer
- Identify the iconic moments: the important storytelling images.

Soon you will find the shape of your animated short and be able to move it from a generic, free-form story to the artfulness of a universal tale.

IN CONCLUSION

***The Kite* by Gwynne Olson-Wheeler**

Acting is truth. It calls upon the artist to create the specific emotions of a character in the moment that are honest and true. Whether your character is a penguin, a rat, a tomato, or a Prince, they are imbued with *anima*—the breath of life of the human condition. Through the study of acting, the animator can access important tools to breathe a vital emotional and physical dimension into their characters.

First, by employing the Stanislavski technique of Psycho-Physical Action we learned that:

- Images create emotion
- The physical body—its movement and gesture—are a reflection of one's inner feelings and emotion.

Moreover, in order to build an authentic character we must use the acting technique to discover:

- How a character truly *feels* moment to moment
- How a character *moves* moment to moment.

Thus, we come to the realization that both the mind and body must be employed to make a character come alive. And remember, a cliché gesture does not really express the character's feelings and does not generate empathy from the audience.

Second, the essential elements for Scenes are as follows:

- Objectives/Goals
- Intentions
- Tactics/Actions
- Resolution.

The characters must want something with their heart and soul. They then work to get it by using their tactics until there is a resolution.

Finally, Improvisation will help you get on your feet, think outside of the box, and discover new ways that a character might behave. And, as a finishing touch, the Iconic Moments will shape the piece so that it is accessible and familiar to the audience.

Acting is truth. It is the exploration of the human condition in all its authentic joys and sorrows. Your characters will become vivid and unforgettable when infused with this concept at every given moment in your script. By learning the art of acting, your characters will be able to better communicate to us, the audience, and the more we will feel what we are supposed to feel at any given moment in the film.

Summary

- Capture "true" emotion that is authentic and specific to the moment.

- Use the Psycho-Physical technique.

- Psychological Process: Images in the mind create emotion. Use Emotional Recall and Empathy to remember a personal experience or find an emotional connection to others by asking: "What if . . ."

- Physical Gestures inform the audience of the character's emotional state.

- Avoid Cliché: generalized emotion that is not specific to the moment robs your characters of emotional truth.

- Mask/Shell: decisions regarding culture, upbringing, or personality that will determine how much of a character's emotional core is revealed.

- Scene work involves three essential elements: Objectives, Intentions, and Tactics.

- Emotion infuses gesture, which infuses your Intentions and Tactics.

- Dialogue must be imbued with the character's Objectives and Intentions.

- Improvisation is unscripted, uninhibited play to discover something "new."

- Iconic Moments are the important story telling images in the scene.

- Acting is truth: the portrayal of a character that is true to the depth of the emotional reality they are trying to express.

Recommended Reading

1. Ed Hooks, *Acting for Animators, Revised Edition: A Complete Guide to Performance in Animation*

2. Keith Johnstone, *Impro for Storytellers*

3. Charles McGaw, *Acting is Believing: A Basic Method*

4. Sonia Moore, *Training an Actor: The Stanislavski System in Class*

5. Viola Spolin, *Improvisation for the Theatre*

6. Constantin Stanislavski, *An Actor Prepares*

The Importance of Play: An Interview with Jack Canfora, Playwright

"Play" is essential in idea and story development. It is never too soon to begin to improv your initial script, talk out your story, generate options, try things on and throw things out—allow for happy accidents to occur. In the interview below, Jack Canfora shares some of his ideas about the importance of play.

Jack Canfora is a playwright whose award-winning and critically acclaimed plays have been read and performed throughout the United States and England since 2001. *Place Setting* was named one of the best plays of 2007 by the *New Jersey Star-Ledger*. *Poetic License* recently finished an acclaimed run Off-Broadway at 59E59 Theaters. *Jericho* was named a winner of the 2010 National New Play Network. In addition to his plays his comedy writing has been seen in Greenwich Village and on the main stage of the world famous comedy club "Caroline's."

Q: What role does "play" have in the development of your ideas?

Jack: When you're playing, if you're doing it well, you're hopefully open to things. Ideas that leap into your head, and actions and words from other people. Play is our way of understanding ourselves and the world, which is of course why children do it so often and are so good at it. It's our point of entry to understanding the world and ourselves in the world. So how could play *not* be the central factor in developing ideas?

Q: When should "play" start? When does it begin with you?

Jack: I think it *is* the start. I was trained in improvisational acting, and a lot of its tenets are excellent guides for creative endeavors in general. There's a rule in improv, for example, that you can't say "no" while you're doing a scene. That's not to say you can never abandon an idea that isn't playing out, but you have to follow each impulse, without reservation and judgment, until it's been given a chance to grow and assert itself. Self-consciousness has no place in the creative act—it has a vital role, of course, in redrafting and editing, which are essential components of the finished product, but in the moment of creating, you need to be open to anything and everything as long as it feels natural and fun. Which is kind of the heart of "playing."

Q: When you are building a narrative, how does play help in the investigation of that story?

Jack: It's actually how I discover the narrative. For me, I think it's essential to be incredibly kind to yourself and non-judgmental when you're writing.

Don't second guess. There'll be plenty of time for that later, when you're editing, when I would argue you need to be nothing short of ruthless with yourself. But when building the narrative, discovering what shape it wants to take, what its textures are, that's hard to do unless you're committed to the idea of playing around it with it.

Playing is another way of saying being open to possibilities, and that's the only I way I can find out what I'm writing about.

Q: What is the role of an "accident" in your play?

Jack: Huge. There's a sharp difference between creating and editing; the two together equal writing, but they're in many ways antithetical on their own. Accidents are what you hope for; there's no other way to discover what's interesting and memorable without it in my experience. The crafting/editing is essential, but that's *later*. It's important not to let that contaminate the fertile period which is the creating part. You (hopefully) are always open for bringing creativity into all you do, but it's important to keep the self-conscious, self-editing process *out* while you're creating. Because then you are prone not to make mistakes, which is the same as saying you're prone to staying predictable and uninteresting.

Q: Anything else you would like to say?

Jack: Be a magpie. Take as much as you can in from everywhere and everything. And don't be afraid to cross-pollinate ideas/genres/techniques.

Illustration by Karen Sullivan, Ringling College of Art and Design

Chapter 4
Building Character and Location

Stories are about people. The people (toys, fish, aliens, cars, dragons, etc.) are the characters through which the story is told. The story belongs to the character. Without a good character you don't have a story.

Character Explorations for *Defective Detective*, by Avner Geller and Stevie Lewis, Ringling College of Art and Design

WHAT IS A GOOD CHARACTER?

A good character is one that is both believable and memorable.

A believable character is an ordinary character (in relation to the world that he lives in) who finds himself in extraordinary circumstances and *reacts* to those circumstances truthfully.

A memorable character has the ability to move an audience emotionally through the events of the story. It is a character that elicits a *reaction from the audience*.

Appeal is something different. Appeal refers to the visual design of the character. Ollie Johnston and Frank Thomas originally coined the term *appeal* in their book, *The Illusion of Life*. To them, appeal meant that "your eye is drawn to a character and you appreciate what you are seeing."[1] You immediately identify with the character. The character can be beautiful or ugly, intricate or plain, good or bad. The character's appeal makes you *want to watch* and find out more about him.

An appealing design is complemented by a captivating personality. A good character is imbedded with strong personality traits with which an audience can identify. These traits are constructed to either aid or impede the character in the pursuit of his goal. As you watch and get to know more about the character, he engages you. You begin to hope for the character's success or failure. At each event in the story, the emotional investment becomes greater.

A good character is one that is right for the story.

CHARACTER PROFILES

A good character is also a character that you understand. Knowing your character well allows you to construct believable reactions to conflicts faced in the story. These reactions are what will move your audience through the story. To engage the audience, you need a fully developed character.

What does that mean? In films there are many types of characters. There are main characters, supporting characters, opposing characters, minor characters, and extras. The term *flat* is often used to describe minor characters or extras. As an audience we don't get to know them very well. They are singular in both function and emotion. Sometimes they are more like props used to move the story forward. Main characters are fully developed. We engage with them because they have a history complete with a full range of emotion, strengths, weaknesses, idiosyncrasies, and faults.

In feature films, character development is called a *back story*. A back story is an extensive biography of the character. It includes everything from physical attributes, education, professional history, family, relationships, lifestyle, and hobbies to past diseases, disorders, strengths, weaknesses, fears, and phobias to a myriad of other traits that determine a character's success or failure in a situation.

For the short we just don't need to know that much. There is not much time, in the few minutes your film will last, for deep character development. Instead, your audience needs to know immediately—within the first ten seconds of your film—who your character is and what he wants. As the animator, you need to know a bit more to progress the story. But what you need to know can be limited to a few major traits determined by the following definitive questions:

1. What is your character's ethical perspective? Ethics are the means by which we make decisions. Knowing—or assigning—an ethical baseline to your character will help you keep him consistent in the way that he approaches conflict. Paul Lester, author of *Visual Communication*, outlines six ethical baselines:

    a. *Categorical Imperative.* This character would have a strong sense of justice. Right is right and wrong is wrong.

    b. *Utilitarianism.* This character believes in the greatest good for the greatest number of people. The focus is on consequences. He would sacrifice one life to save many.

    c. *Hedonism.* This is the pleasure principle. This character just wants to have fun. He is selfish.

    d. *Golden Mean.* This character compromises and negotiates. He will try to find the middle ground to reach a peaceful agreement.

    e. *Golden Rule.* Do unto others as you would have them do unto you. This character has empathy and compassion.

    f. *Veil of Ignorance.* This character blissfully goes through life wearing rose-colored glasses. Everything is good, everyone is equal.[2]

2. Is the character dominated by emotion or logic?

3. What is his greatest strength?

a. What might help him in the face of his conflict?

4. What is his flaw?

   a. A Hero will be flawed, but the flaw will be redeemable.

   b. A Villain is fatally flawed. Whatever is flawed will be his downfall.

   c. What would be something that would be an impediment to your character's success?

5. How does he see himself?

6. How is he seen by others?

7. What is this biggest secret?

   a. What is at stake for the character?

8. What does the character want?

9. How far will the character go to get what he wants?

10. What does the character need to learn?

These questions build what is called *a character profile*. The character profile forms the personality of the character. It is best if these questions are answered with the story and story conflicts in mind. Then you can construct a character that meets the conflicts and drives the story in the way that you intend.

Let's look at a possible profile for Chunk, the main character of the short *The Animator and the Seat.*

Concept: There are no breaks during crunch time.

Premise: An overworked, tired animator wants to take a break, but is forced back to work by an unexpected authority.

Chunk:

1. Ethical Perspective: Golden Mean.

2. He is dominated by emotion.

3. Greatest Strength: Chunk usually has an unwavering work ethic, incredible talents and the ability to sound cooler than he really is.

4. Flaw: He is bored with his job.

5. He sees himself as complacent and law abiding.

6. He is seen by others as weak, but a great workhorse. He will go the extra mile to get a project done.

7. Biggest secret: He has decided he needs a change in employment.

8. What does the character want? A break.

9. How far will the character go to get what he wants? Not very far. He is a pushover. He is extremely excitable when faced with physical threat. He will use all of his willpower to avoid a physical situation and will give in rather than fight.

10. What does the character need to learn? There are no breaks during crunch time.

Chunk by Eric Drobile, Ringling College of Art and Design

Chunk is an animator who starts to take a break, only to be forced back to work by his chair. His chair has clearly been charged with the task of keeping him in his place—working.

The Animator and the Seat, **by Eric Drobile, Ringling College of Art and Design**

The character profile makes sense when put in relationship to the story and how the character emotionally reacts to the situation in which he finds himself. If your profile doesn't help your character progress through the story, then you need to change your profile or change your story. Don't think of the profile as something that is set in stone. Think of it as a working document that can be refined as you go through the story development process and learn more about your character(s). Characters are constructed. Their personality traits may need adjustment for the good of the story.

Note that the profile defines internal character traits. This is because there is a difference between character and characterization. When most people begin to define characters, they talk about physical traits, occupations or hobbies. This is characterization. What really defines a character—and why we watch—is to see how he reacts under pressure. Two characters might have the same build, work at the same company, like the same girl and drink the same coffee from Starbucks, but can react very differently when the Starbucks they are at is robbed. One might confront the robber while the other one flees. This is when we see what the true character is made of and, from this, what life lesson he/we might learn.

WORKING WITH TWO OR MORE CHARACTERS

***Gopher Broke*, directed by Jeff Fowler, Blur Studios**

When working with two or more characters, there is additional information you need to add to the profiles:

1. *What is the relationship of your characters?* Characters have relationships. Did they just meet or do they have a history? Are they strangers, acquaintances, friends, foes, family members, lovers, siblings, enemies? How do they feel toward each other? How does that affect the way they act in the story?

2. *What is the status of each character?* Status is defined by how much power you wield in a relationship. The power in a relationship is negotiable. We negotiate status all of the time. In a restaurant the customer is of higher status than the waiter. It is the job of the waiter to serve the customer. But that power shifts if you ask the waiter for a recommendation. Characters will negotiate power by being aggressive, passive, pleasing, assertive, or manipulative. Who has the power in your story and how is it negotiated with the other character(s)?

3. *What do they want from each other?* This is slightly different from the original question, "What does the character want?" In *Gopher Broke*, all of the characters want the same thing. They want vegetables. The gopher wants the other characters to leave the vegetables alone. After all, he has done all the work. The other characters simply don't care. In fact, they are willing to threaten and fight the gopher for the vegetables. This defines the relationship between the gopher and the other characters and becomes the primary conflict.

4. *Who is the story about?* This may seem obvious, but frequently when there are two strong characters, you sometimes lose sight of whose story you are telling. Make sure that you keep it clear who the main character really is. Often the main character is the one who arcs—or learns—the most.

CHARACTER ARCS

A character arc is the transformation of the character(s) through the course of the story.

In *Gopher Broke*, the gopher starts out clever and hopeful as he digs holes to dislodge vegetables from the produce truck. As his efforts are continually foiled and his frustration rises, he buries the vegetable sign causing a huge crash and ultimately his own demise.

In *The Animator and the Seat*, Chunk begins the story as a bored, overworked employee looking for a break. In a bizarre occurrence, his chair refuses to let him leave and he ends up trapped, despondent, and still working.

Character arcs can be:

- Physical: life to death, rich to poor, fat to thin, weak to strong, drunk to sober
- Mental: sane to crazy, foolish to wise, naive to enlightened, confusion to clarity, forgetful to remembering, positive to critical
- Spiritual: bad to good, wrong to right, stingy to generous, out of love to in love, nonbeliever to believer, intolerant to tolerant, revenge to forgiveness.

All transformations include an *emotional* arc. There cannot be a transformation in character without a corresponding transformation in emotion. Determine how your character changes and identify the emotional arc in your story.

In terms of design, determine if there are any physical attributes that change as the character arcs. This would give you the ability to express the arc in the design of the character. This is the Pinocchio principle. In the beginning, Pinocchio has a small nose. The more he lies, the bigger his nose gets until he learns his lesson. This is not something that is necessary; it is just a possibility that is often overlooked.

CHARACTER DESIGN

A well-designed character has the following characteristics:

- It will be immediately recognizable and relatable.
- It will be have a recognizable shape or silhouette.
- It will reflect the personality of the character.
- It will have physical attributes that complement the content of the story.
- It will be able to complete the actions that are required by the script.
- It will be interesting to watch.

Searching for the right gopher. Sean McNally character design sheets for *Gopher Broke*, Blur Studios

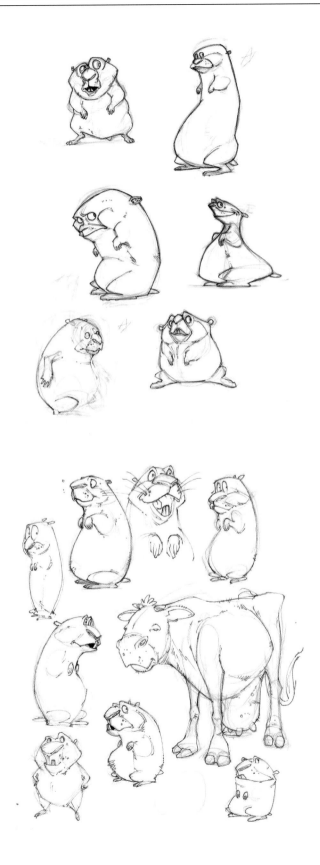

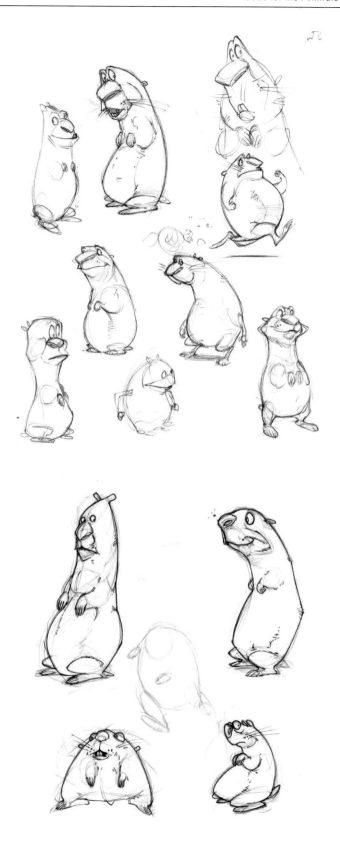

Recognizable and Relatable

In the animated short, we need to set up the story, tell the story, and get out. There is precious little time to get to know your character. Therefore it helps if we understand the character's personality and function the first time we see him. If your character is a weird part-alien, part-human, part-machine creature, we need to know immediately if we are for or against him, if we like him or hate him, how he works and why. If this isn't clear you will either lose your audience or waste time trying to explain the character. The point is to engage your audience, and to construct empathy, concern or at least curiosity about the character as soon as possible in the story.

Shape

Shapes have inherent meaning. Circles are organic, cyclical and innocent. Squares are human-made and solid. Inverted triangles are strong (think of the chest on a superhero). Upright triangles have a lower center of gravity. They can be subordinate, complacent or content (think of the nerdy scientist). Sharp angles and diagonals are dynamic suggesting tension or danger.

Most characters are constructed from a combination of basic shapes. The relationship of the shapes to each other will determine the visual interest that your character will command. The goal is to have a nice contrast of size, shape, and proportions that will express the personality of the character and meet the needs of the story. If you have more than one character, you want each one to have visibly distinctive traits. You will need to put them in contrast to each other, each made out of different combinations of shapes, proportions, exaggerations, and details.

For example, in *The Triplets of Belleville*, Sylvain Chomet created distinctly different and geometric figures:

Of the characters, many have geometric silhouettes because it is a silent movie. The characters cannot be recognized by their voices. So when they are far away or even when they appear in a scene very fast we need to know, okay, that is this character. So the audience doesn't get too confused. So when they see something that looks very small like a yogurt pot, they know it is Madame Souza and an enormous square-ish character in black, they know it is the Mafia. This is also something you can do with animation which you cannot do with live action.

The characters are quite convincing because of their shape and also probably because they have lives on their own. They have a story and they are just like us—they live, they suffer, they exist, they can get hurt, and they are so natural.[3]

Mme. Souza in Belleville. Sylvain Chomet, *Triplets of Belleville*

Mme. Souza in Belleville. Sylvain Chomet, *Triplets of Belleville*

When you begin a character, begin by thinking in shapes. Style and details can come later. What are the basic shapes that communicate the essence of your character?

Personality and Function

After you have identified the basic shapes for your character, it will need to be pushed further. Why? Whether you're designing a gopher, a computer animator, a grandmother, or a robot—there are hundreds of similar designs out there. Your character will be generic unless you express their unique personality and style.

The best character designs have personality. They pop off the page. You'd love to meet them. So how do you do that? Achieving personality means combining two things: originality and function.

To make a character original, you need to look closely at its character profile. Who are they and what makes them unique as a character? Find this trait and exaggerate it in the design. If your character is a great intellectual, exaggerate the cranium. Give him a big forehead. If your character is a habitual eavesdropper, give him big ears. If a gopher is highly optimistic but slow, give him big eyes, but a heavy lower body. Define what visual attributes are necessary to effectively tell your story.

Sometimes these attributes are defined by what characters have to *do* in the story. What they have to do gives cues to their visual design. In *The Incredibles*, Elastigirl is not just an interesting design for a superhero; she stretches because she is a mother and must always multitask. Dash is fast because he is a little boy with so much pent-up energy. Violet disappears and has a protective shield because she is in adolescence. Elastigirl is organic and loose in the joints. Dash is solid, low to the ground with strong legs. Violet is slim and has hair that perpetually hangs over her large and watchful eyes.

Another way to find a unique character design is to look at the characters' goals and the conflicts that they must confront. In *The Triplets of Belleville*, Mme. Souza's goal is to save her kidnapped grandson, Champion, from the French Mafia. She is small and old. Many obstacles are put in her way: an ocean, lack of money, the city of Belleville, and the Mafia. You would think that this would be enough. But Sylvain Chomet designed her with one leg shorter than the other. She wears one elevated shoe. Because of this, she can only move slowly. There is, in her physical design, an impediment to her goal: to quickly rescue her grandson. It is not enough that she is small and old. We expect grandmothers to be small and old. That is ordinary. Her foot makes her different and memorable. The first time we see her we see her foot. It creates intrigue and we want to know more about her.

Similarly, Chris Perry's little girl in *Catch* is made of simple geometric shapes. Her environment is also made up of shapes. The shapes represent the simplicity and innocence of childhood. They contrast sharply

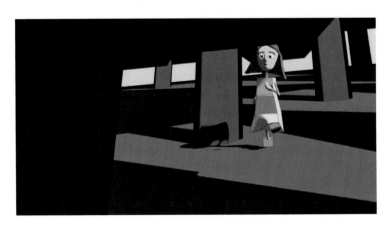

***Catch*, Chris Perry, University of Massachusetts at Amherst**

with the photographic reality of a grown, well-developed woman in a billboard. The little girl must confront her future and decide what is worthwhile at that time in her life. The design of the character is in direct contrast with the conflict she must face.

Creating originality and function can be simpler than that. It can be as simple as designing a character who wants to sew on a button but has extremely fat fingers, or a character who needs to scratch an itch but has very short arms.

Finally, there may be times when it is necessary for the design to contrast with the personality traits or functions of the character. In Meng Vue's *The Dancing Thief*, the policewoman is defined by her overbearing size and her badge. These are cues that signal how seriously she takes her job and the threat that she poses to the thief. We are surprised and delighted when we discover that she is graceful, loves to dance, and is capable of love.

The Dancing Thief, Meng Vue, Ringling College of Art and Design

Remember that the short film needs to deliver more in a smaller time frame. Carefully constructing your character design to immediately convey strong personality traits or character functions will communicate the essence of your character to your audience faster.

Actions, Gestures, and Additional Attributes

The final step to designing your character is to test it against the actions and gestures it will need to perform in the story. If you have designed your character with a big head and short arms, but the story requires him to cross the monkeybars in a playground, you might be in trouble. If you need his mouth to drop to the floor and his tongue to roll out across the room, make sure he is designed in a way that will allow him to do so.

Look at the extremes of the emotional expressions your character needs. The face and the hands are the most expressive parts of the body. How far do they stretch? What kinds of exaggerations are necessary? This becomes a bigger consideration when you begin to model, but at the design stage, you want to make sure that the expressions are readable.

Also think about how detailed the character is and how the design will affect the time it will take to animate it. Things like flowing hair, loose clothing, big bellies, and large feet all have additional considerations when you model, rig, and animate the character. Make sure that you will have the time to execute what you have designed. Consider leaving out unnecessary attributes that do not drive the story forward.

The bottom line is that your character design is driven by the story. It needs to match the tone of the content. That is the goal of your character design.

Model Sheets

Once the character design is finalized, a model sheet is required to begin the production process. The model sheet will be used to create your 3D model. If you have more than one person working on the film, it will help keep everyone consistent. The model sheet is a detailed drawing of the character that shows exactly the style, proportions, costuming, and all anatomical details in front, back, three-quarter and side views. It is also the first step in guaranteeing that your character is appealing and animatable from all angles.

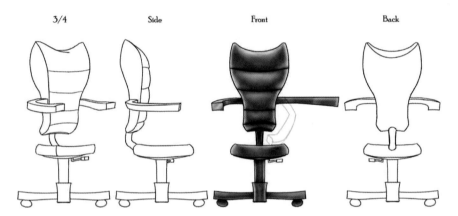

The Animator and the Seat, **Chair Model Sheet**

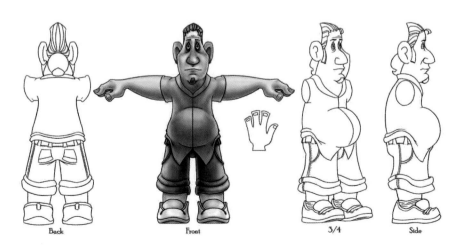

The Animator and the Seat, **Chunk Model Sheet**

BUILDING LOCATION

A good location:

- Sets the stage for the animation
- Determines the mood of piece
- Supports the story.

Setting the Stage

Some of the most cutting-edge work in animation is in the design of the environment. We only have to look at the ballroom scene from Disney's *Beauty and the Beast*, the vast, frozen terrain of Blue Sky's *Ice Age*, the underwater world of Pixar's *Finding Nemo*, the complex kitchen in *Ratatouille*, or the islands in *Avatar*, to see how environments have been innovative in pushing both visual and technological progress as essential storytelling elements. The location is not just a background for a piece. It is not just a space in which the character acts. The location is the world in which the character lives.

Props

Props are objects that populate the environment that the character uses to drive the story forward. A landscape is never just a landscape, a town just a town, a building just a building, or a room just a room. The location, and the objects in it, is specific to the character and the story. They give the audience many visual cues that provide instantaneous information about the character, the back story, and the situation.

For example, in *Gopher Broke*, we begin the story on a dirt road in the middle of a wheat field. The first thing we see is a sign that points in the direction of the Farmers' Market, posted in the rocky dirt on the side of the road. Next, we see dandelions. Then we see the dandelions disappearing into the earth until the Gopher runs into the sign and gets a better idea as a pickup truck loaded with crates and tomatoes (identical to the ones on the sign) drives by. We learn from this introduction that we are in the country. There is a critter who ordinarily eats dandelions but now has an opportunity for something better. The make and model of the truck tells us the time period. Because the story involves several iterations of vegetable displacement from various trucks that drive by, we need to consider the other props we need for the story: trucks—making them the same but different colors will help with feasibility; types of vegetables; types of crates.

***Gopher Broke*, Prop Concept Art by Chuck Wojtkiewicz, Blur Studios**

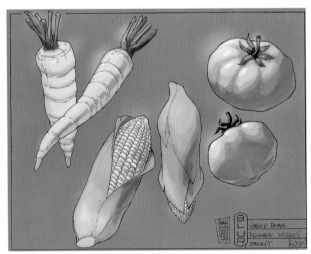

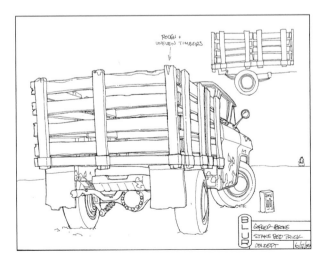

Important props, like the sign and the dandelions, need to be prominent. The sign is of particular significance because it is the prop that ultimately causes the demise of the gopher. The gopher, in frustration, throws the sign on the road where it is hit by a truck that careens out of control, catapulting a cow from the back of the truck, which lands on the gopher. The lesson here is that a prop is also never just a prop. It must be used to convey information or drive the story forward. Be careful not to overpopulate your sets with props. Use only what you need to tell the story. Make sure the props don't steal the scene from the character.

Props give us important information about time period, geography, character personality and history. If a piece is set in the present, props become especially important, providing specific and unique information about the character and space that distinguishes them from the rest of modern society.

The Animator and the Seat, by Eric Drobile, Ringling College of Art and Design

Space

Space is the empty area in a set that must be big enough for the characters to do what they need to do. Whether this is a claustrophobic interior or a vast expansive exterior, the design of the space should direct the viewer to the important action in the scene. Therefore, great care needs to be taken to analyze the action and compose the props in such a way that they do not visually interfere with the action and so that they are where they need to be when the character needs to use them.

Look at the space in the design on p. 91. In this story, the animator needs to move from his desk toward the entrance to his cubicle. As the entrance is blocked by his chair, he tries to climb the bookcase as an alternate route of escape. He is pulled off the bookcase and forced back to work at his computer. The space is designed with a direct route from the chair to the door. The desk is placed against the far wall of the cubicle. The character simply needs to turn his chair around and head for the entrance. When the entrance is blocked, the bookcase is to the left of the character so he can turn and begin to climb. There is, then, the same direct route back to the computer from the bookcase, allowing for maximum action, minimum interference from other furniture, and minimum movement of the camera.

Imagine the difference if the desk was turned around facing the entrance and if the bookcase was located behind the desk on the far back wall. The space would require the character to run around the desk, creating a barrier between the character and the chair, stopping the action.

Too often, beginner animators create their locations from something they have seen or something they know. They then move the characters to the props rather than position the props where they are needed for the story. They waste valuable animation time making the character move around obstacles or walk or run great distances—movements that with good design are avoidable. Analyze first the function of the space, the action that takes place, where the camera will be placed, and then design for maximum efficiency.

Defining the Mood of the Piece

What is the mood you want to create for your piece? Is it night or day? Are we in a happy place or a scary place? What is the atmosphere, the weight of the air, the temperature of the space? As soon as the film fades up from black and begins, an impression, emotion, feeling, or dramatic effect is created by the texture, color, lighting, and design elements of the location.

Texture

Everything in a location has a texture—the hard surface of a desk; the smoothness of a flower petal; the coarseness of a brick street. Texture is the fabric, material, fiber, grain, pattern, flexibility, or stiffness that gives a tactile surface quality to the objects in the world. The amount of texture defines the level of detail and reality in a scene. The more texture and detail present, the closer to reality the scene becomes for the viewer.

In *The Animator and the Seat*, there is a relatively low level of texture. This supports the boredom of the cubicle and desire of the animator to leave the space. The lack of texture also means there is a lower level of reality present which supports the believability of the unusual occurrences that take place in the space.

On the other hand, *Respire, Mon Ami*, is filled with semi-realistic, heavily textured locations. The reality of these spaces magnifies the weak grasp the boy has on his own sense of what is real.

High texture and detail give a sense of realism. *Respire, Mon Ami,* **Chris Nabholz, Ringling College of Art and Design**

Color

Some colors that we use in a scene are dictated by what is called local color. These are colors that have natural associations. Grass is green; the sky is blue; the wood floor is brown, etc. Other colors are used to create emotion through visceral, psychological, or cultural associations. For example, green is associated with nature, growth, and rebirth. But it can also mean lack of experience, good luck, greed, envy, jealousy, or sickness. How can one color generate such a range of possibilities? The range of emotion often has to do with the value or saturation of the color. Yellow-green connotes sickness. Dark green is the color of ambition. Pure green symbolizes healing, safety, and nature. Colors have finite emotional associations. Reds and yellows are warm. Greens and blues are cool. Grays are neutral. Good design requires that you understand the range of emotion that a color can create so you can apply it thoughtfully in your work.

- Red—warmth, richness, power, excitement, eroticism, romance, anxiety, anger
- Orange—hot, healthy, exuberant, exhilarated, ambitious, fascinated, exotic, romantic, toxic
- Yellow—happy, energy, joy, innocence, caution, cowardice
- Green—vital, successful, healthy, fertile, safe, inexperienced, jealous, ominous, poisonous, corrupt
- Blue—stable, calm, dependable, tranquil, loyal, sincere, passive, melancholy, cold
- Purple—wise, dignified, independent, mysterious, mystical
- White—innocent, good, pure, clean, cold
- Black—elegant, formal, strong, authoritative, powerful, dangerous, evil, grief, death.

For every location in your piece, you will have a color palette that will define the emotion in the scene. The color of the scene may set one mood that remains constant throughout the scene or the color may change with the emotion of the character or the rising intensity of the action to support specific moments in the story. A color key or color script is used to plan the color scheme of a given film.

Color Script for *Defective Detective*, by Avner Geller and Stevie Lewis, Ringling College of Art and Design

In this story, an old woman is making tomato soup. When she hears a mouse, she screams and drops her pot. Some of the soup leaks through the ceiling to the apartment below where an inept detective decides to save her. The color script shows the difference between the monochromatic world of the detective and the bright high key world of the old woman. Both color and light contrast their worlds.

Light

This is the most important element in creating the mood of your piece. Many cinematographers refer to light as the paint for their canvas—the screen. Light is what shows or hides important details, defines shapes. Light sets the atmosphere, the tone, color and the drama of the scene through the quality and intensity of the light. Light determines what we see. It sets the composition.

Below is an excerpt from an interview with Bert Poole, CG Supervisor at DreamWorks. Bert describes the use of lighting situations to support different types of narrative content.

Q: How is light important in setting the mood of a piece or helping support the narrative of a scene?

Bert: Lighting serves two masters:

It is in service to story in that it conveys important information like the time of day or the mood at the current moment in the film. Color is an obvious example, where it can reinforce the emotional beats in a sequence. Reds convey passion whether it be anger or love, blues convey fear or sadness, yellows convey nostalgia or sentimentalism, etc. A more subtle yet equally important device is the quality of the light. An overcast soft quality can convey either an apocalyptic or a mystical tone where direct harsh light can bring out action or comedy. The lack of light or playing something in silhouette can either create a feeling of suspense or help emphasize the action in a given beat.

Lighting is also in service to the readability of a shot or a series of shots. Each shot is a compositional puzzle. Given the space through and the time over which a shot takes place, you're determining where and what the audience will see. If it's a quick shot with a lot of action you may need to simplify the lighting so the basic shapes read quickly. If it's a shot where the character is delivering a key line, you'll need to be sure that the face reads well at the right beats.

The tricky part is that you're dealing with cameras, layout and surfacing that, when brought together, fight the two-dimensional composition of a scene. Through lighting, you can completely counter all of those other elements to make a more compelling composition. We use our core illustrative tools, the relationship of value, hue and saturation, to push and pull the viewer through the scene.

An example of knocking down visual complexity to create a strong simple read would be the sequence in *How to Train Your Dragon* where Hiccup finds Toothless for the first time in the woods. Throughout the sequence, we used pockets of fog and a diffused soft-lit quality to simplify the plants in the forest which could have easily cluttered the image. By grouping these using subtle value, hue and saturation relationships, we could direct the viewer's eye to the important aspects of each shot.

Q: What are the different types of lighting situations and when might you use them to support different types of narrative content? (high key; low key; high contrast; low contrast, etc.)

Bert: High key often involves the quality of the light, where the scene is a bit more directly lit and shapes the character of the core areas. Midday lighting can be thought of as high key. Typically high key is used in situations when readability is important. For instance, comedy is one situation where a character's facial gestures are important. Action can also benefit from a high key situation. High key is meant to overstate something. An example of high key lighting would be the opening fight sequence in *Kung Fu Panda 2* where Po rescues the village. In that case, you can see how the comedy plays out easily amongst a lot of action.

Low key features a softer quality to the light. It's meant to be more moody or suspenseful, involving mystery, reflection or ominous tones. Mystical is another word which comes to mind. An example would be in *How to Train Your Dragon* when Hiccup encounters Toothless for the first time bound in ropes in the foggy forest. You can see how it creates a feeling of mysticism and suspense.

High contrast can involve high key lighting, but it can also be characters in full silhouette in a low key situation, such as in the wide shot where Stoick is hunched over Toothless when he fears that Hiccup is dead. In that case, it is high contrast because of the bright atmospheric quality but Stoick himself is in a low key scenario where it's more overcast and apocalyptic in quality. The high contrast in that shot makes Stoick easily readable where we need him to read amongst a lot of debris and destruction from afar. The crowd is then entering from the right with the primary characters having a little more hue and value contrast making them the secondary read. Using the atmospherics also allowed us to desaturate the scene and diffuse the light giving it a soft quality for the tender contemplative moment.

***How to Train Your Dragon*™ and © 2010, DreamWorks Animation LLC All Rights Reserved**

Low contrast is often used to play something down and is typically juxtaposed against a high contrast situation for pop and excitement. An example of this would be in the original *Kung Fu Panda*, the close-up on Tai Lung when he is waiting to escape his prison. As he lies in wait to escape, the lighting relationships are played down to help build the suspense and mystery. Upon his escape the contrast is boosted to emphasize the action and excitement, which also services the quick cutting action making things easily readable over just a few frames.

When lighting a scene make sure it is the image you want. Be deliberate. Remember that the computer always gives you an image. Make the image you want to make rather than being satisfied with what is given to you. Never forget that you are designing an image.

Design Elements

The line, shape, scale and directional orientation of the elements in a scene communicate meaning and create style. An environment composed of organic shapes has a very different feeling than one created with geometric shapes. Curves, right angles and horizontal orientations are calming and stable. Diagonals, pointed edges, repeated verticals and whacked perspectives create energy and tension.

In *The Animator and the Seat*, the perspective and shape of everything in the environment from the doorway to the bookcase to the desk is off kilter, creating an environment that is tense—like a bad dream. This reinforces the idea that the chair could come alive in this environment. It walks a line between reality and hallucination.

Catch uses primary shapes to evoke a sense of the simplicity and childhood. The beginning of the piece is open and round. The forest is large, vertical and sharp. The scale of the forest creates danger. The billboard scene uses hard verticals to create a feeling that is industrial and cold.

Gopher Broke is more realistic. The design elements reinforce the story of a gopher in the Midwest.

In *Defective Detective*, the design elements used in the characters place the height and angularity of the detective against the compact and curved elements in the old woman. Likewise their apartments are equally contrasting. Everything in the detective's environment is square and slightly at an angle. It communicates the detective's need for control and his inability to get it. In contrast the old woman's environment has a lot of circular elements and rounded edges. Just from the environments, we know that the woman will control the situation when these two finally meet.

Supporting the Story

Everything about the location—the props, space, texture, color, lighting, and design combine to support the story and communicate the time period, genre, and style of the piece. Styles range from general categories such as realistic, abstract, caricatured, cartooned, exaggerated, organic, and geometric; to specific recognized styles in art like *Art Deco* or *Film Noir*; to very specific times or locations like Muncie, Indiana, in the 1950s. Don't copy styles from other people. Don't make the style of the piece the way it is because "that is the way you draw." Choose a style that will best enhance your character and tell your story.

Locations are developed in concept art called master sketches or master backgrounds. This is art that is produced to accompany story pitches. It should communicate the atmosphere, lighting and design of the piece. These pieces should create intrigue, curiosity, and interest in your audience. For the short, you want the visual of your location to get your audience into the story quickly. Just as with your character designs, the location design needs visual interest that makes us want to know more.

The following drawings show two possible variations for a scene that takes place in a grandmother's house. The first is a perfectly acceptable drawing of the living room. It sets the stage, has room for action to take place, and gives a sense of who lives there. It is a passive but functional space.

However, the second drawing has intrigue and implication. It is a location where something has happened and more could happen. It is an active space. The furniture and accessories have been carefully moved to the edges of the room. The rug has been rolled up, the mirror taken off the wall. Tools lie prominently in the foreground and a hole has been broken through the floor. It creates questions in the mind of the audience. Who has done this and why?

Gary Schumer, Ringling College of Art and Design   Gary Schumer, Ringling College of Art and Design

The first drawing sets the stage, but the second drawing is what you want to sell the piece and to start the story.

Summary

Character:

- A good character is one that is believable, memorable, and right for the story.
- Understanding your character will allow you to create believable reactions to the conflicts in the story.
- Knowing your character comes from creating a back story or character profile.
- The character profile forms the personality of the character.
- When working with two or more characters, you must also establish their relationship, status, and individual goals.
- You must establish which character the story is truly about.
- That character will arc or change, physically, mentally, spiritually, and always emotionally, throughout the course of the story.

A good character design will:

- Be immediately recognizable and relatable.
- Have a recognizable shape.
- Reflect the personality of the character.
- Include physical attributes that complement the content of the story.
- Be able to complete the actions that are required by the script.
- Be interesting to watch.

A good location:

- Sets the stage for the animation through props and space.
- Defines the mood of the piece through texture, color, light, and design.
    - Texture determines the level of reality.
    - Color evokes emotion.

- ○ Light creates atmosphere, tone, and drama.
- ○ Design communicates meaning and creates style.

- Supports the story.

- A good location design creates intrigue, getting the audience quickly into the story.

Additional Resources: www.ideasfortheanimatedshort.com

- *Telling a Story with Light: An Interview with Bert Poole, DreamWorks Feature Animation*

- *Visual Design: An Interview with Kendal Cronkhite, DreamWorks Feature Animation*

- *Visual Design: An Interview with Kathy Altieri, DreamWorks Feature Animation*

Recommended Reading

1. Tom Bancroft, *Creating Characters with Personality For Film, TV, Animation, Video Games and Graphic Novels*

2. Eric Goldberg, *Character Animation Crash Course*

3. Marc McCutcheon, *Building Believable Characters*

4. John Alton, *Painting with Light*

5. Patti Bellantoni, *If It's Purple, Somebody's Gonna Die*

6. http://www.salon.com/ent/col/srag/1999/08/05/bird/: This is a great interview with Brad Bird that explains how everything in an environment supports the story. If it is still available online, you should read it.

Notes

[1] Ollie Johnston and Frank Thomas, *The Illusion of Life*, rev sub-edition, Disney Editions, 1995, p. 68.

[2] Paul Lester, *Visual Communication: Images with Messages*, 4th edition, Wadsworth Publishing, 2005. The names of the six ethical perspectives come from Paul Lester's book. The definitions have been modified for simplicity and space. For deeper definitions of these terms, please refer to this book.

[3] Quotes from the *Making of Belleville*, by permission of Sylvain Chomet.

Personality, Goals, Shapes and Variance in Character Design: Tom Bancroft, Funnypages Productions, LLC

Tom Bancroft is a partner in Funnypages Productions, LLC, a company that provides illustration, character design and artistic animation development for clients like Disney, DC Comics, Big Idea Productions, Warner Brothers, CBN, Scholastic, NavPress, Thomas Nelson, and Zondervan. FP Productions has also developed many original properties for film and television and illustrated over 30 children's books. Prior to Funnypages, Tom worked for Walt Disney Feature Animation on both shorts and features films including *Beauty and the Beast*, *The Lion King*, *Aladdin*, *Mulan*, *Lilo and Stitch*, and *Brother Bear*. He is author of the book, *Creating Characters with Personality*.

Tom: For this book, I was asked to contribute some of my thoughts on the subject of character design.

I don't have much room here to go into all the nuances of character design, but I did want to hit four main principles that you should think about when designing a character:

Personality

You don't want a bland, generic character, right? So, don't just think: "I want to draw a cute, little bear." Think: "I want to design a bear that is kind of lazy and only motivated to go fishing (his one true love). He knows everything about fishing, but won't do anything around the house for his wife. In high school he was a football champ, but has since let himself go because he doesn't need much strength for fishing. He is a likeable guy though." Now you're ready to design a character with a personality. Knowing what you are designing is job one.

Goals

It's important to know what, why, and how you want to design this character. Make some goals. If this character is not just for fun but for a client, then you will have a lot of the "goals" of what you need to design given to you. Is it for a certain age group? Do you want it to be cute or just appealing (there is a difference)? Does it have to do anything special, like: run fast, look pretty/sexy, look a certain age, etc.? Is there a style that you are trying to accomplish? Should it look realistic or extremely cartoony? All these things should be thought about or discussed before pencil hits paper. After all, without goals, how do you know when you are done?

Shapes

When I start drawing, the first things I start thinking of are what shapes will make up this character. If it's a happy, thick character, I will start working with circle shapes. A strong, firm kind of character would get squares. A thin, wimpy kind of character might be rectangles or ovals. You always want to be able to break your character down into basic shapes so that you (or others) can duplicate that character in a variety of different angles, poses, or expressions.

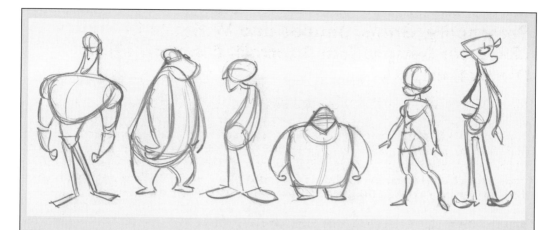

Variance

Below are some designs that I created for a made up assignment. First, let me state my goals:

I am trying to design an extremely cute girl character, around six to eight years old, that has a "devilish" side to her. Stylewise, I'm going for a pretty cartoony style too. It's for TV, so it needs to be a fairly simplified design also.

As you can see by the designs (and they are numbered in the order I produced them), that I didn't decide I "had it" after the first design. I kept refining and trying different shapes and sizes of things. One will have longer legs and a short torso. The next: a big head, medium torso, and short legs. One has small eyes that are close together, another, large eyes that are farther apart. In short, I am adding "variance" to the designs. That's variance—using shape and size in various ways to create different designs. Which one would I pick as my favorite? I'll let you decide which one met the above goals the best. Enjoy the challenges of creating characters with personality!

Visual Design: Interviews with Kendal Cronkhite and Kathy Altieri, DreamWorks Feature Animation

Kendal Cronkhite graduated from Art Center College of Design in Pasadena, California, with a major in illustration. After working for magazines and newspapers, a former instructor recommended her for work on *Tim Burton's The Nightmare Before Christmas*. Kendal then art directed on *James and the Giant Peach* before coming to DreamWorks to art direct on *Antz*. She was production designer for *Madagascar* and is now production designer for *Madagascar: The Crate Escape*.

Madagascar™ & © 2005 DreamWorks Animation LLC. All Rights Reserved

Q: Some animation studios seem to have an identifiable style or "look" to all their films while DreamWorks seems to develop a new look or style for each film. Do you agree this is true? And could you talk a little bit about how content influences design?

Kendal: It's absolutely true. It's a standard that we try to hold to studio-wide. I remember sitting down with the *Antz* directors and producers, and saying, "All right, do you want us to design for the computer?" And they said, "Absolutely not, we want you to design what's right for our story and we'll figure out how to make it technically later."

By designing what is right, visually, for the story, we end up pushing the technology. We don't want to do what's been done before; we don't want to repeat ourselves. It's more exciting, and it's more interesting creatively for all of us. And it kind of moves us into the future.

Q: How you begin to come up with the design for the film?

Kendal: We read the script, the treatment, and then break it down and start to design the movie that visually tells that particular story. I often start by doing the visual structure on the film. This is a visual map that follows the drama. I use line, shape, space, and color to enhance what's going on in our story.

For example, if it's a movie about coming home again I may use circles as a design element throughout. If there are emotional highs and lows, I may enhance those moods with light and darkness. If it's a traveling film, I may choose to use deep space and focus. After this visual map is created, we go into each set and sequence in greater detail. We also look for the style for the film. Is it a comedy or drama? Is it a certain time period? All these questions are asked and answered visually.

I can take you through how *Madagascar* happened. Initially, what was really striking about the story was that it was a real New York-style comedy. The characters came across as real New Yorkers with a definite East Coast sense of humor. There was a lot of physicality to it.

In talking with the directors, we felt strongly that here was our chance actually to do something we had thought about before—to make a real 3D cartoon. It just seemed to suit it.

One of the first things we did was hire a character designer, Craig Kellman, whose strength has been to take retro 2D character styles and infuse them with a modern edge. He came from Cartoon Network and had designed characters for *Powerpuff Girls* and *Samurai Jack*.

He initially nailed down our four lead characters. They have a stylistic point of view that was based in the design of the 1950s and 1960s. A strong design element is contrast between straight edges and curves.

The humor in the design is in the pushed proportions. Alex the lion has a huge head on a really thin body. Gloria has a huge body with tiny hands and feet. When you look at something that has those extreme proportions, it's funny and that was really important to the tone of our film. So we took those elements and then designed our world around them.

When you look at our world, everything is also designed with straights against curves and pushed proportions. It also has what we call a "whack" factor—sort of a cartoony design element. Let's say you had a building. You would never design a straight, linear-shaped building. You would do what we call "whack," which means you would angle the sides, the tops and windows off kilter to each other. Additionally, every leaf on every tree—all the vein patterns, the bark on the jungle trees—everything is stylized the same way.

In most other films, jungles have been mysterious, disorienting, claustrophobic, and for our film we couldn't have that. Our jungles needed to be cheery, and fanciful and slightly childlike, because our characters were new to this environment—like children seeing it for the first time.

The director said, "Well what about Henri Rousseau? His jungles have that oversized, childlike, naive quality. They have primary colors everywhere." So, we combined Rousseau with our stylistic concept to get that childlike, beautiful, sweet jungle out of *Madagascar*.

Q: So, when you design, a lot of what you choose is based on the point of view of the character in the story—what and how they would see things, correct?

Kendal: Yes. Try to put yourself in the character's shoes, and then move through the story. In *Madagascar*, we wanted the characters—in the moment they hit the beach—to feel like they were in a world unlike anything they had experienced before.

In New York, we tried to make everything feel very manmade. The plant life is very manicured and contained within metal chain-link fences because we also wanted the feeling of containment. Not trapped necessarily, but that our characters were contained within this atmosphere. So even when birds fly up, they can't get out of the surrounding cityscape. You never see them escape. We also took out the sun, moon and stars, even though we have night and day. Everything is linear and straight. There are few curves in that world. We tried to strip all of nature *out*.

So when we hit Madagascar, it was all nature *in*. Madagascar is all about curves, the sun, the moon, the clouds, the stars, and the bounty of nature. We wanted the audience to have the same experience that our characters had when seeing Madagascar for the first time—complete awe. These designs then, are character-driven and that is very important.

Kathy Altieri has been working in the animation industry for more than 25 years. She began as a background painter in television animation, and then went to Walt Disney Feature Animation as a background painter and supervisor on *The Little Mermaid*, *Aladdin*, *The Lion King*, and *The Hunchback of Notre Dame*. At DreamWorks, she was an art director on the *Prince of Egypt*, and production designer on *Spirit: Stallion of the Cimarron*, *Over the Hedge* and currently on *How to Train Your Dragon*.

Hammy (Steve Carell) has no idea that he's about to be "booked" by a Trail Guide Girl in DreamWorks Animation's computer-animated comedy *Over the Hedge*. *Over the Hedge*™ & © 2006 DreamWorks Animation LLC. All Rights Reserved

Q: Could you talk a little bit about how content influences design in *Over the Hedge*?

Kathy: There's no question that the scenarios in *Over the Hedge* could be happening, at least in some part, right now in our very own backyards, in real life. It's a film about how critters have learned to adapt to our enthusiastic development of the wilderness.

Since the film is meant to reflect our lives and homes as they really are, the film's style is basically realistic. The homes are "set dressed" to look like our own backyards, complete with doggie toys and old lawn chairs, beat-up grass and barbecues. The lighting and atmosphere are realistic; the homes are built in the computer to imitate the homes that are built in the Midwest.

In addition, one of our directors, Tim Johnson, felt that we have a strong emotional connection to the photographs we all have in our albums—so we re-created a similar lighting environment that we recognize in photographs. It has to do with the behavior of light in the lightest lights and darkest darks. The average viewer won't notice these choices, but they add to the feeling we were trying to create of familiarity, of home.

Q: You had some interesting copyright issues when it came to designing some of the elements of *Hedge* that, I think, beginning storytellers wouldn't consider. Could you talk about those considerations a little bit?

Kathy: You have to be really careful when you're working on a film that's set in a contemporary environment. Any product you use in your film that's recognizable from "real life" has to be carefully examined for possible copyright infringements. Any product you design or logo you make cannot bear any resemblance to the real product without first "clearing" it from the manufacturers themselves. In addition, any spoof of an existing product also has to be considered.

For example, we had girls in *Over the Hedge* delivering cookies door to door. Of course, these were originally meant to be Girl Scouts, but the Girl Scouts of America had objections to what we had "their" girls do in the film, basically smash a squirrel with a Girl Scout Handbook. Of course, this is a cartoon, and no squirrel was really hurt—but we completely understood their concern and went about designing our own fake girls' organization, the Trail Guide Gals. Every last detail of the Trail Guide Gals had to be passed through legal for clearance—the color and style of their uniform, their logo, the design of the handbook, the type of bow they had at their neck, even the name itself.

Q: Where does this type of thing come into play for young animators?

Kathy: In any creative undertaking, we all strive to be as original as possible. In doing so, it's really important to be aware of and respect copyright and trademark laws. Being a student or young professional does *not* exclude you from responsibility to this, so be aware that all of your work should be truly original and unique to you.

Closing: What are the important things to remember when designing a film?

Kendal: One of the most important things is that you're a filmmaker; you're not just an illustrator or a painter. So how a film turns out on the screen is the most important thing. Learn the process, and immerse yourself in the filmmaking. Learn about camera and camera composition, line and shape, space and light, and how it all comes together to create a strong cinematic point of view. When you decide on a visual point of view for a film, the best way to get it across is to be consistent through every aspect of it, from the character design to the design of the world to every element that goes into that world, and it should work with the story and the tone of the story.

We start designing in art, but then it goes through many departments before it ends up on screen. From art to modeling to surfacing to lighting to animating, you have to make sure you are staying true to what is important in the design. So that when you get this image on screen and your characters are moving around in it, it says what you want it to say, throughout the movie.

There are a lot of voices and a lot of stress in the kitchen, and it gets hard to juggle it all. You have to feel pretty passionately about it, and stick to your guns. That can be challenging over a two- to three-year process. Have a strong point of view and see it through.

Chapter 5
Building Story

Concept Art for *Defective Detective* by Avner Geller and Stevie Lewis, Ringling College of Art and Design

Basic story structure seems pretty simple:

- It is an ordinary day
- Something happens that moves the character to *action*
- A *character wants* something badly
- He meets with *conflict*
- The conflict intensifies until
- He makes a *discovery*, learns a *lesson*, or makes a *choice*
- In order to *succeed.*

But storytelling is hard. Each story is unique and has its own puzzles to solve. What gets tricky is figuring out how to raise the conflict, or in what order to place the events of your story to engage and entertain an audience. In this chapter we are going to discuss some strategies that will help you do that.

THE JOURNEY OF THE AUDIENCE

An audience trusts you to take it on a journey and bring it back safely. What this means is that the audience is expecting an experience. It wants a certain amount of intrigue, engagement, difficulty, problem solving, heartbreak, hope—and even pain with a payoff that makes it all worth the time they spent watching your film.

What happens to the character, the events of the story, is what happens to the audience. The character is really a stand-in for the audience.

As a storyteller you are in service to the audience. Everything you do is for the good of the story to deliver an experience for the audience, move it emotionally and bring it back transformed through the theme, the life lesson.

It's the hardest thing to remember when you are building a story—that it isn't about you and what you want—it is about the audience and if what you deliver is a satisfying experience. Will they want to watch your film again?

PITFALLS IN THE PROCESS

When creating a short some of the biggest pitfalls have to do with two things:

The terminology we use. When we start talking about things like "life lessons" or "delivering an experience that transforms the audience" the tendency is to go to something that is "big" or "important." Shorts are small. They are single situations, a single conflict, a memorable moment or a slice of life. Sometimes they are just jokes. And a good joke has everything we ask for above.

When a story isn't working, instead of identifying what is wrong with the story, new shorts producers tend to add more: another character, another event, more props, more dialogue. It usually doesn't fix the story. It is just more, not better.

PREMISE AND THEME

With most ideas you will start with your premise and your theme. Remember that the premise is one or two sentences that introduce your character and the conflict. The theme is the life lesson that your character and audience learn as it watches your film.

Let's use *Defective Detective* as an example:

Theme: Don't jump to conclusions

Premise: An inept detective wrongly assumes a notorious killer is harming his neighbor.

Defective Detective **by Avner Geller and Stevie Lewis, Ringling College of Art and Design**

The premise is the first step to see if we have anything interesting to pursue. It is really just a sketch of an idea. It provides the basic framework but lacks details on how that situation will play out.

WHO, WHAT AND WHY? WHERE, WHEN AND HOW?

If you look at the premise above, all you really have is a situation. It sounds like fun, but we need a little more clarity to really know what we are working with and before we can start.

Usually there is something more than the premise already in the back of your brain. You may have even begun to envision what happens—what the character does. But it will make it easier to build a successful story if you take the time to make sure you know more about the toys you've brought to your sandbox and how you think they function. These are the story elements you're going to be playing with for a while. Let's get to know them before we use them.

- Who is your character? What does he want? Why can't he get it? What is at stake?

- Where are we? When does it take place?

- Who are the other characters? What do they want? Why can't they get it? What's at stake for them?

- Who is the story about? How does that character arc? What else do you need to know?

In *Defective Detective* we know that the detective tends to jump to conclusions—that comes from our theme. We know there is a notorious killer who he thinks is harming his neighbor. We know that, since the lesson is "don't jump to conclusions," the neighbor is probably *not* being harmed—or not in the way that he thinks. This is about all we can muster from the premise.

Here are where your questions come in—and it might take a lot of brainstorming to find the answers.

If you have done your initial character profile, you probably know that what is at stake is the detective's reputation, he acts more out of emotion than logic and that he has some self doubt about his capabilities. We know he wants to save his neighbor. He can't do that because no harm really exists.

Where and when does the story take place? The characters are neighbors. How do you determine that they live in an apartment and that her apartment is above his? How does he know something is wrong? What does he see or hear? If she screams: what is she really screaming at, what's the situation and problem in her apartment?

In this story, the detective imagines the absolute worst. And we know that we have to teach him how his assumptions are wrong. So whatever is going on above him needs to be rather mundane. What is something simple that could make an old woman scream? Geller and Lewis came up with a brilliant solution with the mouse. A mouse might also help define the time period, condition or age of the apartments. Wait—how do know his neighbor is an old woman? What type of neighbor would be the most vulnerable and in need of his help?

The scream is probably enough to move the detective into action, but then what? You can't just scream all the way through your piece. You could, but put that against the experience of the audience—is that building the suspense, or the humor, that you want? If the detective imagines the worst, and we know he thinks the threat is a killer, then the best evidence of physical harm and possible death is blood. What could the old woman be doing that would also give the impression of this type of physical harm? This is how you might begin to think through the questions that will lead you to tomato soup.

Remember that you need to do a character profile for the old woman, too. What kind of personality do we need to teach the life lesson we want to deliver? Using an old woman is great because the detective (and the audience) can jump to conclusions (or stereotypes or generalizations) about her needing help. But if the life lesson is to *not* jump to conclusions, then you need a character that can take care of herself.

You want to identify as many of your assets as you can before you start building your story, but as you get to know the story better, these may swap out and change.

We still don't know how the story unfolds but by taking the time to define a few details we have a better understanding of what we are trying to do and how we might do it.

When you have gathered all your toys you can start building your story. The place that you begin—is at the end.

ENDINGS AND BEGINNINGS

If you are taking your audience on a journey, you have to know the destination.

How important is this? Did you ever tell a joke and forget the punch line? The whole thing falls apart. In storytelling the ending is everything. If the ending doesn't work, the story doesn't work.

This is so important that James Mercurio, screenwriter and teacher, believes that until you know the ending, you can't really understand how to write the beginning. In order to know your ending you must understand what your piece means—the theme.

This is because the theme or meaning of the piece directs the resolution. In story structure, the theme is realized in the crisis of the story. This is where your character makes a discovery, learns a lesson and/or makes a choice. Whatever your character learns or discovers communicates the theme of the film. The decision he makes, how he chooses to act against the opposition, determines the ending.[1]

The ending that you are looking for is the transformation of the character, the audience, or both. In the very best endings, you give the audience what it expects, but not in the way it expects.

In feature films the lesson usually happens when the character is at their lowest point. When Shrek sits heartbroken in the swamp, Donkey convinces him to tell Fiona he loves her. Shrek realizes at that moment that he both wants and deserves love (realization of the theme). He goes to defeat Farqaad and win his girl (the act that determines the ending). And quite a bit happens before we get the ending we expect—but not in the way we expect it.

When Fiona finds true love, she is supposed to take true love's form. Both Fiona and the audience believe that she will assume the beautiful form of the princess—because pure love is beautiful. Instead she turns into an ogre. And she is fine with this because it is the form of her true love. In the film, the audience has known for a long time that Shrek and Fiona will end up together, but this ending does it in such a way that it is both perfectly aligned with the story and unpredictable.

From here we can write the beginning which shows Shrek in his swamp using a fairy tale book with an illustration of Fiona as toilet paper. If you don't know that Fiona becomes what is highest in Shrek's esteem you can write this moment that shows when she is at his lowest. It is in these first few moments of the film that you define the arc of the character and begin to lead him to what he needs to learn.

In the short film, as you know by now, we don't have a lot of time. So when you are defining your ending it is usually a combination of the crisis and the resolution. And in the short, it may not be actually be a crisis—it may just be a pivot that changes the direction of the story or a climax that you have been moving toward. And the character may not have been brought down emotionally—the climax may be a moment of joy that propels them toward the resolution.

Likewise the beginning usually includes both the set up and the inciting moment. The setup is your *ordinary day*. And the inciting moment is what *propels the character into action*. These combined begin and define the arc of your character in your piece. Sometimes in a short, you won't even have an exposition. You get right into the story at the point of action.

At the end of *Defective Detective*, the detective shuts his eyes and musters the courage to shoot what he believes is the Butcher—the notorious killer—to save his neighbor. What he shoots is a pot of soup that drains onto the floor. And thankfully, he has not shot the old woman. He learns he was mistaken. Because you know this is the ending, in the beginning you have to start with the soup. The detective hears a scream and sees what he thinks is blood—but it is the soup that has been dropped, draining onto the floor above. You can't set up the inciting moment unless it is tied to the lesson learned at the end. Anton Chekhov says, "If you put in a gun in the first act, you have to use it by the third." And in this case the "gun" is a pot of soup.

Defective Detective by Avner Geller and Stevie Lewis, Ringling College of Art and Design

So for a story you have to know your ending. Whatever happens at the end has to be set up in the beginning. These parts of the story relate. If your ending isn't working, the problem is in your beginning.

BUILDING CONFLICT: THE JOURNEY OF THE CHARACTER

We know our beginning, we know our ending, we know how our theme is realized and now we just have to get there. This is where you get to have some fun. Between your inciting moment and your pivot, climax or crisis we have what Brian McDonald calls *ritual pain*.[2] This is where you take your character through enough challenges and pitfalls to allow them to make their discovery and change. And the change makes everything they have gone through worth it. Francis Glebas says during this time the character will toggle emotionally between hope and fear.[3] The character will think he can do something (hope) and then he can't (fear). The emotion is fear because if the character cannot overcome the obstacle, he will fail. The trials that the character endures as the conflict builds is the journey of the character.

Progression of Conflict

Often when beginning storytellers think of conflict, they default to the catastrophic. They think about *big* problems. Problems don't have to be very bad to greatly affect us and cause conflict. An itch, the common cold, or a bee sting can all have great effect and be wonderful inspiration for a story. But if you scratch an itch, take medicine, or put ointment on your sting, the story is over. These are single events that cause a problem and can be easily resolved. To build story, the conflict has to get worse. Scratching an itch leads to itching all over that leads to a spreading rash that lands you in the hospital where you meet a pretty nurse who catches your rash . . .

In story, the progression of the conflict for the character occurs in a pretty predictable way. In the short, most conflicts are what we call *compounded* conflicts. A compounded conflict is a *single* problem that builds in layers upon itself through similar or related events.

For example, in *Defective Detective*, the conflict for the detective is the imagined harm of his neighbor. At the inciting moment he hears a scream and sees what he thinks is a drop of blood. He springs into action (hope) climbing on her balcony when the window is splattered with what he thinks is more blood (fear) but he gets in a side window (hope) and makes it down a hallway where he smells something "dead" (fear) only to choose to turn and shoot (hope) and realize that he just shot a pot of soup (fear). So the compounded conflict is about the perception of increased physical harm—a drop of blood, a large splatter of blood, and finally the smell of death.

Defective Detective **by Avner Geller and Stevie Lewis, Ringling College of Art and Design**

Increasing the Intensity of the Conflict

One of the common problems in story development is that sometimes multiple events are created for the character to overcome, but the events do not rise in intensity. The story doesn't really go anywhere.

Increasing intensity has to do with raising the magnitude of a problem in a specific way. Some of these ways to raise the magnitude of the conflict include raising the:

- Physical obstacle
- Physical jeopardy
- Mental jeopardy
- Amount of activity
- Expenditure of energy
- Acquisition or depletion of strength
- Competition
- Degree of completion
- Volume or quantity of the problem or obstacle.

These problems compound as the need for the character to resolve the conflict becomes greater.

The Character in Conflict

The story is the character's story. The plot is driven not by the action required by the conflict, but by the reaction of the character to the problem. Depending on whom your character is, what their strengths and weaknesses are, their history, moral position and whether they operate primarily from a position of logic or emotion it will cause the character to react to a problem in one of four ways:

1. Physically
2. Emotionally

3. Strategically

4. Critically.

The character may react in just one way or in all of these ways as they explore different tactics—ways the character attempts to resolve the conflict. These tactics include:

- Avoiding
- Preventing
- Controlling
- Negotiating
- Attacking.

These tactics are driven by the character's thoughts and emotions. Thought and emotion drive their action and reaction. Emotion is evoked in the character because there is something at stake for the character. What is at stake for the character usually has to do with loss of status or power:

- Control
- Acceptance
- Reputation
- Freedom
- Self-esteem
- Health.

Emotional changes in the character occur as each event in the story puts what is at stake in jeopardy. These emotional changes are called a character arc. Every character, at every point in the story, is thinking and feeling something. This is called *internal monologue*. When you understand what the character is thinking and feeling you can determine the most truthful way for the character to react to the conflict. You can also alter the internal monologue by trying tactics to find which are most entertaining to your audience.

If you are having trouble writing conflict events, it is helpful to write out or talk out what the character is thinking. This helps clarify where the story needs to go or identifies when the character or conflict has deviated from the focus of the story.

If you know what your character is thinking or feeling, you also know what they are doing—and the intensity of emotion with which they are doing it. This gives you the weight and force of the action. And when you know this, you can animate the scene.

NARRATIVE QUESTIONS AND NARRATIVE STRUCTURES

By the time you've figured out your conflicts, reactions and tactics you probably have your events in some kind of order. This is where you want to see if it is creating the experience for your audience that you want. Sometimes you have all of the elements for a story but it still isn't entertaining. Often this is because the story is laid out and the audience can see what is coming. It makes it boring. We already know how it will end.

What engages an audience and keeps it engaged is carefully laid out narrative questions. Narrative questions set up curiosity, intrigue or suspense in the mind of your audience. Some questions you will answer immediately—they are setups. For example in *Defective Detective* the first thing we see is an apartment building when a light in one window is on. Immediately your audience is wondering—who's in the apartment? And then we can show them. Other times, when answers to the questions are given too quickly the audience loses interest. So the key to good storytelling is to make the audience wait. But it is also important to determine what it is waiting for.

In any story, your audience will be located in one of three places:

1. With the character. The audience learns as the character learns. This creates suspense. Neither knows exactly what will happen.

2. Ahead of the character. The audience knows more than the character. This creates tension and drama. Think of the classic horror film where the audience is screaming at the character, "Don't open the door!" This location of the audience can also sometimes create humor—usually when the character is inept or clueless to the real situation that is going on around him.

3. Behind the character. The character knows more than the audience. This creates intrigue and curiosity and those lead to surprise.

Where the audience is located in relationship to the character changes the journey for the audience.

For example, when we looked at the rising conflicts in *Defective Detective*, we only looked at the conflicts that the detective was facing. This *could* be the story and all that we see. If that were the case, the audience would be located with the detective and completely believe that his neighbor is in peril. The story is a drama.

If we go this route, the audience will be asking if the detective will get there in time and if the neighbor will be saved. After all that suspense, is the ending satisfying or will it fall flat? Will the detective learn his lesson?

Is there more information that the audience needs to know that will make the story more entertaining? When we add the additional story of the neighbor, we now place the audience ahead of the character. The question that engages the audience through the story is: What will happen when the two meet? The audience knows the old woman is safe so each time we raise the conflict we create humor by his reaction instead of drama. And the ending works better because he finally knows what we know. Geller and Lewis take this one step further in an epilogue to the story. While the detective and old woman eat soup, we pull out to discover two things: the old woman is in control, and that her apartment is nearly the only apartment where a crime is not being committed. The detective is not so inept after all. This unexpected epilogue puts the audience behind the character and the story giving it a moment of discovery.

Defective Detective **by Avner Geller and Stevie Lewis, Ringling College of Art and Design**

The order of the events in your story determines where your audience is located and how it moves through the story.

In feature films, where the audience is located varies through the different events of the story. In the short the audience is usually only in one place. Think about where you want it to be.

The audience will think and feel something at every event in your story. What it is thinking and feeling is called the *external monologue*. This can be the same—or in opposition to—what the character is thinking and feeling—*the internal monologue*. By writing exactly what you want your audience to think and feel through the events of your story, you can pinpoint, construct, and evaluate your narrative questions and edit the order of your events to guide (or move) your audience through the story, what you want it to know, where you want it to be and how you want it to feel.

Thankfully, there are a few standard story structures against which you can put your events to help find the most entertaining and engaging journey for your audience. Often—not always—the structure you want relates to the lesson you want your character and audience to learn.

Linear Narrative

This structure is the one that we find at the beginning of the chapter. In the short, this is the closest approximation of the Hero's Journey commonly used in most feature films. In a linear structure, the arc of the character tends to move from one extreme to another. What the character learns or where he moves to by the end of the film is in contrast to or is the opposite of where he started out. For example, Shrek thinks he likes being alone but finds out he needs and deserves a love and friends.

***Beware of Monster* by Meghan Stockham, Ringling College of Art and Design**

The short, *Beware of Monster*, largely follows this structure:

Theme: Sometimes what you think is a monster is really a friend.

Premise: An adventuresome young tomboy finds a monster and must convince it that she is really a friend.

- *It is an ordinary day:* A little girl who likes monsters goes out every day and finds something—an insect—and draws a picture of it in her sketchbook looking ferocious, and shows it the picture. It is scared away.

- *Something happens that moves the character to action:* She comes across a sign that reads, "Beware of Monster" and looks around with great anticipation.

- *A character wants something badly:* She wants to meet a monster.

- *He meets with conflict:* She sees one eating flowers, but when she giggles, she scares it into hiding.

- *The conflict intensifies until:* Because she is standing beside the sign, the creature thinks she is the monster. To clarify matters she draws him as ferocious—and it scares him more.

- *He makes a discovery, learns a lesson, or makes a choice:* She gets an idea.
  - It is at this point that the little girl figures it out. Drawing creatures as ferocious scares them. She has to change her method if she is going to make a friend. Remember however, that storytelling is story delaying, so instead Meghan Stockham has her little girl lure the creature out with his favorite food—flowers. And she even draws him one—but it doesn't taste very good.

- *In order to succeed:* When the creature is close enough she shows him a new picture—one of her hugging him.

At this point Stockham could end the story with a hug. But remember what we said about props—if you put a gun in Act One . . . —so we need to get back to the sign.

As part of the resolution, the little girl shows the monster how to draw so he can respond in kind. The last image is back at the sign. Together they have made a drawing over the words that shows us (not tells us) that there are no monsters, only friends.

In this film, the audience learns as the character(s) learn.

Other films that use linear structure are:

- *Dancing Thief:* A jewelry thief gives up both his treasure and his freedom in exchange for a dance—and through dance he also finds love.

- *Fantasia Taurina:* A bull is mad when a girl steals his apples but learns he needs her when he gets in a crisis.

- *The Kite:* A little creature tries again and again to fly a kite, only to learn that when it flies too well, he has to let it go.

- *Noggin:* A mutant and outcast in a world of Bellyfaces learns that being different is really a gift.

Parallel Structure

With parallel structure, more than one event is going on at the same time during the story. Usually these events eventually converge at the crisis or the climax. In this structure the audience is ahead of the character. Because it can see both simultaneous events, it knows more than any individual character. The primary narrative questions involve wondering when and how the character(s) will find out what the audience already knows. This structure is often used in horror films or mysteries creating suspense; it is often used in scenes with high action like car chases; and it is sometimes used in comedy—in all of these situations the main character doesn't know what is really happening, but the audience does.

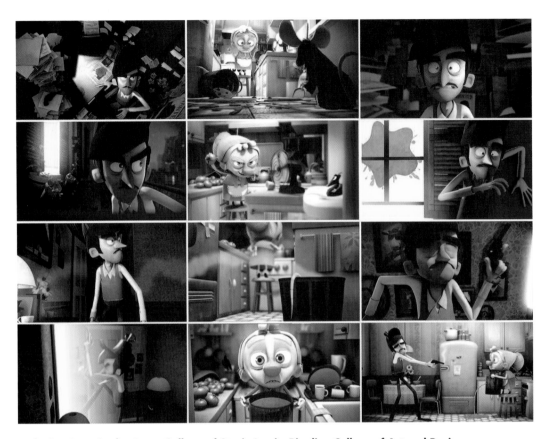

***Defective Detective* by Avner Geller and Stevie Lewis, Ringling College of Art and Design**

Clearly our primary case study in this chapter, *Defective Detective*, follows this structure. When we enter the story, the audience is with the detective. We too believe the drop of "red" is blood and something horrible must be happening upstairs. But very quickly, we learn that the old lady saw a mouse and dropped her pot of soup. The questions that drive the story next are:

- When will the detective find out he is wrong?
- Will the old lady kill the mouse?
- When she does and the detective thinks he smells something dead—will he actually harm the old lady in attempts to stop the killer?
- And finally—did he learn his lesson?

The attempts of the old lady to kill the mouse are perfectly timed to propel the detective forward in his quest.

Another short that uses parallel structure is:

- *Ritterschlag:* A young dragon has been in training to kill knights. While his trainer sleeps, he tries to do this on his own.

Zigzag or Ping-pong Structure

In this structure, the character moves back and forth between similar but escalating obstacles and similar attempts at resolution. Often the obstacles are new characters, objects or challenges that arrive as the old ones leave.[4] The difference between this structure and a parallel structure is that the events are not happening at the same time but in sequence, like a card game. The events do usually converge at the pivot, climax or crisis. These stories frequently involve competition, cause and effect or conversations. Games of strategy like poker or war where one side delivers and the other responds are also a common use of this structure.

***Bottle* by Kirsten Lepore**

Bottle is one example of this structure.

Theme: Friendship is worth the risk.

Premise: A snowman and a sandman become pen pals and decide to meet.

On the surface you might think that this is a parallel structure but the events in the story are not happening simultaneously. Instead the sandman finds a bottle of snow, and sends one back out with sand. Then the snowman receives it. The snowman sends out a bottle, and the sandman receives it. The events ping-pong back and forth between the characters in conversation. The characters in this piece come from very different environments that neither could ever hope to visit and survive. In the bottle, they send objects from where they live. So the narrative questions have the audience asking, What will be sent next? And how will that strange object be interpreted?

In *Gopher Broke*, a gopher digs holes in a road, causing a Produce Truck to bounce, and making vegetables fall from the truck. Each time the gopher successfully gets vegetables on the ground, some other creature steals them before he can get to them: first a squirrel; then a mean chicken; and finally a flock of crows. Each event sends him back to try again. He ping-pongs between the same attempt to get vegetables and similar but escalating defeats. The narrative question in this piece is, Will the gopher ever get some vegetables and, once the pattern is set, What will be waiting to eat them at the next stop?

In this structure, the audience usually learns as the character learns. Narrative questions involve what will happen when we try again.

Other shorts that follow this structure are:

- *A Great Big Robot from Outer Space Ate My Homework:* A boy tries to explain to his teacher that his homework was eaten by an alien robot, but at each explanation the teacher misinterprets what he is describing.

- *Poor Bogo:* A storybook creature tries to act out what is in the imagination of a child as her father tries to end the story and get her to go to sleep.

Circular Structure

In a circular story structure, the character ends up back where he began. Sometimes he changes and sometimes he doesn't. This structure is commonly used for serial cartoons where, at the end of the day, the hero must be restored to himself to start another adventure tomorrow. Roadrunner, Scooby Doo, Tom and Jerry, and Ben 10 go through a series of adventures in every episode. These characters may arc within the episode itself, but by the end, they are essentially unchanged.[5] *Lion King* is a feature film that uses this structure—it is even reflected in the main theme of the movie. This is often the case.

Origin by Robert Showalter, Ringling College of Art and Design

Origin is an example of a short that uses the circular story structure. And look at the theme.

Theme: Where you are is where you need to be.

Premise: A small robot takes a journey to find out where he came from.

In this story a small robot skips happily on leaves in a colorful forest. He's happy, but has a longing to know where he came from. One day he gets that opportunity and hops on a train to visit that place. What he finds is a place that is monochromatic, mechanical, cold and unfriendly.

Pivot: As the character backs away from the cold environment he steps on a leaf on the ground.

As he turns toward the light of the forest we see him remember. He picks up the leaf and begins his journey back to where he originally started and again, he is happy.

In this structure the audience usually learns as the character learns. Sometimes the audience will be ahead of the character where it knows more than the character knows.

In *Our Special Day* a little girl is waiting for her father to come and pick her up. She's all dressed up, her bag is packed and her favorite doll is ready to accompany her on her trip. She waits all day. She sits on the steps, she swings on a tire swing, she pulls petals off flowers—he loves me, he loves me not—when she hears a car coming down the road. It's not him and she ends up sitting on a fence at sunset waiting. "I don't know where he is, but I know he's out there."

Other shorts that use this structure are:

- *Eureka*: There is more than one way to solve a problem.
- *The Animator and the Seat*: There are no breaks at crunch time.
- *Catch*: Stay a child as long as you can.

Bus Stop Structure

Stan Howard, animation writer, describes this structure as one where an essential secondary character arrives and leaves during various parts in a story. "It is a bit like people getting on and off a bus." The example he gives is Cinderella's godmother, who arrives, solves a problem and leaves.[6] In addition these characters might also arrive to deliver a message. In *Shrek*, the mirror on the wall serves this purpose. He introduces Fiona as just one among the classic fairy tale princesses that we already know.

***Das Floss*, directed by Jan Thuring, Filmakademie Baden-Wuerttemberg, Germany**

Das Floss is a short where a seagull plays this role but here he creates a problem. Two men have been adrift on a raft at sea for many days. They watch as a seagull catches a fish and lands on their mast to eat. The seagull drops the fish onto the raft causing conflict for food between two hungry men and then flies away. Because they can't share, the conflict leads to the demise of both men.

In all of these examples, this character is used to move the story forward. You want to be careful about introducing a new character at the end of your story that solves the problem. This is usually not your best ending because the life lesson is—usually—imposed by this character instead of having your other character(s) learn through the trials of the story. This character has not experienced any pain.

If you are doing 3D animation you will want to make sure this character is essential—that there is no other way to propel the story—because you will have to model, rig and animate another character for just a few seconds of screen time.

With bus stop characters the audience is learning or discovering with the main character because it rarely sees these other characters coming. But these characters always create a pivot and change the narrative questions to something like—What now? Which one? Where is that going to take us? Or as simple a reaction as "Uh oh!"

Slice of Life

This story structure is used when the situation doesn't appear to have a lot of conflict, when the problem seems inherent in the story.

Treasure by Chelsea Bartlett, Ringling College of Art and Design

Chelsea Bartlett's *Treasure* is such a story. In this film a homeless woman is living in a junk yard. She is rifling through the refuse looking for items of use or value to her. She seems pretty happy. Other than her inherent situation, there isn't a lot of conflict. We watch as she searches through items, picking some up and keeping them and putting others back. The story question for the audience becomes, Why is she being so selective, and what is she going to do with what she chooses? At the pivot of the story she finds a diamond ring. We think that that she has finally found a treasure of real value. And from her reaction, so does she. But we find out that in this world, the diamond has no monetary value—at least not to her. It is just *the* item in her collection that will help transform her tent into a beautiful place. We learn that happiness is not about what you have but what you do with what you've got.

In Robin Casey's *Flight of Fancy*, again we have a story where the only problem is that a young debutant is getting ready for a dance and refuses an offer for a ride. The only real question here is, How will she get there?—which turns out to be a little bit of magic involving a flock of bluebirds who fly her there, and her gratefulness to them for the ride.

In the slice of life structure the audience is almost always behind the character. The character knows more than the audience. As we enter, they already have a plan. The story is almost always propelled forward because the audience wonders exactly why they are doing what they are doing and the life lesson is learned when we find out.

Flight of Fancy by Robin Casey

Summary

There is no magic formula for making a good story. Good story is a combination of a strong character and the appropriate choice of structure, conflict, emotion and reaction for that character. Knowing the options allows the storyteller to experiment, search and find the best way to tell the story.

When building story, remember:

- The goal of storytelling is to create a satisfying experience for an audience.

- Stories begin with a premise and a theme.

- To flesh out your ideas, ask questions: Who, what, why, where, when and how.

- When you begin to build your story, start with your ending.

- Beginnings and endings relate. The beginning is really just the ending in the form of a question. If your ending doesn't work, the problem will be in the set up.

- Most shorts have compounded conflicts.

- Conflicts in a story need to intensify.

- The character in conflict will try different tactics to resolve the conflict. We watch a character to see how they will *react* under pressure.

- The reaction of the character to the conflict is driven by thought and emotion. This is called *internal monologue.*

- The audience is also driven by thought and emotion. This is called *external monologue.*

- Your audience will be located in one of three places in relationship to your character: ahead of the character, where it knows more than the character knows; with the character, where it learns as the character learns; or behind the character, where the character knows more than the audience.

- The audience is led through the story by a series of narrative questions.

- The location of the audience in relationship to the story determines what questions the audience is asking.

- You don't want to answer story questions immediately. To engage the audience you have to make it wait.

- There are a few standard story structures that are often determined by the type of story you are trying to tell and the type of life lesson your character learns:
  - Linear
  - Parallel
  - Zigzag or Ping-pong
  - Circular
  - Bus Stop
  - Slice of Life.

- Successful storytelling requires the exploration of possibilities until you find the most entertaining way to tell the story.

Additional Resources: www.ideasfortheanimatedshort.com

- See additional information for story development in the Case Studies.

- See also Designing for a Skill Set, with interviews from the creators of:
  - *Flight of Fancy*
  - *Bottle*
  - *Beware of Monster*
  - *Treasure*
  - *Origin*
  - *Defective Detective.*

Recommended Reading

1. Brian McDonald, *Invisible Ink*

2. Francis Glebas, *Directing the Story*

3. Robert McKee, *Story*

4. Jeffrey Scott, *How to Write for Animation*

5. James Mercurio, *Killer Endings* (DVD)

Notes

[1] James Mercurio, *Killer Endings*, DVD, Screenwriting Expo Seminar Series #027, Creative Screenwriting Publications, Inc., Los Angeles, CA, 2006.

[2] Brian McDonald, *Invisible Ink*, Libertary Edition, Seattle, WA, 2010, p. 55

[3] Francis Glebas, *Directing the Story*, Focal Press, Elsevier Inc., Burlington, MA, 2009, p. 275

[4] Stan Howard, *MakeMovies: AnimationScriptwriting*. http://www.makemovies.co.uk/. This structure is not a new idea, but I have not found the term "zigzag" used in any other source.

[5] Stan Howard, *MakeMovies: AnimationScriptwriting*. http://www.makemovies.co.uk/.

[6] Stan Howard, *MakeMovies: AnimationScriptwriting*. http://www.makemovies.co.uk/. This structure is not a new idea, but I have not found the term "bus stop" used in any other source.

Making It Visual: *The Fantastic Flying Books of Mr. Morris Lessmore*

An interview with Brandon Oldenburg and Adam Volker, Moonbot Studios (excerpt)

Brandon Oldenburg was a co-founding member of Reel FX Creative Studios (1995), doing a combination of design and special effects for television and film. Serving as Senior Creative Director for 15 years, he worked with such clients as Troublemaker Studios, Pixar, Disney, DreamWorks and Blue Sky Studios. From 1998 to 2009 Mr. Oldenburg oversaw a joint venture with William Joyce and Reel FX. This working relationship led to the creation of Moonbot Studios in Shreveport, Louisiana, which Oldenburg and Joyce co-founded in 2009. Their first animated short, *The Fantastic Flying Books of Mr. Morris Lessmore*, won a 2012 Oscar for Best Animated Short.

Adam Volker is an illustrator from the Midwest. He studied illustration at the Ringling College of Art and Design and got his start as a concept artist in the video game industry. He has worked on multiple AAA titles for companies such as EA Tiburon, Bioware, and Midway Home Entertainment. In 2009, Volker moved to Shreveport, Louisiana, to work with William Joyce on a series of children's books. He transitioned into art direction on Moonbot's first short film, *The Fantastic Flying Books of Mr. Morris Lessmore*, and has been a story/concept artist for the studio for several years. Volker is now a creative director at Moonbot's fledgling Moonbot Interactive branch. He still draws in his sketchbook whenever possible.

Q: How much does Buster Keaton influence the character development of Mr. Morris Lessmore and the way that he does things?

Moonbot: A lot! There is almost a one-to-one influence. For instance, there was a rule about his eyelids, that his eyes would always be half-lidded on the top. Like Buster Keaton, Morris is a silent character, so his physicality and emotions have to tell the story. We almost took the mouth out of him totally so that he was emoting only with his eyes, and poses, instead of his mouth.

Morris Lessmore poses - Joe Bluhm - moonbot

Q: It seems like that means you would have to become more creative visually. How do you come up with some of the visual things that Morris does?

Brandon: It comes from a lot of thought about each particular interaction or moment in the story. What would that moment mean to Morris? For instance, Jamil [Lahham] went through a lot of paces with his guys about the way Morris would run, or the way Morris would turn a page, or the way Morris would sit, instead of having just *somebody* sit down and make the pose appealing. It had to be specific.

For example, in the hurricane scene there is a moment when Morris is being swept away and he catches his cane on the light post. He holds onto the cane with his teeth as he watches his book hanging on a wire. The cane in the teeth was one of those moments. We had to make sure that it was Morris' teeth that were biting on the end of the cane and not just anybody's teeth . . . or that even he would do that.

We took the things we liked from *Singing in the Rain* or *The Wizard of Oz* and translated those to Morris' actions. We knew we had a storm, and mostly it was the fun of trying to wedge those moments in. How could we put in a light post in the city and have it blow away? Let's try this, and let's try that. We would board and re-board until it read right.

Sometimes the moments weren't even in the script or the animatic per se. They became the sort of thing that just occurred in reviewing the animation performances.

Adam: Right. Another time is when the storm is over and the house lands upside down, the door opens and Morris tumbles out. Then his cane comes down, his hat floats to his head and then his book drops in front of him. I did the storyboards for that and they were atrocious. Really the reason that moment works is because of the animator—Bevin (Blocker)—did the fall. And that's why that moment is so appealing to watch. Someone was given the freedom to express whatever they wanted— not what I boarded out—but how they felt it should go. And Bevin made it way better.

Not only that, but the over-the-top fall contrasts really nicely to the quiet moment when Morris realizes that his book is empty. The fall gives you an "up"—a small lift—in the middle of a catastrophe.

Q: There is another scene later in the film when Morris is in the library fixing an older book. In that scene there is a montage where Morris flies through a series of letters. Can you talk about that, and the use of letter gags throughout the film?

Moonbot: Using the text was a thematic decision. We knew we were trying to tell a story about books and about words, so every little idea we had about what would be in a letter-themed world—that would be in a word-centric world—we tried to inject it. So there are letters on some of the clothes of the characters, and the books eat alphabet cereal in the morning. We also toyed briefly with Morris having a letter too but as we thought about it later, that became a bit too contrived and it gave away where he was going too directly.

In the medical scene montage, there was just something appealing to us in the graphical sense of just how beautiful letters are when they are taken out of context. How beautiful is a question mark, right? It's a beautiful shape. And you can think of letters in terms of objects or actions. An "S" is like a slide.

We were trying to capture what it is like to get sucked into a story. For production reasons, we didn't have Morris go on a journey between stories, landing on a pirate ship and flying over a castle, only to find him somewhere else. We actually had boarded that a long time ago. It could have been beautiful but also difficult because of all the environments you would have to build. We thought the simplicity of using only words just seemed like the right thing. We were able to create a visceral, adrenaline-rushed flight through the words for Morris. And it was also a very happy accident in that it was very simple to build.

Q: What advice would you give for first-time filmmakers?

Brandon: Your craft needs to be good (that is something you could spend hours and hours learning), but you really have to tell a story that is true. And if you can have at least one true moment in your story, then it's going to be good. Then you can ride on that for a while. That's really the most important part I think.

Some people called it heart, some call it character. I think it comes from speaking from something that really resonates inside of you, something that you personally experienced. And that's what you can latch onto. This particular show was good enough to have so many things that we could latch onto even if we were not all around for the initial nugget of inspiration. The curative power of story was really big.

Additional Resources: www.ideasfortheanimatedshort.com

See a complete case study of this piece under Case Studies on the web:

- Character and Environment Designs
- Scene Clips
- The Making of *The Fantastic Flying Books of Mr. Morris Lessmore*

Chapter 6

Off the Rails: An Introduction to Nonlinear Storytelling

What happens to content when the linear roadmap is thrown away? Suddenly you find yourself without standard continuity, without narrative editing, perhaps without plot and character too. How do you develop ideas under such circumstances without ending up in the ditch? Is it even possible?

In this chapter, we will discover that not only is it possible but that, in quite unexpected ways, releasing animation from the structure of narrative storytelling can open up a new world of possibilities, some first cousins to linear narrative and others like nothing you've ever seen.

WHAT "NONLINEAR" MEANS

The only definitive thing that can be said about the meaning of nonlinear storytelling is that it is not linear. This means it doesn't follow a linear timeline with a predictable beginning, middle and end. Neither does it work within the overall rules of narrative structure. Instead, nonlinear storytelling works with a variety of rules and encompasses many approaches to storytelling including abstract, non-narrative and experimental.

These categories are often associated with challenging content—abstract squiggles or obscure dancing objects—but surprisingly, they also include work that you've been watching your whole life. Animated commercials, music videos, TV or film credits, sports and news bumpers, internet graphics and musical numbers in your favorite Disney and Pixar films frequently use a nonlinear approach.

Notice that some of these examples, such as TV ads and music videos, act as freestanding pieces. Others function as adjuncts to linear narrative, offering alternative ways to present key aspects of story within the context of an otherwise straight-line plot. Think here about the opening credits for *Spider-Man 2*; the pink elephant scene in *Dumbo*, or the overview of Carl and Ellie's life together in the opening of *Up*.

Also notice how different these examples are from one another: the photo-album structure of *Up*'s opening montage could hardly be more different from the wild, free-form imagery in the pink elephant sequence yet they are both solidly nonlinear in approach. Nonlinear can achieve this kind of range simply because it has been freed from the boundaries of narrative story. As we've said, this doesn't mean that there are no rules, only that the rules tend to change according to circumstances, governed by such factors as the main idea driving the project or the primary mood that needs to be established.

Within those ever-changing guidelines, nonlinear storytelling can:

- Jump freely from location to location or between past and present without regard for narrative continuity, for example, in a scenario where a confused witness is struggling to describe a crime

- Mash together a variety of shots linked only by a common theme, design element or movement, as you might see in a travelogue or the opening sequence for the World Series

- Stay firmly focused on a single repeated movement within a single, static shot, like a fish trying desperately to snatch a worm dangling on a hook in a piece about misplaced ambition.

It's important here to mention one last distinguishing feature: where meaning comes from in nonlinear. Unlike linear where we look for meaning first in plot, character, dialogue and performance, nonlinear communicates primarily through such factors as context, contrast, symbolism and the abstract qualities of movement (speed, rhythm, direction and so on).

For example, in the witness scenario above, the jumpy editing sells the idea of confusion as much or more than the witness's dubious testimony. And in the fish scenario, the sense of misplaced ambition is not in the fish's very basic performance but rather in the never-ending repetition of that performance (the ambitious bit) combined with our recognition that catching the worm means certain death (the misplaced bit). This hallmark approach to creating meaning in nonlinear storytelling can take many forms.

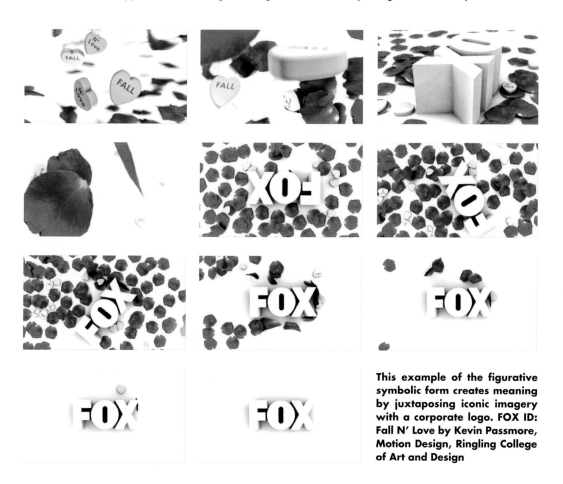

This example of the figurative symbolic form creates meaning by juxtaposing iconic imagery with a corporate logo. FOX ID: Fall N' Love by Kevin Passmore, Motion Design, Ringling College of Art and Design

Given all these options, it may be that the best way to truly define what makes a story nonlinear lies in looking at a variety of models. Through the examples we study here, the beginnings of a new roadmap will emerge on which we can trace various routes for how nonlinear ideas can be developed.

THE NONLINEAR CORE IDEA

Released from the strictures of narrative storytelling, the nonlinear concept is free to roam over a vast territory. It can explore issues ranging from politics to philosophy or play with an emotion without worrying about plot or character. Also included in that range are:

- Interpretation of music, poetry, short stories

- Studies of a single subject including the arts, sciences or visual subjects

- Portraits of a person or place

- Creation of a mood

- Study of an aspect of the medium itself.

At first glance, some of these models look like they would work for either linear or nonlinear. And that is true. As it turns out, a lot of what distinguishes nonlinear from linear work lies in the interpretation: how the idea intersects with technique or the use of camera angles, for example.

Take the interpretation of music. Music can easily be given a linear interpretation, as in *The Sorcerer's Apprentice* from *Fantasia*, or can just as easily be interpreted in a loose, even abstract nonlinear manner, as in the *Toccata and Fugue in D Minor* that begins the same film.

On the other hand, the creation of mood is territory owned almost exclusively by nonlinear. Here the ability to dump all the trappings of story to concentrate on cutting speed, sound-based atmosphere, evocative color palette and imagery connected by theme rather than by narrative gives nonlinear a huge advantage over linear.

For example, a sports network might create a football segment that includes quick cuts of passes, fumbles, injuries and touchdowns that when mashed together communicate all the highs and lows and tap into the visceral emotions of the competitive sport in just ten seconds.

This is not to say that the range of nonlinear excludes story. Actually, nonlinear can tackle all manner of story including the kinds of concepts that drive linear narrative. But don't look for those linear-style beginnings, middles and ends to suddenly make an appearance here. Instead, the nonlinear version might only show the end of the story with beginning and middle implied. Or it might even collapse past, present and future into a single time frame.

So we might end up with a core idea based on "The Three Little Pigs" in which three main actions—the pigs building their houses, being threatened by the wolf and defeating the wolf—are all shown on the screen at the same time.

Notice that this core idea includes interpretive/structural factors (how the material will be shown) right alongside what we normally call "content" (the various actions of the pigs). This is because interpretation is not only a carrier of nonlinear elements, it is also an integral part of nonlinear story.

Our linear fairy tale reinterpreted has the advantage of a fully realized plot with which to work. Now watch what happens when nonlinear tackles a linear concept at an earlier stage, before the details have been fleshed out. Here we can pull in not only all the nonlinear tricks we have discussed so far but also break down story possibilities into the following forms:

- Option 1: Characters engaged in an emotional, though still nonlinear performance

- Option 2: Characters whose performance and function are primarily symbolic

- Option 3: Figurative elements in symbolic performance

- Option 4: Fully abstracted elements in symbolic performance.

In this example of the character symbolic form, the use of silhouettes helps make the performance feel more symbolic/universal than emotional/personal. Reel SFX, Sarasota Film Festival Trailer, Nicole Gutzman and Alex Bernard, Motion Design, Ringling College of Art and Design

These options exist for all aspects of nonlinear. Applied to one starting concept they produce an interesting variety of story approaches. Let's say the concept were "It may be futile to pursue an impossible dream but it sure is fun trying." The linear version could follow the exploits of a character—whether human, animal or object—who looks for love in all the wrong places using the classic "boy meets girl, boy pursues girl, boy loses girl" plotline.

By contrast, nonlinear Option 1 could feature a boy who literally leaps from romance to romance with growing determination. Note that the hero's performance here would be emotionally driven but might be delivered in random order and placed in randomly changing settings.

Option 2 could show our hero on an endless rollercoaster ride with a series of different girls. Here the character performances would be driven more by ritual than emotion and the setting would be highly symbolic.

Option 3 could be based on the symbols of love—valentines, jewelry, love notes, roses—in progressive states of freshness and decay. In this option, the objects—in terms of what they are and how they move—would be chosen for their symbolic connection to the theme and the setting might be equally symbolic or simply neutral.

And Option 4 could simply show a pair of lines, one (perhaps the male) intent on weaving and the other (perhaps the female) on unraveling. This last option would therefore present nonfigurative elements moving in symbolic ways, set in either a symbolic setting or a neutral one.

Take note where meaning might come from in these scenarios. For example, the first could derive meaning by balancing the constant bouncing from setting to setting against the hero's reaction to his ever-changing circumstances. Meanwhile, the second option nicely combines the emotional ups and downs of failed romance with the fun of a carnival ride (the two sides of our theme) in one symbol—the rollercoaster—which can easily carry this message without an emotional character performance.

Option 3 banks on our shared knowledge of acceptable romantic gestures. And finally, Option 4 builds on the stripped down language of movement.

It's very important in nonlinear to be sure you have embedded the potential for meaning into your core idea before you go any farther. Nonlinear has fewer options for this essential task. If potential isn't built in at the very start, it may be impossible to add later.

Just as important is ensuring that your idea is actually nonlinear. Again, what isn't there from the beginning will be hard to add later and will have a weak relationship to your theme at best, rendering it little more than a gimmick.

NONLINEAR VISUAL CONTENT

What might we see on the screen while watching a nonlinear piece?

Unlike the character with a mission acted out in various locations with various supporting characters who dominates the content of linear work, the visual content of nonlinear work is highly varied. It might focus on the movement of light and shadow across an old tree or consist entirely of a pile of objects—ranging from kewpie dolls to jelly donuts—being flattened frame by frame. At the other end of the nonlinear spectrum, you may see familiar elements mixed with some decidedly unusual ones—characters in an emotional performance set within a fractured version of time and space, for example.

In our "boy meets girl" scenarios, we have some interesting options along these lines to explore. How exactly will our first hero leap from one romantic adventure to the next, for example? Since this idea is based on an emotional performance that grows in determination, giving the boy both means and reason to leap higher and higher might provide a good way for his determination to be expressed. The girls in each setting could be placed ever further out of reach, progressing from a second-floor balcony to the top of a mountain fortress perhaps, forcing the hero to resort to pogo sticks, then trampolines, and finally cannons in his vain attempts to reach his goal.

In the second option, everything depends on the rollercoaster since the character performance will be very minimal, so finding ways to vary the rollercoaster's tracks with twists, turns and visual gimmicks while still maintaining the essential ups and downs could be effective here.

Notice that in both cases, neither the abrupt shifts of location nor sudden appearances of superficially illogical props are an issue. This is because nonlinear works almost entirely on deeper logic—such as the symbolism of the rollercoaster. So as long as they stay within the boundaries of that deep logic, the visual elements can move around freely.

Notice also that these highly varied visuals, from the mainstream to the most experimental, all share the same strengths. They are all built around one simple visual idea such as the tree in light and shadow or the rollercoaster. They all have movement built into them. At the same time, they all manage to be both evocative and unexpected. And by surprising us in multiple ways, they all provide the foundation for creating memorable work.

NONLINEAR SOUNDTRACKS

What might we hear on a nonlinear soundtrack?

Sound can function in nonlinear much as it does in linear work but it can also take the same components—dialogue, narration, effects, music—and use them in unexpected ways. For example, if linear sound usually supports the visuals, nonlinear sound can be used to oppose the visuals, creating meaningful contradiction.

This contradiction could take many forms. It would be unusual, say, for a linear soundtrack to be deliberately irritating at the expense of the visual. But a nonlinear track might intentionally consist of one continuous irritating sound. Paired with a beautiful image, the purpose might be to distort our reaction to that image—perhaps leading us to question why we value beauty—by taking advantage of sound's dominant role in generating emotion.

Nonlinear sound can also take an active role in storytelling. In our rollercoaster story, for example, the constant click of the cars on the track could set the rhythm for the whole piece, reminding us of how the tracks will force the hero to repeat his actions again and again unless he works up the nerve to get off the ride.

Finally, some nonlinear soundtracks consist primarily of music or spoken word such as narration. Here sound becomes a main source of continuity. This approach would work well with our first option, allowing the narration to buttress the bouncing visuals with its steady, straightforward structure.

NONLINEAR STORY STRUCTURE

Beginning, middle, end: the structure of linear storytelling is a sturdy and dependable thing. As a structure, it always leads somewhere and therefore comes with a guarantee of at least minimal success built right in.

By comparison, nonlinear storytelling has no such absolute structure on which to rely. Instead, story structure must grow outward from the core idea. As always, this grants both the freedom to invent new structure and the responsibility to use that freedom well. To do well here, you'll need to dig deep to uncover a structure that truly serves your story and then work hard to stay inside its boundaries.

There are existing story models that can be taken on wholesale or adapted to the needs of your project. These can also be used as jumping-off points for creating brand new models. There are no set rules for why this particular model best matches that particular story. Instead, plan to begin by considering the potential meaning built into each model and how that meaning will intersect with your themes.

Nonlinear story models include:

The Cycle (Circular or Pendulum)

Applied to nonlinear work, this model may mean that we see one pass of the cycle, ending the story where it began, several passes or even multiple rapid-fire passes. It may soon become clear that the whole film will be nothing but endless passes of this one cycle. So where is the meaning here?

Often, meaning comes from the repetitiveness itself combined with a particular context. We've already seen that a fish jumping continuously for a hooked worm could make a statement about misplaced ambition. That statement could be intensified not by making the fish's performance more elaborate but simply by toying with the speed of his cycle. Greatly exaggerated speed might speak to the fish's frantic state of mind, driven to have the one thing that is out of reach. Varying the pace and even adding pauses between jumps could convey his fatigue or perhaps that he is attempting a strategy to "outsmart" the worm.

The same goes for our fourth romantic option—the abstract one—where again there is room to vary the speed of the continuous twining and unraveling. For both examples, all the suggested approaches could produce a solemn mood or plenty of laughs.

The Puzzle

Here the information, both visual and aural, appears in seemingly random order that gradually reveals the big picture in which all the pieces add up. Done well, this model acts like a detective story, keeping the viewer on his/her toes as they attempt to second-guess where the film is going.

A variation on our third romantic scenario, featuring the objects associated with love, could work with this model. Against a romantic background—full of tokens of a budding love saved by our ever-hopeful hero—scraps of a torn photograph begin to appear, gradually revealing the truth about the hero's new relationship: that he is really a dreamer whose "girlfriend" doesn't even know he exists.

The Clothesline

Nonlinear pieces built on the interpretation of music, poetry or short stories are often a good match with the clothesline structure. When the soundtrack tells a story, it naturally becomes a source of continuity and that creates an exciting option. While not the only way such projects can be structured, the advantage of the clothesline approach is that, with the continuity accounted for in such a reliable fashion, the visual is granted an unusual amount of freedom.

In this model, the soundtrack is the clothesline—a thread carrying the main message that runs through the entire piece from beginning to end—and the visuals are the clothes. Each sequence hangs on the line—a potentially separate entity with its own logic inspired by its moment in the soundtrack, yet tied through the track to the deeper logic of the whole.

By far the most accessible way to create nonlinear work, the clothesline structure is a great way to feel out how nonlinear functions. For example, let's see how our first romantic option, with its leaping hero, could be adapted to work with this model. Already episodic in nature, all that's actually missing here is the soundtrack.

So you just need to add one of any number of love (or lovelorn) songs/poems—each of which would alter the story to some degree—adjust the visuals to work with or against the lyrics/text and away you go. A lonely-guy song might work best if the visual elements—the various situations and performance— upped the ante on the desperation factor. On the other hand, an outright love poem such as "Sonnets from the Portuguese 43: How do I love thee? Let me count the ways" might skew the theme towards the delusional once again. Here the soundtrack could mirror the hero's belief in each of his quests while the visuals make clear that he doesn't stand a chance.

NONLINEAR FILM STRUCTURE

As in every area of production, nonlinear demands a new relationship with film structure. A nonlinear piece can have moments that need linear structure. When it comes to the oddball bits, though, a different approach is required.

This new approach can be expressed in a variety of ways. You could, for example, exaggerate standard film structure to the point where its relationship with content is significantly altered. So now, rather than using fast cutting to build tension between two rivals as might happen in linear, you could push the cutting speed into ultra-high gear, causing the characters to virtually blend into one. The message now expands to include the idea that these two characters are really two sides of the same coin.

Exaggeration is just one of the ways a new interconnection can be created. Options on this list include:

- Standard film structure put to new purposes
- Standard film structure stretched or exaggerated
- Film structure intentionally placed in conflict with content
- Film structure used as active content
- Very complex film structure
- Minimalist film structure
- Animated film structure.

With all these possibilities, it's no surprise that the relationship between nonlinear and film structure is so very different from the traditional relationship. Yet even in nonlinear there is one immutable rule in play: structure has to serve content. So film language can be twisted and turned, stretched and challenged in the nonlinear context but not to the point that it begins to fight the content unless . . .

. . . that is the actual point. Of course, this isn't so much a breaking of the rule as just another twist which is perfectly acceptable as long as it produces meaning. This sometimes links to another important aspect of nonlinear in which film language itself becomes the focus of the work.

You'll find examples of this potent combo in independent works but also in such mainstream work as Chuck Jones' masterpiece, *Duck Amuck*, where Daffy Duck is forced to share top billing with various components of animation and animation film structure. This film is perhaps best described as a linear/ nonlinear hybrid in which the linear aspects (Daffy Duck's performance arc) and the nonlinear aspects (the structural parts which actually represent the offscreen animator) go to war.

Specifically, this film demonstrates the interaction of two options: structure as content and structure in conflict with content. But does this double conflict produce meaning? Yes, in spades. In fact, Daffy's emotional reaction to the structural onslaught—his demented determination to finish his performance in spite of endless obstacles—speaks volumes about the psychology of thwarted ambition.

It's interesting to note here how strongly the second option depends on the audience's knowledge of narrative film language. When we see a distant character begin to talk, we naturally want to get closer to them. Standard language will generally pick up on that wish and cut closer but nonlinear might deliberately hold the long shot for any number of reasons. In some situations, for example, the purpose may be to frustrate the audience while in others, such as *Duck Amuck*, the purpose may be to frustrate the hero instead.

Frustrating the hero could also be the goal if we wanted to adapt this structural duo to work with our first romantic scenario. In a variation on our theme, we could change the hero from a guy who tries too hard to a guy with terrible luck. This decision would allow us to give the film structure an active, contradictory storytelling assignment: it would now be cast in the role of fate. So every time our hapless hero is about to make a leap into love, the structure would get in the way, suddenly zooming in and knocking him off balance, for example.

Minimalist structure is another useful possibility. It can, among various options, work as a form of denial. With the camera nailed down, every other element in the film is then forced into working harder and more creatively to compensate for this loss.

In our abstract scenario of unrequited love, placing the unraveling female line at the center of the screen with the camera resolutely focused on her—leaving the twining male line with only the outer edges of the screen—automatically sets up the power structure of the story. It also provides a hidden point of view (POV)—essentially we are seeing the situation from the male line's POV in which the female has all the power and "he" (though in reality the hero of the piece) is nothing more than a bit player begging for a little attention.

The minimalist approach can also lead to another option in which much of the job of creating structure shifts to the animation itself. This opens the door on a fluid and potentially seamless world in which structure and content truly become one. In this world, we can create a continuous flow of images unbroken by standard editing of any kind.

The third scenario could work nicely with this approach, in yet another variation. Here all the objects could be treated like flowers, perhaps: growing, blooming, fading and wilting away to nothing in a continuous flow of imagery.

This abstract/figurative hybrid combines minimalist framing with free-flowing animated structure. FEELM, Sarasota Film Festival Trailer, Yahira Milagros Hernandez Vazquez and Javier Aparicio Lorente, Motion Design, Ringling College of Art and Design

PRESENTING NONLINEAR SCENARIOS

Storyboards are excellent planning tools, uniquely suited to linear storytelling. In nonlinear, storyboards are sometimes useful and sometimes not, depending on how far the project drifts from the linear model. In some cases, a nonlinear story can be adapted wholly into storyboard language, allowing the board to function as it would in a linear piece, as a full structural blueprint.

In other cases, the storyboard functions primarily as a guide—creating a loose outline of the project within which the creators can improvise. And sometimes, storyboards aren't needed at all. In these cases, an efficient animation technique which allows for a higher shooting ratio might be combined with a highly improvisational approach to content. Here a storyboard may be more hindrance than help and the best choice may be to simply jump in.

Keep in mind, though, that in some situations—such as a meeting where you need to sell an idea—a storyboard may be a requirement. Here the storyboard functions less as a working guide and more as a means of accurately and graphically presenting your concept. In some cases, it may take high creativity to find a way to capture your idea in storyboard form but if it makes the difference between landing your deal or not, there's no question that the effort to create it will be worthwhile.

FINAL THOUGHTS

It's essential in nonlinear work to be aware from the get-go of all potential sources of meaning. This is because there are fewer elements available in nonlinear for this task. Be sure to review the examples in this chapter to get an overview of the full range of options.

Also be aware of the common misconception that, compared to linear storytelling, nonlinear is somehow easier and more forgiving—a kind of free-for-all governed by the whim of the artist. This couldn't be farther from the truth. In fact, nonlinear storytelling is more demanding than linear. It requires more strategy, precision and attention to detail in order to create any meaning at all. However, once you get the feel for how it all works, you'll find that going off the rails is possibly the best ride you'll ever take, one that (bonus!) carries you into a brand new world of animation.

Summary

General Principles of Nonlinear Storytelling

- Nonlinear encompasses many categories including non-narrative, experimental and abstract animation.
- Nonlinear work can also be found in media you watch every day.
- Nonlinear work can stand alone or function as a part of an otherwise linear piece.
- Just like linear, nonlinear storytelling needs rules but the nature of those rules is defined by context.
- Short nonlinear works are often built around one simple visual idea.
- Nonlinear creates meaning through such factors as context, contrast, symbolism and abstraction.
- Nonlinear qualities need to be embedded in your concept from the very beginning of development.

Key Points for Working in Nonlinear

The range of nonlinear core ideas includes:

- Interpretation of music, poetry, short stories
- Studies of a single subject including the arts, sciences or visual subjects
- Portraits of a person or place
- Creation of a mood
- Study of an aspect of the medium itself
- Adaptations of linear concepts.

Nonlinear story forms include stories driven by:

- Characters engaged in an emotional, though still nonlinear performance
- Characters whose performance and function are primarily symbolic
- Figurative elements in symbolic performance
- Fully abstracted elements in an abstract context.

Nonlinear story structures include:

- The Cycle
- The Puzzle
- The Clothesline.

Options for creating nonlinear film structure include:

- Standard film structure put to new purposes
- Standard film structure stretched or exaggerated
- Film structure intentionally placed in conflict with content
- Film structure used as active content
- Very complex film structure
- Minimalist film structure
- Animated film structure.

Additional Resources: www.ideasfortheanimatedshort.com

- See the complete motion design films under *More Films* on the website.

Recommended Reading

1. Norbavah Mohd Suki, *Unraveling Non-linear Storytelling: Case Studies*
2. Jon Krasner, *Motion Graphic Design: Applied History and Aesthetics*
3. Spencer Drate with David Robbins, Judith Salavetz, *Motion by Design*
4. Paul Wells, *Understanding Animation*
5. Ellen Besen, *Animation Unleashed*

Nonlinear on the Edge: An Interview with Deanna Morse

Nonlinear visual content is highly varied. In this film it consists of rubbings made of the interior of a hotel room. Image is from *Help! . . . I'm Stranded . . .*, 16mm, animation, 5 minutes

Our chapter on nonlinear storytelling in animation has focused primarily on its more mainstream applications, with the more alternative side of the field only hinted at. The alternative side is in fact very dynamic and with its adventurous nature has often led the way in building the nonlinear language which finds expression in both experimental and mainstream work. To better represent this area, here is an interview with renowned artist/animator, Deanna Morse.

Over the past 35 years, **Deanna Morse** has been working as a film/video artist, creating experimental and art films and videos, animations, installations, and interactive multimedia pieces. Her films are visual poems, often revolving around a character exploring an environment or situation. This art-film-work has been screened in many different and varied venues: on cable, network and public television, in film and animation festivals, museums and schools. Her films are represented in many international collections including the Metropolitan Museum of Art and the Australian National Film Library. She has also made films for children, including animations for *Sesame Street*.

Q: Where did your work in more exploratory and nonlinear animation begin?

Deanna: As an undergraduate student in the late 1960s, I undertook a broad-based art education. Early on, I became interested in trying to answer this question: How can a specific tool be used in a manner that is unique to that form of expression? For instance, what could an artist do in painting that could not be done in sculpture? How does the tool limit or extend the artist's voice or expression?

My continued artistic pursuit still grapples with that idea. What is unique to filmmaking? What is unique to animation? What is a distinctive visual style, technique, message that you can present in animation, but you cannot create in live-action, or in photography?

Q: Your past work includes such inventive pieces as *Help! I'm Stranded . . .* in which you survive a potentially boring night unexpectedly stuck in less than ideal tourist accommodation with only a pad of paper and a red crayon by creating rubbings of everything in your motel room: hangers, bathroom tiles and all. What are you currently working on?

Deanna: My current work as an animation artist involves shooting thousands of images of nature. I use my camera as the palette to record the subtle differences of shape, color, light and tone. I have an awareness of the frame before, the frame now, and the frame after. Then, I edit the material together, often rearranging the information in those frames, to create a juxtaposition of shots that emphasize their similarity and differences.

I am basically drawn to new technologies. I am interested in how using different techniques, different media, affects the message, and affects my process.

Q: Can you describe your process?

Deanna: My process always has two paths. I experiment, making "animated sketches" which can be drawn or could be created with the camera (like time lapse). I do a lot of this work, like exercising. If a series of sketches begin to have some resonance for me, I continue in that direction, and build a film around them. At the same time, I always have some broad concepts that I research. That research feeds my sketch work, but may or may not be evident to the viewer when the film is completed.

For instance, my current project involves animating tree bark. My current research is around these themes: the benefits of directly experiencing the natural world, how cultures honor growth and decay (like Japanese *wabi-sabi*), how forms and patterns in nature repeat, and what it means to shed skin. This research will go in several different directions before the film is complete. It is part of what feeds the project, keeps me inspired.

Q: Does your work have any relationship to narrative animation and if so, what?

Deanna: An effective element of narrative structure work is how the audience identifies with the characters. Sometimes the character knows something, and the audience is trying to figure out what they know. Sometimes the audience knows something that the character doesn't, and they anticipate when the character will get it. If the audience and the character are too much in sync, things get boring—the tension of either being ahead or behind the character is one quality that keeps us involved.

In non-narrative or nonlinear films, this can happen, too. I try to work for this—to have the audience engaged in a similar manner. For instance, I create a pattern of image and sound relationships (like in my film *Help! I'm Stranded. . .*) and when I feel that I have cemented that connection—I break it. Or I build a visual structure (*Breathing Room*) where we start inside, go outside, then come back inside. That book-ending structure sends a message to the audience that we are coming to the end of the film—when the windows close, and the music changes, I have often heard an audible sigh from the audience. That is satisfying to me.

I incorporate narrative elements, like book-ending, pacing, rhythm, rising and falling action. I apply those structures (or rules) to my non-narrative work. I try to show that, as a filmmaker, I have carefully made choices, that I am in control of the film. I do this through careful editing, structure and change, and through my counterpoint editing and layering with music or sound effects.

Q: What are some of the driving forces behind your work?

Deanna: I always hope that the audience will be aware of things outside the frame, of the moments before and after. I heard that Kurosawa, at age 84, said that he was just beginning to understand how movies work. I am on that same journey—trying to understand how movies work; what is central to the language of film and how we can extend it, re-invent it, make it sing.

As an artist/animator, I find something magical in that space between the frames. My technique of creating films a frame at a time, by analyzing the underlying visual structure, is a methodical manner of generating imagery. It allows me to play with visual creation, with time, with space. The result is akin to a jazz riff. There is an energy that is revealed by animating similar and dissimilar shapes, colors, and forms, and then playing them at "normal" film speed. It's not the actual shapes on an individual video frame that build meaning, but the differences in shape—between the frames—that create the energy. This animation concept continues to enchant me. It drives my current film work.

Q: Given all this, what factors make your current work unique?

Deanna: My recent video work examines nature through the lens of time. Light sweeps across a lawn, a bird dances with a berry in slow motion, flowers erupt in a riot of color, and the seasons change and transform within a single space. These video poems amplify moments and gestures that are not always visible to the naked eye. My videos consider our relationship to the spaces and environments we inhabit. Common surroundings of the natural world are elevated in importance as they are reanimated and presented through media in new ways.

Audiences have told me that this recent work makes them look at nature more closely. Several people have commented on how vibrant and alive the landscape becomes through my lens. The animation technique that I invented for shooting multiples of flowers makes the still environments pulsate with energy.

Many artists have used nature as their inspiration. What makes my work unique is my form. By taking the familiar, and reanimating it, using the lens of time to build a visual rhythm, those familiar elements are elevated in importance, and help to set a public agenda of concern for balance in our natural and managed landscapes. Change only happens through increased public awareness. Art will help drive that awareness and push that change.

Chapter 7

The Purpose of Dialogue

Charlie Chaplin, Buster Keaton, the Roadrunner and Wile E. Coyote (Chuck Jones) were masters of clarity of movement to communicate story without words. Often animated shorts are devoid of dialogue because we don't necessarily need dialogue when we have the ability to exaggerate actions, emotions and reactions, push strong poses and use visuals that are more powerful than words. In fact, we are always encouraged to show, don't tell.

However, there are times when your characters *need* to speak. The audience needs to hear what they have to say in order to maintain the suspension of disbelief, to communicate internal conflict, or to condense and drive the plot.

In Eric Drobile's *The Animator and the Seat*, Chunk, the animator, is trying to escape from his office by climbing a bookcase when his chair grabs him, pulls him down and forces him back into his seat. Chunk cries out, "What do you want from me?!" It is exactly what all of us would do in his situation. If he did not speak at this moment, it wouldn't seem real. It also helps to drive the plot forward. After this line of dialogue the chair responds by showing Chunk exactly what it wants.

"What do you want from me?!" Eric Drobile, *The Animator and the Seat*, Ringling College of Art and Design

Other times it is the character's *goal* that requires speech. In *The ChubbChubbs*, the fumbling, good-hearted, helpful hero, Meeper, wants nothing more than to be a respected karaoke singer. In order to sing, he must also speak.

"Sock it to me! Sock it to me!" *The ChubbChubbs,* **directed by Eric Armstrong, Sony Pictures Imageworks**

"Hey Friends!" *The ChubbChubbs,* **directed by Eric Armstrong, Sony Pictures Imageworks**

"Why can't we be friends?" *The ChubbChubbs,* **directed by Eric Armstrong, Sony Pictures Imageworks**

"A little respect!" *The ChubbChubbs,* **directed by Eric Armstrong, Sony Pictures Imageworks**

And sometimes it is not what you say, but how you say it. In *A Great Big Robot from Outer Space Ate My Homework,* Mark Shirra uses nonsense language to communicate both the desperation of the boy (Bertie Lated) and the disbelief of the teacher (Miss Spleen) as Bertie tries to explain why he doesn't have his homework. But what they say is not as important as the attitude, intonation, pacing, and the passing of the dialogue between the characters. Because of this we still know exactly what is going on.

Shirra said this about his dialogue:

> The dialogue was meant to be largely *visceral* gobbledygook with the occasional comprehensible word thrown in. When I recorded the voices, I pretty much made a lot of it up as I went along, but I had storyboard drawings to look at so I knew what needed to be said, even if in an abstract way!

"Beep! Beep! Beep!" Mark Shirra, *A Great Big Robot from Outer Space Ate My Homework*, Vancouver Film School

Similarly, Chris Nabholz's *Respire, Mon Ami* is intentionally composed in French. It sets the mood of the piece. Intended for a primarily English-speaking audience, the subtitles create anticipation, suspense and control the timing of the release of information.

"Let me help you with that!" Chris Nabholz, *Respire, Mon Ami*, Ringling College of Art and Design

THE PURPOSE OF DIALOGUE

In this chapter, we are going to define the functions that dialogue serves in a story so that you can choose when and how to use it well. Then, we see how these are put into practice in a dialogue analysis of the short script, *The Captain*, by Christianne Greiert and Nick Pierce.

Setting the Mood

A short can begin with dialogue:

- A mother singing a lullaby
- A man yelling at the top of his lungs
- Children telling jokes, playing and laughing.
- A bank teller counting money.

All of these things could almost be defined as ambient sound—the same as wind through the trees, or street sounds and sirens in a city—except for the fact that *what* the mother is singing, *what* the man is yelling, *which* jokes the children are telling, *how* much money is being counted *should* have specific meaning that drives the plot forward, foreshadows the theme of the piece or establishes a story question. How can a good mother sing heavy metal to her newborn infant? The man is yelling for *HELP!* What does he need and will he get it? Where did little children learn jokes like *those?!*

Sometimes dialogue can change the mood. Perhaps there is a boxing match on the TV in a bar. As a fight breaks out in the bar, the boxing match escalates and the voice of the sports announcer seems to be narrating the conflict in the bar instead. The point is that everything that is said in your piece, whether it is background or foreground information, has meaning. What we hear as background information can also set the mood.

Revealing the Character

When dialogue reveals the character it means that what the character says discloses his goals, personality, needs, fears and transformation.

There are four main ways that dialogue reveals character:

1. It reveals a character's goal or motivation.

   Robber: "Money will fix everything."

2. It reveals a character's attitude toward a situation.

   Robber: "Isn't it a little late for this?"

3. It reveals the antagonist's motive.

   Robber: "No one told me there were four guards."

4. It can reveal a character's transformation over time.

   Robber: "Maybe tomorrow."

Driving the Plot Forward

When dialogue drives the plot, it does so by acting on the train of thought and emotions of the audience or reveals information to the character that forces him to act.

There are five main ways that dialogue drives the plot forward:

1. Creates curiosity

   Robber #1: "Did you bring it?"

2. Creates tension (through the exchange of power—social, political, sexual, or physical)

   Robber #1: "Are you sure *you* picked the right place?"

3. Creates conflict by presenting new information

   Robber #2: "No, I'm not sure. My mother would be so disappointed in me."

4. Shows us something we did not expect

   Police: "We're here to check on a disturbance."

5. Builds suspense for what is to come

Bank Teller: "We'll be closing in ten minutes."

Robber #1: "What now?"

Driving the Resolution

When dialogue drives the resolution it implies, reinforces or reveals the theme of the piece. Review the section on themes in Chapter 1. Remember how often, in films, the characters remind us of the theme of the piece through dialogue.

Robber #2: "Getting a job would be easier than this!"

Creating Subtext

Subtext always seems like a difficult concept. But if you link it to emotion it becomes relatively easy. One of the biggest pitfalls of dialogue is that beginning writers mirror exactly what the character is thinking with what they are saying. Don't do this.

"I used to like bears."

Eric Drobile, *The Animator and the Seat*, Ringling College of Art and Design

At the beginning of *The Animator and the Seat* Chunk is tired and needs a break. He doesn't say, "I'm so tired. I think I'll take a break." Instead the audience sees mounds of soda cans and empty coffee pots (not cups . . . pots!). Chunk sighs, "I used to like bears."

And the audience is given the opportunity to view what he has been forced to spend hours animating. His simple phrase, coupled with the visuals, communicates it all in a much more powerful way. He *is* tired. He *does* need a break. But we don't have to hit the audience over the head with the message.

As human beings we rarely, if confusingly, say exactly what we think—and this is because of emotion. Remember that in story, our characters are in conflict and there is something at stake. Therefore, emotions run high. Characters tend not to say what they think because it is either a) too risky or rude to say what they really think or b) the other party already knows what they think.

Look at the simple script below. In this situation, two people are meeting. They used to date. Character A wants to make up. Character B does not. The dialogue itself is benign, but the internal monologues of our characters are emotionally charged.

Dialogue	Internal Monologue
A: Hello.	*I am so happy to see you. I miss you so much. I hope this goes well. Please be pleased to see me too!*
B: Hello	*I can't believe I agreed to meet you. Don't look like such a puppy dog!*
A: How are you?	*Oh no. She doesn't seem receptive. But she's here. Maybe I have a chance.*
B: Fine.	*This is a mistake. How do I make him go away?*
A: Really?	*She doesn't want me here.*
B: Yes.	*No.*

This is subtext. Subtext, in dialogue, is saying one thing, but meaning another. We understand the true meaning of the words through the situation, intonation and the physical interaction and gestures of the characters.

Using Narration

Every time a narrator speaks it is like interrupting the story. Make sure that everything that is said is carefully chosen to move the plot forward and/or condense time without confusing the viewer or giving away too much information. You want to make sure that there is a balance between your narration and your visuals. Too often, the visuals become an illustration of the narration. You can remove the visuals and still have the complete story. We work in a visual medium. The narration must support, but not dominate the visuals. If you find yourself in this situation, find another execution for your story—or maybe find another story.

There is a difference between narration and voiceover. In *Forrest Gump* we have narration that reveals the inner thoughts of the character as he looks back on his life. In *Poor Bogo*, we have voiceover that adds another dimension to the situation. In this short, a father is trying to get his little daughter to go to sleep by attempting to end a bedtime story. But the daughter continues the story. Instead of seeing these two characters we watch the storybook character play as the daughter expands the story and react as the father tries to end it. We *hear* one conflict, but watch another.

"After all his adventures, Bogo was so tired he went right to sleep. . ." Thelvin Cabezas, *Poor Bogo*, Ringling College of Art and Design

"Oh no, daddy, Bogo is not sleepy, he is hungry!" Thelvin Cabezas, *Poor Bogo*, Ringling College of Art and Design

Sometimes the audience needs some set up, or exposition. Instead of using a narrator, the characters themselves can often reveal this information, acting as a narrator, but without breaking the flow of the story.

Moongirl by Laika Studios is a dialogue-driven piece. In *Moongirl*, Leon is a boy from the bayou that likes to fish. He uses fireflies as bait. One night he is taken to the moon where he meets a girl and learns how the light for the moon is sustained. At one point in the story, a creature called a gargaloon steals the jar of lightning bugs. To Leon they are just bugs. But Moongirl explains, "No, Leon. Without fresh lightning bugs, we can't relight the moon. And without moonlight, there'll be no romance—or dreams." This is an example where the character narrates and reveals complicated and necessary information that both the audience and characters need to know but might otherwise be hard to show. Leon doesn't really care about romance or dreams, so Moongirl has to make it meaningful for him. "There will be no more night fishing!" And this line drives the plot.

Leon and Moongirl, Laika, Inc.

Tempo, Pacing, Rhythm, Intonation and Timing

Early in the chapter we looked at the use of dialogue in *A Great Big Robot from Outer Space Ate My Homework* and *Respire, Mon Ami*. Because they use other languages, they are good examples to compare the tempo, pacing, rhythm, intonation and timing or the dialogue in relationship to the content and emotion of the piece.

Listen to them. Try to graph the rise and fall of the intonation of the voices. Pay attention to pacing and rhythm of what the actors are saying as the conflict rises. Focus on the *silences* in the scene. Silence can punctuate a line of dialogue, enhancing both the emotion and impact of the scene. Silence allows your audience time to comprehend what your characters are saying. Silence allows time for other characters to react. Too often beginning animators seem to fear silence when creating dialogue. They do too much, too quickly and without time for the dialogue to support the emotion of the scene.

When creating dialogue write down what you want your characters to say. Then record it a number of different ways. Take the script away and improvise the dialogue. Have many different people do it for you. If you are lucky enough to have a college or theater in your area, see if you can hire an actor to improvise your dialogue for you. It is amazing how much the voice and interpretation of the words can enhance your animation and help you determine the extremes of your poses.

NOTES ON MUSIC AND SOUND

Music and sound do not play the same role as dialogue. As Sonia Moore said, "The words are like toy boats on the water." They reveal the underbelly of the emotion of the character. And sometimes, if the acting is good, the words are irrelevant.

Music and sound, however, play the role of supporting characters. If you do not pay as much attention to the development of the music and sound as you do to the development of your story and hero, it can make or break your piece.

For every footstep, glass clink, pencil tap, rain-on-the-window, and element of your piece that makes noise, you must find or create that sound. You must also create the sound of the environment, the ambient sounds of nature, the city, fluorescent lights in an office, and diners in a restaurant. There are many copyright-free sounds available on the Internet. Make sure that your sound is copyright-free and that it is truly the right sound for your piece. If you need the bark of a German shepherd don't compromise or substitute the bark of a greyhound. Someone will know the difference and it will break your suspension of disbelief.

Too often beginning animators are more interested and experienced in image-making than in creating sound and music. They will find a piece of copyright-free music that fits the rhythm and pacing of their animation and lay it underneath the visuals. Simply finding music that matches the pacing of the piece is not enough. The music must mirror and support the emotional rise and fall, the intensity of the rising conflict as the piece progresses. If it does not, the music flattens those moments and can actually do more harm than good.

The very best thing to do is compose custom music. If you are not good at composing music, find someone to do it for you. As much as you need to get your animation out there to help your career, musicians and actors need to get their talents out there as well. Usually for a nominal fee, credit, and a copy of the finished piece (with permission to distribute on their portfolio), you can find people to help you.

DIALOGUE ANALYSIS OF *THE CAPTAIN*

We can find almost all of the purposes of dialogue except narration in this script for an animated short, *The Captain.*

Script: *The Captain* by Christianne Greiert and Nick Pierce	Purpose of Dialogue
LOCKER-ROOM SCENE	
Characters: Coach Charlie Max	
Concept: There is no "I" in T-E-A-M	
Premise: Charlie, the team captain of the Fighting Lions, has an injury that will keep him from playing in the championship game. He must learn what it truly means to be a leader.	
FADE IN.	
INT. FIGHTING COBRAS LOCKER-ROOM	
Two players sit on benches near their lockers suiting up for the big game. The wall to the front is lined with school banners and pennants from years gone by. There is a trophy case with only two trophies and a series of team pictures. Offscreen there is a band playing, crowds cheering. We hear cheerleaders chanting "T-E-A-M. Gooooo TEAM!"	*Exposition:* "Go Team!" Establishes the theme, sets the mood of the piece
COACH: **(Clapping his hands excitedly)** Alright! Alright! Ten minutes till game time, men. Everything you've got—put it on the field tonight!	The coach plays the role of the herald, bringing information to the story. This inserts the narrator into the story without breaking the story.
Coach and most of the team exit except for Charlie and Max. Charlie is only half-dressed, while Max laces and unlaces his shoes. Max is stalling.	
CHARLIE: **(Sitting in a warm-up suit with a towel around his shoulders)** Nervous?	Sets mood, establishes emotion of characters.
MAX: Um . . . not really.	
CHARLIE: **(Standing up quickly)** You should be. We've been waiting for a championship for the last four seasons.	Reveals character. Establishes external goal.
Charlie opens his locker, tossing his towel inside. He is clearly irritated.	
MAX: **(Finishing tying his shoelaces)** OK, what's crawled up your shorts, dude?	*Inciting Moment:* Drives plot. Establishes internal conflict.
CHARLIE: Nothing. I'm just saying this is a big deal and you need to be ready.	

MAX: I'm ready . . . You know, I didn't choose to start.	*Conflict:* Drives plot. Heightens conflict.
CHARLIE: Well, I didn't choose to bust my knee, either. Life's not fair—not today at least.	
Hangs up the towel and starts to straighten the things in his locker.	
MAX: Is that your idea of a team captain's pep talk?	Reveals Charlie's role.
CHARLIE: Nope, not doing it.	Reveals character.
MAX: So you don't get to play and it's "forget about the rest of us"? We've all worked for—	
Charlie slams his locker door.	Reveals character. Drives plot.
CHARLIE: All I can do is cross my fingers and hope some second-string sophomore doesn't screw it up.	
MAX: Whoa! What's wrong with you? Before you, when a ball flew at my head—I actually ducked. And now, when all I want is to do half as well as you could, you cut me down? Thanks.	
Coach reappears, clipboard and playbook in hand.	
COACH: Alright guys, game time. We've been working for this all season. OK, Max, you loose? **(Starts to rub MAX's shoulders)** Warm? Feeling quick on your feet? Remember, the left side of the defense—there are some holes there.	Breaks tension. Allows plot to stay on course. Refocuses on the game.
MAX: Yeah, I got it Coach. **(to CHARLIE)** I've got some warm-ups to do, see you out there.	Subtext
Max exits throwing Charlie a disdainful look. Charlie turns back toward his locker. None of this gets past the coach, who sighs and shakes his head.	
COACH: Charlie, I hope you've got some words of wisdom for these boys, they need it. See you on the sidelines.	Drives resolution.
Coach pats Charlie with the play book and exits.	
CHARLIE: **(Punching his fist into a locker)** Aargh! What the hell am I going to do now? No speech. No knee. No hope for a trophy. After four years—this is not how I thought it would end.	*Crisis Moment:* Drives the plot.
Coach reappears.	

COACH: Charlie, will you get out here? This punk of a sophomore goalie won't start until you're there. He's saying he needs your blessing or something like that.	Drives resolution.
CHARLIE: What?	
COACH: You're still the captain, Charlie. Get out there and act like it.	*Climax:* Drives resolution. Reveals theme. Throws Charlie into his point of no return. He must make a choice.
Charlie watches as the door slams behind the coach. Grabbing his jersey, he pulls it on as he limps out the door.	*Resolution:* And we celebrate.
END SCENE	
FADE OUT	

Exercise: *The Captain* was written for a group project. If you were working alone, how could you condense the role of the coach into the character of Max? How could you alter what Max says to serve the same purpose?

On first read, *The Captain* would appear to be better for live action than for animation. Brainstorm visuals that would make animation the necessary medium for this story. What if the main characters were not people? What is the game they are about to play? How could these emphasize, change or put a twist on what it means to be a team or a team leader. What is Charlie really leading his team to do?

For example, without changing a single thing in the script you could make the characters Lions (it's the team name) and place this in the Roman Coliseum during the time of Caesar. Takes on a whole new twist, doesn't it?

Summary

Dialogue serves the following purposes:

- Sets the mood of the piece
- Reveals the character
- Drives the plot forward
- Drives the resolution
- Creates subtext.

There are two things to watch out for when you use narration:

- It can interrupt the story and break the flow of your piece.
- It is easy to "illustrate" the narration rather than create unique visuals with meaning of their own.

Music and sound need to be treated as supporting characters to the story:

- Too often new animators use music and sound as filler instead of carefully building sound and music to support the content and rising conflict of the piece.

Often animated shorts do not have dialogue. There are times when your characters have to speak in order to be truthful to the story. Understanding how dialogue functions allows you, as a storyteller, to use it well.

Recommended Reading

1. Linda Seger, *Creating Unforgettable Characters*, Chapter 1: Writing Dialogue

2. Will Eisner, *Graphic Storytelling*

3. Gloria Kempton, *Dialogue: Techniques and Exercises for Crafting Effective Dialogue*

4. Robin Beauchamp, *Designing Sound for Animation*

Note

The purpose of dialogue in this chapter comes from a condensation of the sources above coupled with experience working with beginning animators to develop story. It doesn't cover everything about dialogue, but provides the basics necessary to begin. Use the sources above if you find you need to go deeper.

The ABCCCs of Voice and Dialects for Animators: Ginny Kopf

Ginny Kopf is well known throughout Florida as a voice, speech and dialect coach for actors and singers. For over 25 years she has been a college and acting studio instructor in Orlando, currently teaching at Seminole State, Valencia College, and L.A. Acting Workshop. She has given thousands of workshops nationally and has done extensive coaching for Disney and Universal Studios, and for numerous theaters, drama departments, films and television series. She holds a Masters degree in theater voice and an MFA in vocal science. Ginny has authored two audiobooks, *Accent Reduction Workshop* and *S Drills*, and her textbook, *The Dialect Handbook*, has received international recognition.

Q: What is the importance of finding the perfect voice for a character in an animated film?

Finding the perfect voice for the character you've drawn on the page will complete the transformation of making him, her (or it!) leap off the page and come to life. Through exploration, you want to create a voice that not only fits the look and personality of the character but is also compelling and thrilling to the listener.

Sometimes the voice is an archetype, or even a stereotype: a voice we'd fully expect coming from a person, creature, machine, or inanimate object. But sometimes you want to give the character a voice that is opposite of what the audience expects: a fearsome, scary-looking dragon with a sweet, soft voice, or an adorable, fuzzy bunny with a dark, gruff voice. It all depends on the effect you want to make on the audience, and the style you're going for—comedy, irony, satire, suspense, or maybe the element of surprise.

Just as your pen and brush pioneers the page, you can explore what your voice can do. Play freely and fearlessly. Try all kinds of things with your amazing vocal instrument. To get you started in the right direction, here are some vocal tips. The ABCCCs of voice and dialects for animators are: *contrast*, *consistency*, and *clarity*.

Contrast

Character voices that contrast will be ear-catching and will expose the characters' differences. Even if they are brothers and have the same dialect, they need to contrast to show their different person-alities. Pairs need to contrast so we don't get them mixed up. Explore contrasts in pitch range (high, medium, low notes), tone quality (breathy, scratchy, nasal, whiney, pushed, richly resonant, etc.), rate (slow to fast speech), inflection (their melody, from monotone, to conversational, to using a very enthusiastic, wide, sing-songy range), rhythm (smooth to choppy), and diction (quite intelligently articulate, to casual, to sloppy speech, including dialects and accents), and volume (loud to soft). Play with different mouth shapes, tongue positions, jaw positions. Get some help learning dialects so you have an arsenal of some really useful ones that are consistent and natural.

Be very specific with your choices. Know exactly what you're doing with your voice for each character. Literally map it out, not leaving it to chance: write down next to the character's name what you are planning to do with their pitch range, tone quality, rate, inflection, rhythm, articulation, any dialect, and volume.

For each character, be sure to change your body language (facial expressions, particularly the eyes, posture, gestures, head moves, manner of walking or moving around) when you are voicing for them. You must stay on the axis of the mic when recording, but still must change your body language. This specific choice for body and facial positioning will be the trigger to help you quickly flip from one character to the next. Change the body to change to the next voice. Thrust the neck forward for the nerdy professor, pull it back for the grouchy pirate, strain up for the talking giraffe, down for the shy mouse. Hunch over for the bear, arch your back for the bird. Changing the eyes is particularly effective to change the voice: squint for one character, open them wide for another. Other eye choices are eyes that dart around, a hard stare, soft romantic eyes, lazy half-closed eyes. Memorize the exact body language and facial expression for each character and write it down next to their character name, each time they re-enter. Then you will be achieving not only contrast of characters, but our next technique: consistency.

Consistency

Once you've established a voice for the red-headed soldier, when he comes in twenty minutes later he must sound like the same guy. This is consistency of character. You must develop a good ear and good muscle memory to have a number of consistent voices. Changing your body language for each character and knowing exactly what choices you've made for each voice is a great start. That's why mapping it out and writing it down will be so important.

Each character must also be consistent in terms of staying in the same pre-determined "style" (whether action-adventure, comedy, mystery, satire, or even a style you've invented). Carefully pick the appropriate vocal style you're going for, from naturalism to highly exaggerated, just as you do with the drawing, and then stay in that style throughout.

Consistency also means you must score out how characters within the same family, species, and locality would speak. It has to make sense, and not be forced. Unless you can justify it in the script, you don't want the audience thinking, "Why is the son speaking in an American accent when the rest of his family is speaking in a heavy Scottish brogue like the rest of their village?" Or, "Why is that tiger the only one with the British accent?" And don't choose a funny or funky voice or dialect just because you can know how to do it. The point is not how clever or skilled or amusing you are: it's about telling the story through the characters. You don't want the voice to call attention to itself, at the risk of the audience's mind wandering away from the story to think about how cool you sound.

Don't have too many wild and crazy dialects or voices either, or the audience can get confused. If they have to think too hard, to decipher characters, and muddle through a sea of audial overload, they will lose the storyline.

Clarity

This is an absolute. The audience must be able to understand you. What good is a funny or provocative character voice or thick dialect if they can't understand it? This means you must work hard every day to get your articulation up to speed. It won't happen just by thinking about it. In order to get your mouth wrapped around all the different dialects and character voices you are doing, your tongue, lips, and jaw must be able to move like an Olympic gymnast. So read aloud every day, do tongue twisters, read Dr. Seuss books, repeat road signs, sing. You want there to be an ease and fluency in your enunciation, especially for fast-talking and highly intellectual characters. Don't try to talk too fast. Stretch out the stress words, or it will all run together. And keep your volume up, not fading out at ends of lines or you'll mumble.

Any dialects you do should be light enough to be understood by a wide range of listeners. The "authentic" or "street" dialect of a region may not be clear enough. Bring it back. Get a dialect coach's help to make it light, consistent, and natural-sounding, while still quite clear. The same goes for if you're inventing your own language in a piece.

If the audience doesn't completely understand the speech of a new character that comes in—if they have to work too hard to listen and decipher your speech—they will click off and just watch the pretty pictures go by. They will miss the story. They will miss key plot points. And all is lost.

The bottom line is always about telling the story. The story unfolds through the character's actions, thoughts, and emotions as they work through conflicts in a particular locale. The voices augment and reveal the storyline.

So, be *clear*, be *consistent* within the character itself and within the style and locale of the piece, and aim at *contrasts*. Lastly, my friends, *be bold*. Often a voice actor thinks they are using a character voice and it isn't a bold enough or clear enough choice. Be fearless in exploring what your voice can do, to bring those characters leaping off the page to brilliant life.

Creating Music to Support Narrative: An Interview with Perry La Marca

Perry La Marca is a Film Scoring instructor at California State University Long Beach. He is also an active film and television composer, orchestrator, songwriter and music producer whose credits include feature film scores (*Area Q, Big Game, The Morgue*); programmatic music (*The America's Cup*); and numerous radio and television commercials. He has also contributed additional music to animated productions such as *Balto 3* and Disney's *The Buzz on Maggie, Kim Possible* and *American Dragon: Jake Long*.

Q: Sound, including music can make or break a short film. What does a director need to think about when selecting and creating music to support the narrative?

Perry: Really, there are several issues and I'll try to list them in the order of importance:

First, find an intimate and unique relationship to the story. The music chosen or composed needs to fit on both a superficial (relating to certain visual aspects) and a contextual level. It may also make sense to have the music convey a sense of time and place. For instance, if the project takes place in a certain locale, the music can convey that. If it takes place during a certain period in time, the music may be able to suggest that as well. There are many different angles by which a director and composer can approach how music will complement the project. In any given scene, the director needs to be able to communicate to the composer not only what is happening in the story but also what emotion or subtext the director wants the viewer to comprehend.

At times, these two ideas can run in perfect alignment—where the music contributes directly to what the viewer sees and/or feels. At other times, the music can contribute something less direct or even counter to what is taking place on the screen. It can also play a different layer of the piece. For example, there are times when the viewer may know something about the story that the characters don't yet know, so the director may want to enhance that aspect through the scoring process. This is why it is so important for the director to be able to communicate exactly what he/she wants to say and to understand at any given point, what the most important emotion is. Consequently, it's important to choose a composer who has a good dramatic sense, not just one who creates the kind of music a director happens to like or thinks would be appropriate for the piece. A truly good composer is always trying to find a way to simultaneously make some sort of organic connection with the viewer and contribute something that isn't already being stated on a more superficial level.

Second, consider your target audience. As music can really help to draw empathy from the viewer and also help to hold their attention, some consideration should be given to demographics. Even if the music is trying to purposely convey something incongruent to the story, or an ethnic or periodic style, a good composer will attempt to find ways to creatively incorporate stylistic elements relative to the demographic of the viewer. This can often lead to a score sounding somewhat eclectic (hence, unique) and more closely tied to the project.

Third is tempo. This is more of a consideration for individual music cues rather than the overall score. A great deal of consideration ought to be given to the tempo of the music and its effect on the scene. If the music is running faster than the action in a scene, it can help push it along or heighten the tension. However, composers should use caution not to overplay their hand and cheapen the moment. If it's running slower, especially in an action scene, it can slow it down or force the viewer to think about something other than what they are seeing at a given moment. There are many fine and effective examples where the composer chooses to play music that reflects the overall story as opposed to mirroring the action.

Lastly, if the music runs in sync with the speed of the action, the viewer will tend to experience both elements simultaneously. This can have a cumulative effect on the impact of the scene.

Q: Could you name a few examples of the above tempo strategies?

Perry: Off the top of my head, it would be difficult. I know I've employed these techniques many times in the past—especially in some of the work I've done for Disney TV Animation. Certainly, one would find usage of these techniques in any serious action picture and in comedy—especially older comedies where a composer might keep the music light and comedic, even under seemingly serious dialogue. The main idea is that it is a dramatic technique—employed through the language of music—a director can utilize to control what he/she wants the viewer to experience at any given moment. By having the music play something incongruent to what the viewer sees, you either divide or shift their attention. This is primarily done when a director wants the viewer to focus on a larger or more macro idea than what is being presented visually at that particular point in time.

Q: What is the advantage of working with a composer as opposed to using generic copyright-free music you might find on the Internet?

Perry: The advantage of working with a "composer" is that his/her contribution will be unique and exclusive to a particular project. You won't hear the same music in something else down the road. This alone can lend great value to a project. Along with that brings the opportunity to create music that subtly blends with the dramatic momentum and direction of the piece. The greatest contribution music can make is to help enhance the emotional experience for the viewer. This happens most effectively when the music can get under the surface of the piece, perhaps play subtext, play from multiple dramatic points-of-view at the same time, etc. This is rarely accomplished with a piece of library music. Especially in terms of certain types of animation, it would be very difficult to hit everything visually and also play elements of the story without specifically designing that piece of music for the scene.

Q: Would it help if the animation is timed/edited using a beat structure? Or a temp-track?

Perry: If the scene is an action scene, it can be helpful if it is cut to a specific tempo as that will allow the music to hit certain points more organically. However, a skilled composer can often adjust the tempo and meter structure of the music without having it feeling unnatural. Sometimes too, it is better if the music doesn't really hit anything but rather serves as the dramatic pulse for the scene, helping to hold the energy and/or tension at a certain level.

In terms of temp-tracks, while many composers have a disdain for them, I think they can be a valuable tool—especially when either the director or composer is less experienced. If a director is unsure of what music would be most appropriate or effective for a piece or scene, he/she can lay some pieces of existing music against the visual and judge how well it works. Likewise, a composer can demonstrate different musical points of view to a director without having to go through the effort of composing several audition cues. The most important concern is that both parties understand and agree upon what the tone and point of view of the score should be prior to the investment of time and other resources. After this exploratory work is completed, the composer can use the temp-track as a guide to determine the appropriate musical style and tempo as well as noting where the music should shift dramatically and what moments need to be addressed. Directors should refrain from asking a composer to directly replicate moments in the temp score as this would constitute copyright infringement.

Q: How would an animator find someone to compose their music?

Perry: If the animator is in school, they should look to the school's music department. Even if they are not currently studying, most local universities have music departments that have composition or even media composition programs. These composers (and their faculty) are often very enthusiastic about the collaborative opportunities borne by these kinds of projects. This is also a good way to go as the composers will have someone more experienced to turn to (their professors) should the process become difficult. Also, the composers will quite often have friends who are very fine musicians that they can recruit to perform on the score. Even having one or two live players on an otherwise synthesized score can add so much life and emotion to the music—which, in turn, will have a positive effect on the dramatic impact of the piece.

Q: And what if you are not a student or associated with a university, where could you find composers?

Perry: I've seen several of my composition students obtain projects by responding to classified listings, in both trade magazines and online sites. Going this route will provide an opportunity for a director to hear music from several composers before making a choice. Nowadays, it's not even necessary for a composer to live in the same city or state. However, I would caution any director not to make a decision based solely upon a musical preference. It's very important to choose someone you can connect with on a social and intellectual level and who can demonstrate an understanding of what your film is about. A good composer should be more concerned about the dramatic effect and momentum of their music than what kind of music should be used to accomplish that.

Additional Resources: ideasfortheanimatedshort.com Under Designing for a Skill Set/ Working in Collaboration, you will find an interview with student director George Fleming and student composer Stavros Hoplaros, who discuss their collaboration developing a musical score for the short, *The Hoard*.

Chapter 8

Storyboarding

Above drawing and the rest, the greatest single attribute of a successful story artist is imagination. Applying imagination to storyboarding is easier said than done but ultimately the imaginative storyteller will see more of their work on the screen. Movies, comics, graphic novels, and Manga are great starting points to see what others are doing, but the goal is originality.
—Barry Cook, Animator, former Disney Story
Development artist, and Director of Disney's *Mulan*

Storyboards are a way for the filmmaker to pre-visualize the film-story as a series of still drawings in order to chart visual flow and continuity as well as to plan for stylistic integrity and story clarity. Storyboarding is a blueprint and a way of visualizing the whole of your film by depicting its individual shots. In larger productions, this blueprint is an essential form of communication to the many artists and technicians who need to know what is expected in the film. The storyboards for a film are not usually seen by the public, but their importance in making a story idea visual for film is vital. Storyboards need to capture the essence of an image's storytelling power. Learn to recognize powerful storytelling images.

I saw this situation on my way home from work one day. I didn't see the accident but I did not have to ask, "What happened?" The image tells the whole story.

DRAWING

Storyboards are created to plan one's own film. Other times they are created in collaboration with story teams to "work out" and realize how a film is going to play. These "process boards" can be simple thumbnails one creates to keep things ordered. Scribbles, stick figures with words, diagrams, and arrows may suffice as long as everyone who needs to know what is going on can understand their meaning. "Presentation storyboards," on the other hand, are made to show others how the film is expected to look. Presentation boards may need to be drawn well enough to be understood by people who are not artists or filmmakers.

Presentation boards carry information about style and content of the film. One may need to create a sense of volume, structure and weight in the drawing but detail is not usually important. Simplicity and clarity are important. Frank Gladstone, a 35-year animation veteran, Producer and Training Director at several major animation studios including Disney, DreamWorks and Warner Brothers said, "I actually find that finely detailed boards are often difficult to read. Better to be clear than polished."

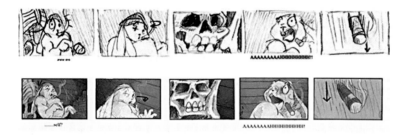

VISUAL IMAGINATION

Those who have learned to draw well have not trained their fingers so much as they have trained their minds. Drawing requires heightened visual powers. Those who draw well are usually more able to visualize and imagine images and are obviously more capable of communicating their vision to others. Those who struggle with drawing sometimes struggle with visual ideas and have difficulty illustrating those ideas clearly.

It is important that the storyboard artist can show form and descriptive detail with clarity. The ability to draw varied perspectives and spatial relationships is also critical. Storyboard drawings need to communicate specific and often complex angles and action. Drawings of humans and other characters must move and act and be believable. Drawings of landscapes, architecture, machines, props and natural elements such as wind and water may be required. It certainly helps if you love to draw and are fairly good at it.

ANIMATION STORYBOARDS

Despite the advances in technology for animation production, animation is usually a slow, labor-intensive process. Shots lasting a few seconds can take months to execute. Unlike live-action films, animation editing is mostly done up front. Animation shots need to be carefully planned so you know what you want to see in the film before many hours are invested in creating it. Storyboarding is how this planning is done. Good animation storyboards also propel the entire process by inspiring the other artists in the production pipeline. Storyboard drawings of action poses, facial expressions, and environments may become the first "key poses" of an animator's scene or suggest background and layout possibilities.

Animation, Action and Exaggeration

> Pushing action is the essence of animation and of storyboarding. The drawing has to "emote" as much as the animation and more since it doesn't move around.
>
> —Jim Story, former Disney Feature Animation story artist
> and instructor of story, University of Central Florida

Much more than live-action, animation storyboard drawings often need to show exaggeration and caricature. Animated characters can move at lightning speed or have their eyes pop out of their heads, perform impossible physical feats and defy gravity. The storyboard artist is bound only by his or her imagination and ability to draw. Animators have been making animals talk and characters fly long before the live action guys figured out how to do it. Even something as primitive as Pat Sullivan's first animated short of Felix the Cat (1919, *Feline Folies*) shows Felix pulling musical notes out of the air and making them into a scooter in which he rides away. Today and in the future, digital film technology will be providing more choices to every aspect of film, so limitations keep disappearing for the filmmaker. This is where the storyboard artist's creative vision can excel.

Professional Story Artist

Can you express a series of thoughts visually? To be a successful storyboard artist, you need an overworking brain and plenty of imagination—you need to understand acting and staging, mood and lighting. You must be able to write dialogue and create characters. A storyboard artist creates the blueprint for the film. Storyboarding is the foundation of a film—a building will not stand without a solid foundation.

—Nathan Greno, Walt Disney Feature Animation Storyboard Artist and Story Supervisor

Professional storyboard artists are a rather small group. However, there is always a need for good storyboard artists because the heart of a good animated film and many live-action films comes from the visual telling of the story by the hands and imagination of a storyboard artist. Putting the story idea into visual form requires the skills and sensitivities of a filmmaker, a graphic artist, a storyteller and an actor. Of course it doesn't hurt to have a fair understanding of animation, layout and set design, music, dance, comedy and psychology. Large studios will invest many millions of dollars to make an animated film. These studios need good story artists and storyboard artists. All the money will not guarantee a good film. It requires a great story and a great telling of the story and that's what the story artists help to do.

FILM LANGUAGE AND CINEMATOGRAPHY

Even though you may be drawing with a pencil or on a computer tablet you are working to create a film (or a film-like video, digital or computer game story). This requires that you know how films and film-stories are constructed. The thousands of existing films, advertisements, music videos and video games form a library of good, bad and so-so filmmaking. It is important to learn how and why the most effective films work. Learn how filmmakers make the viewers understand complex plots and actions as well as the flow and timing of simpler scenes. Analyze what the filmmaker has done to make you feel the tension and fear, joy and triumph, so that you laugh, cry and squirm in your seat in all the right places. It is not only the fact that the evil zombie is hiding in the closet but it is how the director chooses to reveal this information to the audience that can make us shudder, snicker or yawn.

A novelist may want you to hear the voice inside a character's head telling us how jealous and irrational he is. A filmmaker may choose to convey the same thing through lighting and camera angle. An animator can use deep and shallow space, strong poses and maybe symbolic or referential images such as blazing fire or strong colors. All of these types of images and the way they are put together are the "language" of the film.

Become a student of film. Analyze the filmmaker's choices. Imagine what changes you would make. See if the film has storyboard examples and other useful information in the supplements section of a DVD. Start a journal, do quick drawings of shots and make other notes as you notice interesting things while watching movies. You will not be able to see a film in quite the same way you did before you undertook this journey. However, you will be a better storyboard artist and you will probably find even more reasons to enjoy the films you watch.

CINEMATOGRAPHY

Cinematography refers primarily to the photographic camera work of filmmaking. In live-action the cinematographers are responsible for getting the right shot for the director. Similarly, the storyboard artist needs to "get the right shot" or at least draw the best approximation of that shot so that it becomes clear how that shot will work in the film. In animation, a bright sunny day, a diffused light, depth of field, the focus or a lens' flare may be painted, drawn or created through digital devices. The more aware you are of the possibilities of photography and cinematography the better storyboard artist you will be.

SINGLE SHOT TO SEQUENCE OF SHOTS

A single image or shot possesses a certain amount of energy. A series of images will manipulate the flow of that energy. It can build to a crescendo or stop us in our tracks. It can tease us, irritate us, make us feel the monotony of a long wait or the excitement of an unexpected surprise. This kind of energy comes from the kind of pictures you create and the sequence and pace at which they are presented.

A picture that shows something we recognize will carry a large portion of the message and the energy of your story, such as a crying face, a hand reaching for a gun or an empty chair. Beyond the subject, the storyboard artist must also consider *how* the subject is presented in each shot and sequence of shots. I am referring to the visual design. Balance, shape, line, space, tone, color and texture are elements of visual design and are tools of the storyboard artist. These formal, abstract elements speak more directly to our emotions and cause us to feel a certain way about any subject. The evolution of design elements through a sequence can echo the thematic and emotional changes in your story. It can start with a single image, perhaps an empty chair. After all, an empty chair can make us feel like we are lonely and miss someone who is not there or it can be inviting us to sit down and join in on the activities. It may say someone has just left or that someone is expected. A storyboard artist needs to consider what idea is being communicated and create a design for the shot that sends that message to our emotions. The juxtaposition of one shot to the one before and after can reshape the idea and further condition our reaction. It is the art of knowing what to show and how you show it.

FORMAL ELEMENTS OF VISUAL DESIGN

If you create a scene that shows a landscape with rolling hills and slow undulating horizontal curves, it may suggest a feeling of peacefulness. A shot of a rocky mountain cliff with jagged, pointed shapes might make us feel danger and tension. Certain colors can evoke excitement. Deep and shallow space can make us feel free or claustrophobic. The juxtaposition of these elements can provoke even more heightened emotional responses. There are many good art books about design. Find some and study the principles of design for their own sake. However, it is important to understand how to use these

Soft rounded shapes may seem inviting and comfortable, while straight harsh edges may seem cold and impersonal

principles to tell stories in film. One of my favorite books on this topic is Bruce Block's *The Visual Story*. Remember that you cannot separate what you are showing us from the way you use the formal elements of design to convey an image's emotional content.

THUMBNAILING

Pre-Visualizing the Pre-Visualization

Every storyboard artist I have interviewed, without exception, said they do thumbnails in the early stages of the boarding process. Most every designer or graphic artist uses small thumbnail drawings as the first step to arriving at an image. Why, because they are quick and rough. You may have several versions of an image in mind so you need to "get them out" and down on a piece of paper to compare and evaluate. In other cases, an artist may have no clear image in mind so he or she develops it on the paper, maybe even placing things randomly at first in order to start to see the possibilities for a shot and to consider how a series of shots work together.

Approaches to Thumbnailing

During thumbnailing, one can be experimental, daring, and perhaps even careless. They can let their mind and vision flow without feeling restrictions or the stifling influence of practical concerns. Sometimes the most creative ideas come when you are not worried about being sensible or pragmatic. These early investigations usually have to be adjusted or even thrown out but they can help you conjure up possibilities. Another approach would be to start arranging basic images in an order that seems to follow the simplest and most direct depiction of the narrative. This approach may not produce the most exciting and adventurous results at first, but it may disclose to the storyboard artist a kind of "skeleton structure" upon which more innovative solutions may be built. It is important to be open-minded, imaginative and flexible. No matter how rough, primitive or even ugly these drawings may be, they are the first step toward realizing your film.

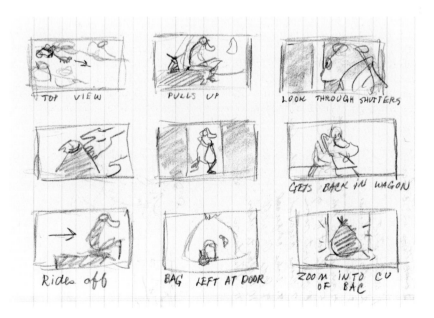

Thumbnails

BEAT SHEET

A beat is one of the smallest elements of a film. It is a single event, action or visual image. Story artists and filmmakers often choose to write out a beat-by-beat description of what will happen in a scene. This is a good way to let the narrative concepts of a story start to form pictures and shots in the imagination of the storyteller.

1. A shot of the outside of a grass hut village.

2. A wagon and driver comes down the road.

3. He stops in front of one of the huts.

4. Inside the house, a mouse is looking out of a gap in the shuttered window.

5. Wagon driver takes a sack from the back of his wagon.

6. Driver leaves the bag on the doorstep and rides away.

SHOT LIST

In addition to a beat sheet, you may also have a shot list. A shot list takes the beat sheet to the next level; it starts to anticipate the cinematic form the beats will take. The shot list will explain how it will look on film by describing every individual shot. A beat, say, a wagon and driver comes down the road, could be one shot or a half-dozen different shots depending on how the filmmaker wanted to present this action.

1. Extreme long high-angle shot of village with a driver and wagon already in scene.

2. Cut to closer shot from same camera angle as wagon slows in front of a particular hut.

3. Medium over-shoulder shot of wagon driver looking at chosen hut.

4. Close-up, three-quarter back view as mouse cracks open shutters and looks through the gap.

5. Close-up of a hand reaching for a dark cloth bag in the back of the wagon.

6. Handheld camera shot from mouse's point of view through the shutters of the driver carrying the bag toward the house.

7. Front view medium shot of driver getting back in his wagon.

8. Same view driver grabs reins and motions to go.

9. Same view of wagon leaving frame, revealing bag at front door.

10. Camera zooms slowly toward the bag.

11. Close-up of bag.

A filmmaker may choose to develop beat sheets and shot lists for the entire film. If you are doing a short this may be a very good idea. These devices can be used to help realize your vision and can be very valuable, but these lists do not necessarily represent the final version of the film. You should approach them as preliminary plans, subject to change.

DRAW AND CHANGE

If you give a beat sheet to ten people you are probably going to have at least ten different versions of how these shots will look. Written and spoken words are not specific enough. You need to make drawings. Imagine your images playing like a film. Ask yourself, "Can they be made better, more interesting?" "How do I want the audience to feel: worried, suspicious or indifferent?" "Who or what is the center of attention in this shot?" The answers to some of these questions may evolve as a series of images develop.

You may be many hours into a project before the best solutions begin to reveal themselves. Revisions will certainly be needed. From shots to scenes to sequences to acts to a finished film, it is important to see the flow of images as malleable and open to reinvention.

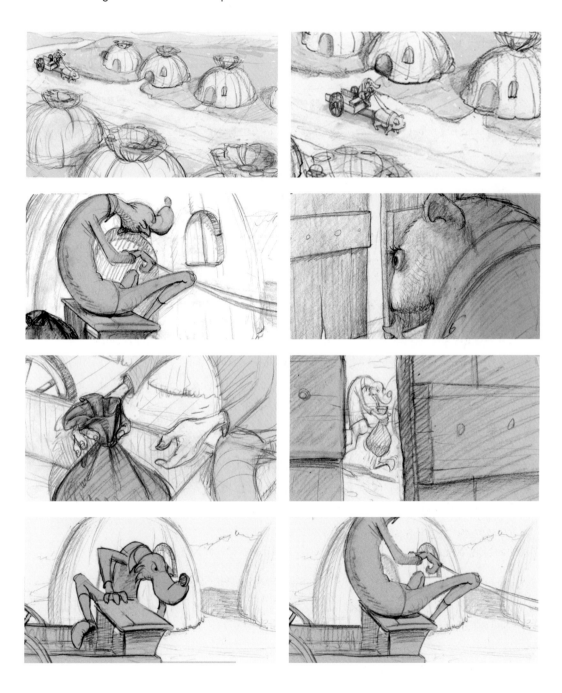

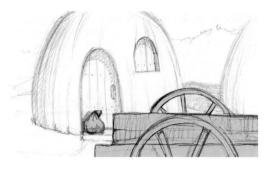 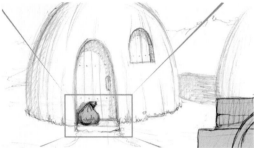

Finished Boards

CONTINUITY

Continuity refers to the logical flow and consistency of the images. Your audience's suspension of disbelief will be lost if it notices a continuity problem. This can pertain to a number of things such as the appearance of objects, the lighting or direction of movement. The viewer will be confused if things are changed too much or are changed illogically from one cut to the next. If the light is casting shadows to the left in the first shot, don't switch them to the right when returning to the original camera angle. If a baseball dugout is left of the batter's mound, do not show the batters coming up to home plate from the right. The storyboards serve as a guide for the film; they need to be correct to prevent later problems. It is advisable for artists to create diagrams and floor plans of a space in order to keep the position of things from various angles clear and logical. If it is not completely clear for the storyboard artist, it may not be clear for the viewer.

180-DEGREE RULE

Steve Gordon, professional storyboard artist for Disney and DreamWorks said:

> I've seen some student storyboards and some test storyboards from non-students. What seems to be most lacking is the understanding of basic cinematography, screen direction and why a scene should cut. Don't get me wrong, I also see some of these things in professional boards as well. The most important thing to learn is the 180-degree rule and how to work around it.

A common "slip-up" in storyboarding and film planning is continuity of movement or screen direction. If a train is moving from left to right on the screen, that train needs to continue moving left to right and not switch direction. If one were to do a cut where the camera appeared to have moved to the other side and the train was now moving from right to left, this could be disorienting for the audience. The audience may feel that it is now looking at a different train or perhaps this is now another time and place. This kind of cut is said to be breaking the 180-degree rule. The 180-degree rule is a guide to maintain a consistent positioning within the two-dimensional frame of the movie.

Eric Drobile's Environment Plans

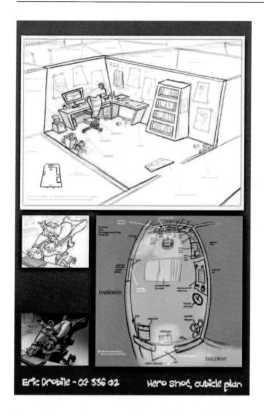

If two characters, say an armadillo and a frog, are playing "tug-o-war," a frog may be seen on the right facing left pulling on the rope. An armadillo may be seen on the left facing right pulling on the rope. The rope represents the 180-degree line. If the camera stays on the same side of that line, the frog will always be on the right and the armadillo will always be on the left even if the camera is shooting down the rope from one end of the action. If the camera crosses the 180-degree line and starts filming from the other side it will reverse the position of the frog and armadillo. The armadillo will then be on the right and the frog will be on the left. Again, this kind of reversal can confuse the audience. So the camera should not cross the 180-degree line or, to put it another way, you should avoid reversing the position or direction of your characters.

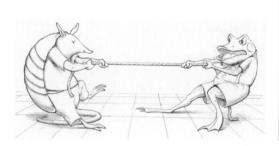

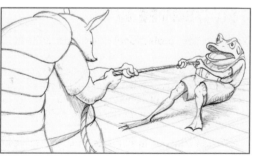

Yes

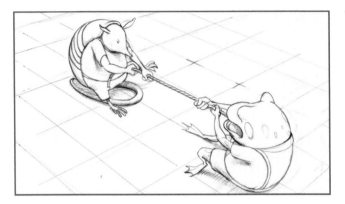

Yes

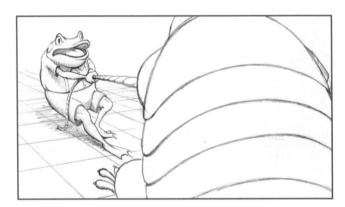

This is Breaking the 180-degree Rule

Diagram of Cameras

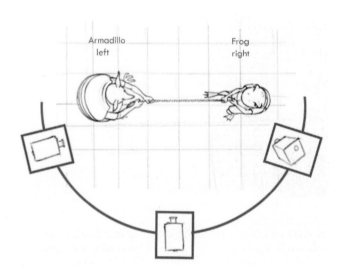

During a fast-action chase or other action scene concerns about screen direction may seem expendable but it is probably not. One could have an overhead shot of a horseman running over a drawbridge and into a fortress, disappearing under the ramparts moving from left to right. The next shot could have the camera inside the walls and at a lower angle as he passes through the gate and across the screen. It is important to realize that this second shot should also have the character moving from the left side of the screen to the right.

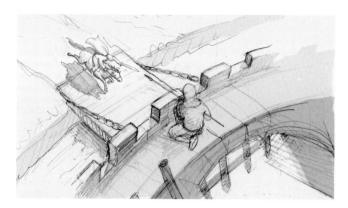

Yes

Yes

No

As we all know, there are exceptions to all rules and times when other factors govern one's choices but usually the orientation of even stationary objects in a shot should remain consistent with other adjoining shots. There is nothing to be gained by confusing the audience or breaking the 180-degree rule when the purpose is to tell your story clearly.

CONTINUITY OF CONTENT

Continuity of content is a general expression of the idea of story clarity. It is important for the storyboard artist to remember that the audience does not know the logic of your story until you show them. This sounds simple but problems often arise because we know our own story and we forget that the audience does not know what we know. The audience will be seeing your shots for the first time and then only for a few seconds. If information is not simple and clear, the audience will miss important story points and end up confused for the rest of the film. There are many ways to confuse an audience. Although I cannot discuss every possibility in this chapter, I would like to point out a couple of common storyboard shortcomings.

Disjointed Shots

Scenes depicting bad drug trips and nightmares, earthquakes, pillaging barbarians and general chaos may show extremely different shots together to instill in the audience a sense of what it felt like to be disoriented. However, the rest of the time you need to provide an uncomplicated flow of visual information to the viewer. Continuity of content requires that you show us all the "pieces" we need to see, usually in a natural, chronological order. It is important that you do not make the viewer work too hard in order to know what is going on. It is your story that should engage the audience. Make the story easy to understand. Storyboards help you to establish both visual continuity and continuity of content. However, since storyboard artists are inherently "too close" to the storyboards to see them objectively, show your boards to others who do not know the story you are working on to see if it makes sense to them. Ultimately, the success of your film will not only depend on whether you understand and like what you see, but rather on whether you have communicated well to others.

Visual continuity also requires the story artist to build an appropriate evolution of shape, color, space, lighting and other formal elements of design as the story develops. The visual design elements can either harmonize or contrast from one shot to the next. Harmonious or similar shapes and colors suggest small changes in the story. Contrasts, big changes in the design or composition, usually suggest more extreme shifts in content, emotion or action. Filmmakers often will show a film for several minutes with fairly constant, harmoniously designed images until the moment when something that will change the story happens, like when the villain appears. When the villain appears his color may be different, the shapes and tones in the background could go from horizontal to diagonal, the camera angle may be very low for the first time in the film and the lighting might be harsh with strong shadows after having been soft and even in earlier shots. It is important to avoid making strong changes in the design from one shot to the next if the story does not have a strong thematic or emotional shift on that shot.

Too Big of a Gap

Story clarity and continuity can fall apart if there is not enough information. Let's say a character is walking down the street and then the scene cuts to that character inside a house sitting in a chair. This could work if the audience believes that time has passed and we are now in some new place. However, if you want us to know that the character went into a particular house that belongs to someone he knows, who the character discovers is not at home, you will have to explain these things. The character may need to be seen walking up to and perhaps into the house, searching for the other character, looking into several rooms and then sit down in the chair. As this character is looking for someone you may need to show him walking through a bedroom door and then cut to a reverse shot showing the character's face looking around inquisitively. Then you may need to show the character's point of view revealing what he sees and does not see as he looks. After that it may be necessary to show the character's face again so the audience knows that the character is surprised or confused and has recognized that no one is there. Then you may need to show him walk over to the chair and sit down. Keep reminding yourself that the audience does not know what's going on in your story or in the character's mind until you show them.

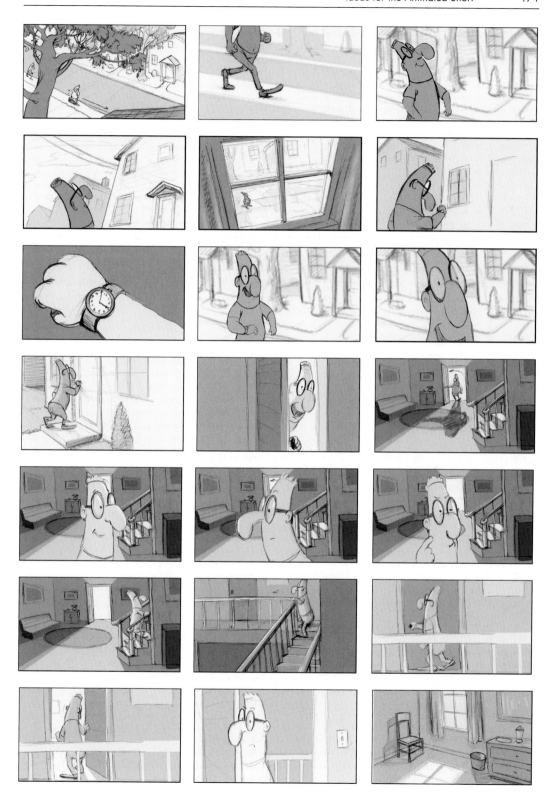

Shot types: Establishing Shot; Reverse Shot; Cut on the Look; POV; and Reaction Shot

ESTABLISHING SHOT

The opening shot in a scene can be used to show the viewer where the story will be taking place: in the woods, in a castle, at the circus or in this case in a middle-class suburb. This is often a long shot that gives a lot of general information about the location or event, the time of day and weather conditions. The establishing shot can also give us a feeling for the story. It could show bright houses with trimmed hedges and a bicycle on the lawn or there could be a dark, ramshackle mansion with an iron gate and dead trees. The feeling of peacefulness or peril could be suggested through the shapes, patterns and lighting. The visual style of the film can be revealed. All of these things set a visual context for all other relationships in the scene making the establishing shot very important.

REVERSE SHOT AND OVER THE SHOULDER

A reverse shot points the camera back in the opposite direction from a previous shot. If we watch our character walk through a doorway and we are looking at his back, the next shot may show a camera view from inside the room he's just entered from a front view. This is often used if two characters are facing each other having a conversation. The camera will show a "front on" shot of one character talking and then reverse the camera and show the other person listening or responding. This kind of shot may also be done "over the shoulder." As the name implies, the camera is behind the character. The character's shoulder and/or part of his head can be seen in the foreground as the audience sees what the character is facing or looking at. Many filmed conversations will use a combination of these shots.

Sometimes students confuse these camera reversals with violating the 180-degree rule but that is different. The 180-degree rule requires that you keep your subjects oriented to either the right or left side of the screen but it does not prohibit you from reversing the position of the camera. However, even when reverse shots are used, as in a conversation, it is often advisable to shift one character more to the left side of the screen instead of in the center and the other person more to the right and to keep these relative positions consistent throughout the conversation. It is also important to keep the camera angled up or down if one character is higher or lower than the other.

CUT ON THE LOOK AND POINT OF VIEW (POV)

When a filmmaker shows the character looking at something and then shows the audience what the character has seen just as if we are seeing it through the character's eyes, this is called a *point of view* or *POV* shot. So, if a character is looking up at the second-floor bedroom window of a house, the next shot will show the window as that character sees it from that low angle and at that distance. If the character then looks down at his watch, the camera may show the character looking at his wrist and then cut to show a down angle shot of the arm and the wristwatch. It is important when your character sees something to show the audience first, that he is looking at something or in some direction and then what he sees. If the audience does not see what the character has seen it will not know what the character has experienced. If the audience does not know what the character has experienced, the plot and the audience's identification with the character's emotions may be lost. The storyboard artist may also want to show us how the character reacts to what he has seen, so that we understand what the character is thinking and feeling.

THINKING, DECIDING, REACTION SHOTS

While the animator or actor is responsible for the final version of the character's performance, the storyboard artist initiates this process by drawing the iconic poses and facial expressions that are appropriate for this point in the story. As Barry Cook, an animator, story artist and Director of Disney's *Mulan*, put it, "I would not advise leaving the acting to the animators for a simple reason, if it is not clear in boards, what your characters are feeling, the scene will never get to the animators." If a storyboard were to show a character looking into an empty room, the following shot could be the character's POV (point of view) of the empty room. Then the next shot should show a close-up of the character's face looking confused

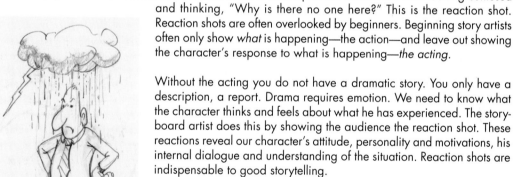

and thinking, "Why is there no one here?" This is the reaction shot. Reaction shots are often overlooked by beginners. Beginning story artists often only show *what* is happening—the action—and leave out showing the character's response to what is happening—*the acting*.

Without the acting you do not have a dramatic story. You only have a description, a report. Drama requires emotion. We need to know what the character thinks and feels about what he has experienced. The storyboard artist does this by showing the audience the reaction shot. These reactions reveal our character's attitude, personality and motivations, his internal dialogue and understanding of the situation. Reaction shots are indispensable to good storytelling.

Although this image may be a bit corny, it would be preferable to having no representation of your character's mood or state of mind

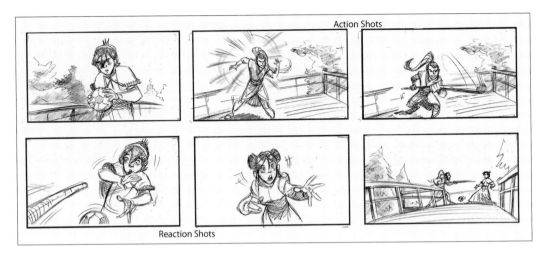

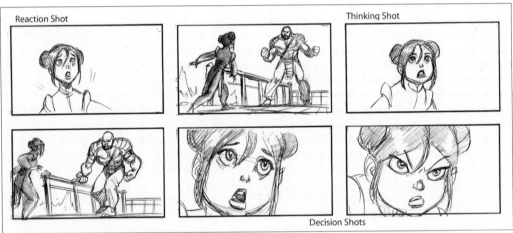

Storyboard Drawings by Steve Gordon

INSERT, CUT AWAY, CUT ON THE ACTION, CROSS CUTTING

In the early days of film, filmmakers often had a camera running continuously from a single location as the action moved in front of the lens, much the way we would see a play being performed on a stage. With experience and artistic vision, filmmakers soon realized that the possibilities of cinematography offered many more exciting choices. Complex angles, multiple views, and simultaneous actions could be shown in a way that the audience could follow when the shots were edited together effectively.

Insert

An insert shot is cut into the flow of an action and is usually designed to show the audience some specific piece of information, often in a close-up, sometimes a still image. If a character looks at his watch you may see an insert that shows a close-up of the watch so the audience knows it is five minutes until midnight. An insert could also be something that the director wants the audience to see but the main character is unaware of. In live action, these shots are usually added, or inserted, during the editing process.

Cut Away

Cut away refers to shots that show images that are not in the main action but are usually happening at the same time. If a knight is fighting a dragon you may see the camera "cut away" to the damsel in distress as she shields her eyes when her hero appears to be faltering in the battle. In a cut away you can show the actions and reactions of these other participants without stopping the main action. The knight and dragon could be fighting near the edge of a rocky cliff and a cut away may show small rocks that have been kicked loose during the battle rolling off the edge of the cliff and falling down into an abyss. Sometimes a cut away is used to reveal the environment to create atmosphere and a sense of what a place is like and feels like. During the knight and dragon battle, a cut away shot may show a pile of human bones and armor telling us that many other knights have tried and failed to defeat the dragon.

Cut on the Action

If an outlaw is going to be hanged in a Western town, a distant shot may show the outlaw's body start to drop through the trap door. A cut away may show a close-up of the rope pulled straight and tight where it is attached at the top of the gallows. Then the camera may return to the distant shot of the outlaw dangling at the end of the rope. This cutting away from the main action to show a detail is sometimes called *cut on the action*. It suggests to the audience that the main action is continuing while the detail was being shown. This same "cut on the action" could happen the opposite way, starting with a detail shot, cutting away to a distant shot and then returning to the original close-up.

Cross Cutting

Another editing device which is similar to the cut away is cross cutting. Cross cutting is used to show two actions that are happening at the same time. This becomes particularly important if the two actions or events are gopping to come together and create one major action. In the storyboard segment of the pirate rabbit by student, Maria Clapsis (pp. 177–8), a lizard captain is above deck and a pirate rabbit is below deck entering a doorway leaving a gunpowder trail on the floor. Later, the rabbit has an encounter with a hanging skeleton that causes him to get frightened and drop his cigar. In the storyboards shown, cross cutting allows the audience to see that the cigar has started a fire that keeps growing next to the gunpowder. At the same time the pirates, oblivious to the fire, are preparing to shoot a cannon ball at a passing ship. In the end, the cigar fire near the gunpowder and the attempt to shoot the cannon simultaneously reach a climax and the pirate ship blows up. The passing ship is unharmed but the pirate ship is sunk.

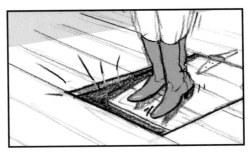

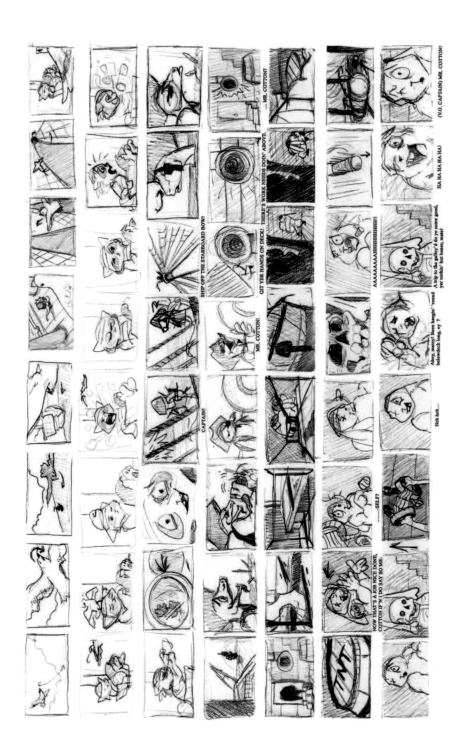

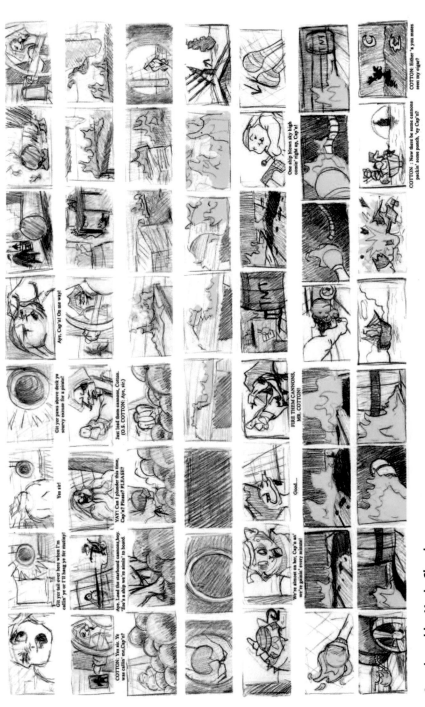

Storyboard by Maria Clapsis

SPLIT SCREEN, COLLAGE, SUPERIMPOSITION, ETC.

In order to clarify simultaneous events or images, filmmakers have tried a number of ways to show two or more pictures on the screen at the same time. These devices can be very effective if used correctly. The problem is that they tend to draw a lot of attention to themselves and may seem artificial or contrived. A split screen is often used when two characters are talking on the phone. The two shots of the two characters are simply shown, each in their own location, on a divided screen.

Split Screen

A similar effect is sometimes created when we see a side view of a character outside of a door and another character on the other side of the door or wall. The cross-section of the wall serves as a natural device to split the screen. A collage technique may show two or more images on the screen together or in quick succession perhaps with cross dissolves as in a montage. Superimposition, another technique, usually refers to a semitransparent image overlaying a primary image. Superimposition is often used to show a memory. A picture-in-picture may have a new rectangle appear on the screen revealing a second image. There are a myriad variations and rare types of shots used in films that I will not cover in this chapter. Books such as *Setting Up Your Shots*, by Jeremy Vineyard, and *From Word to Image*, by Marcie Begleiter, cover types of shots and terminology in greater depth.

TRANSITIONS

Beyond the types of shots, storyboarding also involves transitions between cuts. When I refer to transitions, I am speaking of two kinds. One kind is technical and refers to the mechanical process of film or digital editing, the resulting visual effect and its meaning for the viewer. The other kind is pictorial and refers to the types of pictures you are putting next to one another and how they move the ideas along. These transitions can expand time, compress time and enhance the mood and energy of a sequence. Although this is more apparent in the animatic or final editing stage, the planning and anticipation of transitions is part of the blueprint of any film. As Nathan Greno, Disney story artist and Story Supervisor for Disney's feature, *Bolt*, put it, "I try to keep editing transitions in mind if they help to tell the story I am boarding— otherwise I let the editor worry about the editing. The more you can do up front, the better it will help everyone else . . . ." If you are making your own film, you may be the story artist and the final editor. So it is a good idea to start planning how you will use transitions to help tell your story.

Technical Editing Transitions

Every change from one shot to the next is called a transition. If the filmmaker decides to put some black frames or white frames between shots or fade one shot out as the other simultaneously fades in, the shots will read differently. Common technical transitions are the standard cut, the cut or fade to black or to white, and the cross dissolve. There are many others, like the iris, that are used for special reasons, which I will not go into in this chapter. A fade to black can suggest that time has passed between the end of one shot and the beginning of the next. This can happen quickly or very slowly and the effect is a sense of duration. A cross dissolve will show one shot becoming progressively transparent and fading away as it is simultaneously replaced by the next shot fading in. Such transitions may suggest we are in another place perhaps at another time. Variables such as the type of image, duration of transitions and the story context will have an effect on the way that our audience reacts to our film transitions. However, these transitions will dramatically affect your story so you must often consider your story and the technical transitions in tandem. You can choose to draw these transitions or it may be enough to simply write, fade or cross dissolve, on your storyboards. If you produce an animatic, you can show the transitions between your story panels and reveal the effect more completely.

Cross Dissolve

Fade to Black

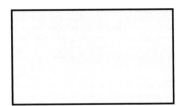

Fade to White

Iris in

Pictorial Transitions, Match Cuts

Unlike a single painting or sculpture, most narrative film is made of a continuous series of changing images. One can put very different images next to each other or very similar images next to each other. When one cuts to an image that is noticeably similar to the previous image, it can be called a *match cut.* If a character is eating and begins to move a spoon toward his mouth and then the camera cuts to

Match Cut

a close-up of him completing the action and putting the spoon in his mouth, this is a match cut even if the camera has moved. The two shots are tied visually and thematically together by the action.

Match cuts like this can be used to create a natural flow of images so the cuts are barely noticed. Match cuts can also be used to relate two different kinds of images. A pair of shots could cut from an image of the round glowing sun to an image of a round glowing light bulb in a room at night. This will not only create a comfortable transition between two similar-looking objects but it may communicate to the viewer that the passage of time has caused the daylight of the sun to be replaced by the nighttime light of the electric bulb. In this case, the two images are matched by content, shape and perhaps even color.

Match Cut

One could also match images by movement, such as a car racing down a road transitioning to a train going down a railroad track. A match cut of a female scientist holding up a test tube in a laboratory dissolving to the same woman holding up a baby bottle just before she feeds her baby could tell the story of a woman giving up her career to be a stay-at-home mother. Match cuts like these are a way of slicing through time and complex details to force relationships between images and ideas. They can often allow us to move through a great deal of story time in a very small amount of movie time. They can often make changes that would otherwise seem harsh or discordant seem more visually agreeable and harmonious.

Clean Entrance/Exit

A clean entrance happens when you show a place and then without a camera cut you see a character or a car or a dog enter the scene. The clean exit will show a character leave a scene and the shot will remain on the place he has departed from for a bit before the camera cuts to the next shot. To show the location before the character arrives or after the character departs, changes the viewer's reading of the passage of time. If you see a girl riding away on a bicycle and the camera cuts before the bike leaves the frame and the next shot is another view of the girl on the bike, the audience can usually assume that the cuts are instantaneous, that no time has elapsed between the two shots.

If the character rides completely off the screen and the camera shows the empty school yard she was previously riding by and then cuts to a shot of the girl's house and the bicyclist comes riding into the screen, the audience may assume that some time had passed between the time she rode by the school yard and the time she arrived at her house.

We will be convinced that these scenes are not taking place in the uninterrupted time of the film, but represent the beginning and end of a journey from which the middle has been extracted, perhaps for the sake of expediency or to more quickly get to the important parts of the story. Showing the girl spending 20 minutes riding from the school yard to her house might be very boring and insignificant to the story. You should not let your story get bogged down with inconsequential information. However, other times the story may require that you show someone doing something that takes a long, long time.

Jump Cut

The boredom or weariness of a long drawn-out action may be a central point in the story. Rather than show the camera on someone as they are in the act of waiting all night you may show jump cuts. Technically, a jump cut is simply a cut where the same character or image moves abruptly from one shot to the next sometimes breaking the flow of time and space. If a person is waiting, there may be a shot of them sitting in a chair. Then the camera cuts to the character slouched back in the chair. A third cut may have them bent over with their elbows on their knees or up walking around in the room. This would create the feeling that we are seeing short excerpts from a long boring period of time. Jump cuts could be used to speed up the portrayal of the duration of time while the audience still understands that this represents a long wait.

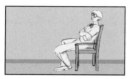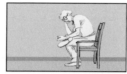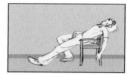

Jump cuts to show passage of time

A film that lasts one minute may tell a story that takes place over many years or even centuries. Storytellers can speed up time, slow down time, move forward and backward in time. The passage of time is manipulated to allow the storyteller to move to the important story points and cut through the less significant events. A storyboard artist makes choices about how the story's time and reality will be communicated to achieve the clearest and most effective telling of the story.

VISUALIZING TIME AND MOVEMENT

Another aspect of revealing the passage of time is the representation of movement. From the earliest cave paintings to the most recent animated film, artists have been trying to create still images that embody an expression of movement. This is because most living things move and to embody movement will bring the artist closer to embodying life. And all great art embodies a sense of life. The history of art is filled with images of flying angels and battling soldiers on running horses. Some modern artists such as the Futurists and Cubists created abstracted representations showing multiple aspects of humans and objects suggesting the images were moving or that the viewer was moving around the objects. When filmmaking came into existence many secrets were revealed about the nature of movement. One of the earliest and still the greatest documentations of the movement of people and animals was conducted by Eadweard Muybridge. In 1877, his technique of creating a series of still images of a horse trotting proved that all four of a horse's hooves were off the ground at some points during the action. The experiments by scientists such as Harold Edgerton in the mid-twentieth century using special lighting devices and high-speed cameras were able to capture shots of a bullet passing through an apple with the clear image of the bullet suspended in air. Some of the photos Edgerton made had shutter speeds of one one-hundred-millionth of a second. So the question is, "What can we learn from this, what do things look like when they move and how do we capture this impression of movement in a still image?"

No Movement

Movement

Storyboard by Steve Gordon

GRAPHIC REPRESENTATION OF MOVEMENT

There are devices of graphic representation that can suggest movement or restrict movement. Buildings are designed to not move. They are typically made of straight lines based on horizontals and verticals like a soldier standing to attention. Therefore, horizontals and verticals may restrict movement. Movement is suggested by diagonals and curves. Humans and animals tilt and turn and bend. We move through space in paths that define arcs and can spin creating serpentine patterns. Drawings of moving things require the application of these elements. A running character may have its feet completely off the ground like Muybridge's horse. He may be leaning forward with his hair and clothing flapping in the wind behind him. Speed lines and multiple images can be used creating a sort of "comet's tail" effect following an object. Storyboard drawings need to look alive. They need to move and act and feel in order to overcome their static reality and to communicate the heightened action that animation requires.

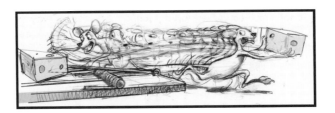

PRINCIPLES OF MOVEMENT: ANTICIPATION, SQUASH AND STRETCH, ARCS, FOLLOW THROUGH AND OVERLAPPING ACTION

Animators have discovered over the years that certain predictable principles can be applied to animated characters and other moving forms. These help to bridge that gap between the time-based dynamics of real-world physics and static reality of the drawn or virtual image. The following five of "the twelve principles of animation" pertain particularly to movement.

Anticipation

Before a character can jump off a box he must anticipate. That means he must contract his muscles, squat down, bend his knees, and maybe bring his arms and elbows up behind him. He may even scrunch up his facial features. Anticipation is the way the character builds up the energy to jump. Through this action, he will also be communicating to the audience that he is preparing to jump. Anticipation is both psychological and physical. One usually anticipates in the opposite direction of the main action.

Squash and Stretch

The principle of squash and stretch is an exaggerated sense of elasticity applied to show how things distort when they move and when they stop. When a character jumps off a box, he will stretch as he falls through the air and squash as his legs absorb the weight of the body collapsing onto itself. Even the head of a hammer may squash when it strikes a board. Though it may not be necessary to apply extreme exaggeration on each movement you depict, the effects of squash and stretch in your still, storyboard drawings may have to be overstated to communicate the force and energy of the movement.

Arcs

Mechanical things such as cars and rockets are distinguished by the fact that they appear to travel in a straight path. However, when most things, especially organic forms, move through space they move in arcs. When a character swings his arm or lifts his head or jumps off a box the path of action will almost always be an arc. If you are showing speed lines, they should reflect the curved movement.

Follow-Through and Overlapping Action

Follow-through suggests that something will keep moving in the direction of its force until some resistance causes it to stop. When a baseball player hits a ball his bat keeps swinging around in its arc until it stops behind his head. If a rider's horse stops suddenly the rider may go flying over the top of the horse. This is closely related to overlapping action, which suggests that different parts of the main body of a character or an object will move or stop at different times. If a person jumps off a box his coat tails may not come down until after the character's feet have hit and perhaps not until the character is starting to stand upright. Follow-through explains that a form keeps moving in its designated path until something stops it like friction or hitting another object. Overlapping action describes the way these different parts may move at different times. So if you draw a character landing from a jump, his knees may be bending from the squash but his coat tails may still be up in the air.

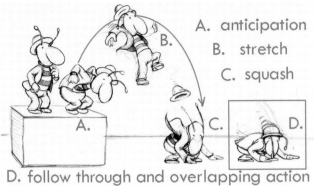

A. anticipation
B. stretch
C. squash

D. follow through and overlapping action

Multiple Images

If a character needs to move through a scene in a particular way, the storyboard artist can either show several panels that represent different stages of the action or one shot that shows multiple, staggered images to describe different positions. The choice is determined by the need for clarity. The goal should be to have one idea in each board so there may need to be many panels to show a shot from a single camera position if, for instance, a squirrel was walking across the counter in a candy store continually searching for goodies. The squirrel may be lifting this and looking under that as he makes his way across the counter. One should probably do a drawing for each action, for each idea.

If, on the other hand, the squirrel is simply walking across the counter, the boards may want only to show the path he takes. In this case a beginning and end drawing with an arrow connecting them in one storyboard panel may suffice. Arrows pointing left and right, up, down, forward, backward and following arcs can "stand in" for movements in the still images of a storyboard and can be very helpful to the direction and clarity of actions.

CAMERA MOVES

One can hold a camera in their hand, put it on a car or an airplane, or push it around on a dolly. Cranes and trucks that ride on tracks have been used to move the audience's vantage point to wherever the filmmaker wants it to be. Digital technology allows cameras to follow bullets into the bodies of victims, be plunged into molten lava and to see through the eyes of an erratically moving dragonfly. Advancements in lenses and internal camera technology also create many options. A storyboard artist should know when and what kind of camera moves to use.

Trucks and Zooms

Truck-in and a zoom-in will produce similar results, but they are not the same. A zoom on a face in a crowd of characters will cause the size of the face to be "blown up" on the screen along with everything else in the frame. In the truck, the rest of the crowd will not grow but the foreground people will be seen passing by as the camera moves toward the face. A truck-in on that character's face will be closer to the experience of walking through the crowd until you are physically close to them and their face is close to you. This is because the zoom is done with the camera lens and magnifies the light coming through, whereas the truck actually moves the camera through the crowd toward the main character. This difference will make a difference in the way you are allowing the audience to experience the action. This physical difference evokes a different emotional response and represents a significantly different way of telling your story.

Zoom

Truck

Representing Camera Moves: Pans, Tracks, Zooms and Extended Frames

If you have decided that it is necessary to show the camera moving as part of your story idea, there are some standard ways to represent this in the storyboard. If a dog sees something good to eat like a pie but the baker is standing guard, the camera may choose to show the character's POV as he looks at the pie and then at his obstacle, the baker. Instead of a cut, you may want the camera to swing or rotate from one view to the other. This type of shot needs to be shown by indicating the movement of the camera. The storyboard artist can draw framing boxes around each of the views focusing on one and then the other view with arrows or lines that connect the two boxes.

This technique can be used for a zoom shot as well. The panel would show the whole scene with framing boxes corresponding to the film's aspect ratio used to show close-up and overview areas with lines or arrows connecting them.

Sometimes the camera moves over such a great distance that it cannot be contained within one standard-sized frame. If the camera follows beside a cat as it walks across a floor and jumps onto a window sill, this is referred to as a tracking shot. It may be necessary to show the distance covered as a storyboard panel that is wider or higher than normal. The character can be shown at two or more positions along the way. A framing box would be shown around several character positions to explain how the camera is framing the character at different points during the action. Once again, these framing boxes can be connected by arrows or lines.

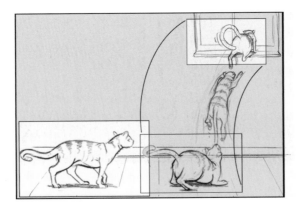

Sometimes zooms and pans or zooms and dollys, called *zollys*, happen at the same time. If camera moves are important to telling your story then you are responsible for showing them. You may choose to show it with framing boxes and arrows or as a series of individual drawings on different panels. You must be clear about what you are trying to show so the storyboards depict how the film version of your story is going to read.

CAMERA PLACEMENT

Where you put the camera is where you are visually and emotionally putting the audience. You can either keep it at a distance watching the action or, make it see and feel like it is in the midst of the events like participants. There is a right time and a wrong time for both of these approaches. It is essential to how you tell a story and a decision you must make on nearly every board. Beginner story artists often do not exploit their options in camera placement. As story artist and teacher, Jim Story, said, "One of the most prominent stumbling blocks in student boards is a tendency to 'lock down' the camera and to view everything at the same size as if it were on stage."

Many boxing movies show the actor swinging punches directly at the camera or waking up from the floor with an up angle of the ceiling lights and the referee counting to ten. This can make us feel as though the experience is happening to us.

Other times we are in the audience looking over the tops of other people's heads. Sometimes the camera takes us completely out of the action and we are looking down from above like a scientist might look at specimens through a microscope. The purpose is not to be fancy with the camera for its own sake. Too many, unnecessary camera moves are surely as problematic as locking the camera down. Your story's appropriate feelings of mystery, intimacy, or indifference can be induced by carefully choosing your audience's vantage point through good camera placement.

HOW MUCH INFORMATION

Students often ask, "How many panels will I need and how finished should they be?" The answer depends on your story and how you are telling it. A filmmaker can show a character going through a door with one shot or ten shots if the situation calls for it. Each board should represent one idea. The camera may cut back and forth between the inside and outside if, for instance, someone is inside watching the door open. If the character hesitates or struggles with the door the boards may be quite involved. If value and light are critical to the telling of your story or something's color is an important element then you may need to show that in your boards. Otherwise, simple line drawings may do the job. If a character comes walking out of the fog then you need to show the fog in the environment where the shots take place. Other times atmosphere and weather conditions may not be a concern.

CLARITY

Nearly every storyboard artist, director and producer I've interviewed mentioned the need to be clear in your storyboards. We cannot go back and re-tell the story in our short film; it has to work the first time. Shots need to be unambiguous and so should your storyboards. Find a simple, clear drawing style. Avoid unnecessary details. Too much detail can actually make the idea harder to read but be complete with the ideas you are portraying. Be bold. Faint graphite pencil drawings that are too weak to see will not work. Use a felt tip or china marker or at least a soft, broad-tipped pencil. More and more often, artists are scanning their drawings into Photoshop or some similar program—or working completely in the digital environment—to enhance the clarity. Contrast can be boosted, tones can be added, cropping and re-framing are easy and layers can allow one to use the same character or background drawing over several times keeping them consistent without re-drawing.

BOARDING DIALOGUE, ACTING

It is often said that dialogue should be like background music. You should be able to turn the sound off and still know what is happening in the story. This is mostly true and it suggests that it is the visual information, a character's gesture, facial expressions and environment that do the communicating. Imagine a wife is waiting for her philandering husband, who is three hours late for supper. She may say, "Oh, I'm so glad you decided to join us." Of course what she really means is, "You thoughtless jerk, you don't care how much inconvenience you cause me." The words are only part of the story and sometimes a fairly insignificant part. Your storyboard panels need to show us that a character's body language communicates their true mood or state of mind as the words are being spoken. Animation tends to use exaggerated body gestures and facial expressions.

Make a video of yourself or another actor delivering the lines or get a mirror and try to find the primary facial expressions you need and then caricature them. In animation all the acting is created on paper, in the computer or with clay, and so forth. As Frank Gladstone, producer and animation artist said,

> This is one of the reasons many board artists were animators first. Like animators, storyboard folks have to understand acting . . . and how acting choices help to establish both narrative context and subtext. Of course, like actors and animators, board artists should develop good and consistent observation skills.

Observation skills mean paying attention to real life and how people behave. Watch how a parent scolds a child. Watch two children negotiate over a toy. Watch someone talking on a phone. Become a student of acting, become a student of human behavior.

What?

Forgot What?

Oh!!!

Hee hee . . .

PITCHING

Pitching is the process where storyboard artists show and explain the boards to others. During the pitch, the storyboard artist will point to individual panels and tell us what is going on, often making sound effects or speaking in the different voices of the characters with the appropriate expression. The pitch will indicate the pace of events by going through the boards faster or slower. It requires that one is not shy and perhaps even has a bit of acting ability. The pitch is presented to inform other members of a story team or the director and clients. A pitch can help "sell" the storyboards and get them approved for animation. Not because they have been made to seem more entertaining than they actually are but because they have been brought to life a bit more. In story teams, such as the major studios have, you can expect that your pitch will result in your story being changed, rearranged and even thrown out sometimes. As Nathan Greno, supervising story artist at Walt Disney Feature Animation put it,

> A successful storyboard artist is one that is open to new ideas. You *can't* fall in love with your boards. Your boards are not the final film—they won't be on the screen. Don't spend too much time on your boards—they will most likely be completely thrown out at some point. If that sounds too depressing, you best find another department to work in.

> Story is subjective. Your director is going to ask for changes. To be a great story artist; you will have to be open-minded to throwing your work away. Even if you completely disagree with your director, you are going to have to make the changes. It doesn't matter if you think the director is crazy.

Stories can be told many different ways. Be willing to change your plan often while searching for the best solutions.

PACING

Pacing defines the rate of the action and the cuts. A dry, flat story presentation may have the cuts at even intervals. A stronger presentation may linger lazily on some images and present others in rapid-fire succession. The number of film cuts may increase as the tension and action build. The audience will feel a sense of urgency even if it is not aware that the cuts are coming quicker. The best way to know if the pacing is working is to see the images change during the pitch or to make the boards into an animatic or progression reel. However, from the very beginning you must anticipate the pacing of your film and imagine the timing of the cuts.

PROGRESSION/STORY REELS

In large studios, the animators will see what is called a *story* or *progression reel* at several points during the production of the film. The first version would be made almost entirely of the storyboard drawings with a scratch track, a substitute dialogue and/or sound effects track. This is how the hundreds of people working on the film can be kept informed about the kind of film they are making. As the project progresses, artists see updated versions of the reel. The next version may have some of the storyboards replaced by animation.

Perhaps a few color scenes would be cut in. Maybe some of the actors' recorded dialogue would be inserted to replace the scratch track and some of the final music score may be heard.

ANIMATIC

Digital technology has provided nearly every story artist with a number of computer programs that allow them to make a progression reel from their storyboards. This digital, video version of a storyboard is usually called an animatic. One can photograph or scan their drawings and play them back with the correct timing and many of the editing transitions that will be used in the final film. Sound can be added as well as text and even some camera moves and simulated effects. This is very useful for the independent filmmaker. The process brings one that much closer to the full realization of how the film is going to play before making the final version. During the animatic stage, it is easier to see if transitions are working, and if rhythm and pacing feel correct for the story. One can coordinate the soundtrack with the images and generally have a clearer vision of the film. How far one goes with the animatic varies. Some of the animatics on the website that comes with this book show a basic skeleton of the shots, while others are nearly films in their own right.

DIGITAL STORYBOARDS

Some video game studios are doing all their storyboards and story presentations digitally. Feature animation studios are beginning to change as well. As Paul Briggs, a relatively new member of the Walt Disney Feature Animation story team said,

> I personally start out by thumbnailing on paper and figuring out the major beats in the sequence. I'll then work all digital on a Cintiq, drawing all my boards in Photoshop. I usually work straight ahead but once I'm done with the sequence, I'm always going back into it and reworking it. Whatever you feel comfortable using and best conveys your ideas is what's important though. A lot of artists still draw on paper and use chalk, crayon, marker, pens, etc. Others work all digital using Photoshop or Painter.

Paul Briggs also said that he presents his work to the directors by projecting the drawings using a computer program which allows him to move and delete boards as well as change dialogue. This will surely become more prevalent in the future, so it is a good idea to become familiar with these programs and the digital drawing tablet.

Summary

- Storyboards plan and communicate the shots and transitions of a film.
- Drawing skill and versatility are essential to professional storyboard artists.
- Knowledge of film language and cinematography is essential.
- Design elements embody the emotional messages in a film.
- Thumbnailing is how we start the visual process.
- One must work to achieve continuity of direction, content, and design.
- There are a number of standard shots and transitions that are used most often.
- One can manipulate the passage of time with the right cuts and transitions.
- Storyboards can represent both the movement of objects and of the camera.
- Camera placement can help determine the audience's emotional attachment.
- Boarding dialogue involves special issues.
- Pitching is how storyboards are often presented to others.
- Animatics reveal the pacing and transitions as a filmed version of the boards.
- The storyboarding process is becoming progressively more digital.

Additional Resources: www.ideasfortheanimatedshort.com

- Films and animatics
- Industry Interviews on Storyboarding with Steve Gordon, Paul Briggs, Jim Story, Barry Cook and Frank Gladstone

Recommended Reading

1. Don Bluth, *Don Bluth's Art of Storyboard*
2. John Canemaker, *Paper Dreams*
3. Wayne Gilbert, *Simplified Drawing for Planning Animation*
4. Will Eisner, *Comics and Sequential Art*
5. Frank Thomas and Ollie Johnston, *The Illusion of Life*
6. Walt Stanchfield, *Drawn to Life*

Storyboarding: An Interview with Nathan Greno, Walt Disney Feature Animation

Nathan Greno attended Columbus College of Art and Design and later completed a Disney Animation Internship in Orlando, Florida. Nathan began working full time as a clean-up artist in the Disney traditional animation studio in 1996 and in the Disney story department in 1998. He served as Story Supervisor at Walt Disney Feature Animation on *Bolt* and was co-director and voice actor on *Tangled*.

Q: What background skills do storyboard artists need to be successful? What would you tell a student?

Nathan: To be a successful storyboard artist, you need an overworking brain and plenty of imagination. You need to be able to express your thoughts visually. You need to understand acting, staging, mood and lighting. You must be able to write dialogue and create characters. A storyboard artist creates the blueprint for the film. Storyboarding is the foundation of a film.

Q: How can one become a better storyboard artist?

Nathan: You get better at drawing by *practice*! Board your own ideas and pitch them to friends. Find a script of a movie you haven't seen and draw a sequence from it—then watch the movie and see what choices the filmmakers made. You will get better—and your drawing skills will quickly improve. Draw different kinds of sequences. If you feel you are better at action—board a sequence with subtle acting and dialogue. If you are better at subtle acting—board a chase sequence. Challenge yourself.

One thing to avoid: "stock" expressions. Unless your project calls for it, stay away from 1930s hammy acting. Act out your sequence before you draw it. Have a mirror sitting on your drawing table. Natural expressions are an amazing tool to have in your belt. The trick to drawing natural expressions: Less is usually more.

Q: Are there special characteristics that you find professional story artists have in common? What makes the successful ones successful?

Nathan: A successful storyboard artist is one that is open to ideas. You *can't* fall in love with your boards. Be willing to change. Your boards are not the final film. Don't spend too much time on your boards—they will likely be thrown out at some point. If that sounds too depressing, you best find another discipline to work in. Story is subjective. Your director is going to ask for changes. To be a great story artist, you will have to be ready to throw your work away. Even if you disagree and you think the director is crazy. At the end of the day you must respect your position. It's your job to make the project as great as it can be. But it's not "your" project.

Q: Have you looked at any student storyboards? What do you think is most often lacking in them?

Nathan: Recently we had a student portfolio review. Many had a similar problem: it was hard to follow their boards. Many students don't like to draw backgrounds, they don't set their characters in an understandable environment. You should be able to follow boards without reading the dialogue. Try this: watch a movie with the sound off. Usually you will still be able to tell what is going on because of the environment, staging and lighting—and expressions! Your boards should work this way. At a portfolio review there will not be enough time to look through every single panel of your boards, and read every single line of your dialogue. Within a dozen drawings a reviewer should be able to know what is going on in your boards.

There's a series of graphic novels that I can't recommend enough: *Bone* by Jeff Smith. They have started coloring them—but they were originally printed in black and white. Buy the black and white editions. It's amazing how much mood Smith can get without the use of color or gray tones. His acting is incredible—learn from what he's doing.

Q: Can you describe your process?

Nathan: There is no "right way" to storyboard a sequence. I always start with thumbnails. Sometimes I "straight ahead" my sequences and sometimes I board a bunch of key shots (that usually helps me with a big action sequence). What works best for you is the way to go.

Q: What do you find are the main obstacles you have to overcome when you are storyboarding a scene?

Nathan: A good thing to keep in mind is one new idea/action per drawing. Don't have too much going on in one panel or you'll confuse people. Clear simple drawings are a good thing.

Q: How would you describe the difference between storyboarding for film and other kinds of sequential artwork like comic books or book illustration?

Nathan: Comic books and storyboards are cousins—not brothers. I have learned a lot of shorthand drawing tools from comics (rain, simple cityscapes, thunder and lightning, blizzards, underwater or splashing effects, characters or object moving very fast, outer space sequences, etc.), but comics follow different rules than storyboards. The "camera" jumps around a lot in comics. What works for a comic book story will not work for a storyboarded sequence.

Q: Do you re-draw your panels many times?

Nathan: Don't fall in love with your drawings and don't sweat over them—they need to read clearly, but they are not the final image you will see on the screen. Make sure you are getting your sequences done on time—and make sure they read clearly.

Q: Do you think of yourself as actor, cameraman, editor, designer and/or all of these things in your job? Have I left anything out?

Nathan: A storyboard artist is an actor, cameraman, editor and designer—but you also must remember you are a collaborator. You work with others.

Q: How important is presentation? Do you refine your drawings a lot before they are presented to the bosses?

Nathan: That depends on a number of factors. You might throw in a few clean drawings if you've never worked with the director before—you want them to know what a "final" looks like. Rough is usually a good idea if you are exploring a sequence. Tighter, prettier drawings will help sell your sequence—directors like nice drawings. Each case is different—talk to your director and find out what they are looking for. Look at the kind of drawings the other artists are doing on their first passes.

Q: Do you find you have to overstate the action, acting, etc. in order for it to read in the storyboard or do you leave that problem to be solved by the animator?

Nathan: The more you "leave to the animator" or the layout artist or whoever—the less you'll see "you" in the film. You are making the blueprint of a building—if you don't design the windows, someone else will. You have a deadline so there will only be so much you can accomplish—but the more info you can give, the better the final film will be. People will take your boards and run with them—if the process works correctly, the film will improve with each department. It all starts with the storyboard artist—you are creating the map that everyone else will follow. You better make sure it's a damn good map!

Chapter 9
Staging

Staging in film refers to the way we present an image or an action for our audience. We plan how something is seen and experienced so that the audience gets the story point. You have probably heard people say that something was "staged." This may refer to planning something so it happens a certain way or that something is not a genuine incident, it is artificial. If something happens on stage—as in the live theater—it is art, but it is still artificial. Film is also art—and artificial—so it is important for the filmmaker to offer the audience a moving aesthetic experience, while providing the essential storytelling images. It is this marriage of the aesthetic and the narrative that should guide our decisions about staging.

DIRECTING THE EYE

Directing the eye refers to using visual devices to get the audience to look where you want it to look in the shot. When an image comes on the screen, the audience may be looking at the lower corner, the center or the upper third. Perhaps if an object is in the center the audience will look at that. However, if everything is placed in the center all the time it will get monotonous. Sometimes a moving image will draw more attention to itself than a stationary one. A strong color or anything that has greater visual attraction can direct the audience to look at that place on the screen.

Because our images may show for only a short time, we must make sure the audience sees what we need it to see while making the visual experience captivating. We have all seen group-shot photographs where someone would put a circle around someone or draw an arrow to get us to look at a certain person in the group. A spotlight is used on a live stage to accomplish the same thing. Spotlighting solutions are used in many films as well. In addition to light, graphic shapes, lines, and alignments can similarly lead the viewer's eyes to see what you want them to see.

Place a character in front of the vanishing point in a one-point perspective shot of a room and the receding lines of the vertices toward the vanishing point can direct our eyes to that person, even if there are other people in the room. A case in point is Leonardo Da Vinci's "The Last Supper." Shapes and lines created by foreground objects, shadow patterns, tone and color patterns can point to the place that you want the audience to see, thereby controlling the viewer's attention.

Storyboard by Maria Clapsis Uses Leading Lines to Direct the Viewer's Eye to the Man in the Window

Leading Lines Created by Shadows and Objects

Spotlight Effect to Get Us to Look in the Right Place

Aspect Ratio, Symmetry, the Golden Section and Rule of Thirds

Aspect ratio is the proportions of your screen. Early television screens were about one foot high and one foot, four inches wide. This is expressed as a 1 : 1.33 aspect ratio. Over the years, the ratio has generally changed to make the screen wider relative to its height. There are a number of reasons for this, one of them being to fill our peripheral vision more completely and approximate the experience of seeing things in real life. All good designs need to relate to the rectangle's proportions and the framing edge.

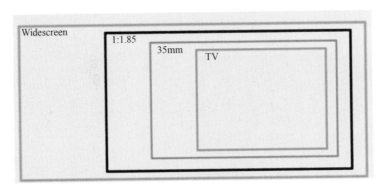

Various Aspect Ratios: Most Images in this Chapter are 1:185

Over the centuries, painters have worked inside of rectangles to build their compositions. The objective has always been to keep the images looking fresh but appropriate to the theme or subject, just like filmmaking. Dynamic images of battles would be designed very differently than portraits. But the search for the best design has led the artist to discover that some relationships seem to work very well and others not so well.

It has already been mentioned that things in the center are boring. Centered things can tend to lack vitality and look inert. It is advisable that you never divide your rectangular frame down the middle either horizontally or vertically unless the purpose is to express division, symmetry, and monotony. The golden section or golden mean is a proportion that would have you divide an eleven-inch rectangle at a place that would split it into two shapes, approximately seven and four inches each. This is a ratio of about 1 : 1.618 and is based on a geometric formula that relates the division to the proportion of the whole rectangle. Artists, architects and other designers had discovered that many things in nature adhere to this proportion so it was considered to be divinely conceived. The golden section is a comfortable, asymmetrical method of organization and is followed by many painters and filmmakers.

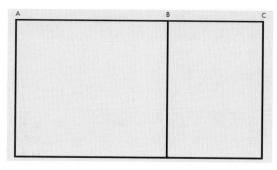

Golden Section: BC is to AB as AB is to AC

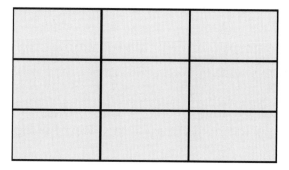

Rule of Thirds: The Intersections of the Horizontal and Vertical Divisions are Hot Spots Where We Should Focus the Viewer's Attention

Many filmmakers use the rule of thirds for compositional choices. The rule of thirds says that if you divide your screen into thirds vertically and horizontally, the intersection of these lines mark critical locations or "hot spots" on the screen. These hot spots are where the filmmaker should put the important information. This is a comfortable place to focus the audience's attention. If you watch almost any well-made film, you'll see the director using the rule of thirds extensively.

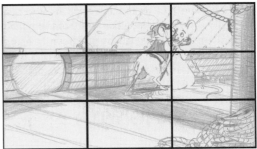

Maria Clapsis, Rule of Thirds

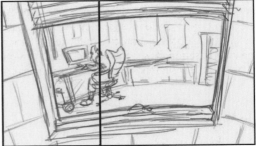

Eric Drobile, Golden Section

REDESIGNING THE RECTANGLE

In the section on storyboarding, we saw how filmmakers can split the screen to show two things happening at two different places at the same time. Montage, superimposition, and picture-in-picture techniques have allowed directors to restructure the film's framing rectangle. Today's relatively widescreen films create special problems for filmmakers as they work to present strong, meaningful visual presentations. It can work to one's advantage to find ways to reshape the area within the larger rectangle to create new and different compositional solutions. We are all familiar with a shot that shows the POV of someone looking through binoculars. This effect is called "mask shot." It effectively changes the shape of the area of interest. "Frame-in-frame" is a similar compositional device that can allow one to reshape their area of interest and provide focus and variation for the audience. If a camera shoots between the limbs of a tree or into the rearview mirror of a car, the shape of the tree limbs or the edges of the mirror will become a new frame inside the overall shot composition. Sometimes these kinds of shots can make the audience

Frame-in-Frame Compositions by Maria Clapsis

feel like voyeurs looking through gaps in foreground objects as if unseen by the main characters. Other times it can make the audience feel that it is intimate and close up, immersed in an environment where one can reach out and touch the foreground elements. Frame-in-frame shots like any compositional device should not be used arbitrarily, but the use of foreground to reshape your area of interest and realign the audience to its experience is an important option.

REDESIGNING WITH TONE

Silhouette

We are often trying to create the illusion of a three-dimensional world in our films. Therefore, we sometimes lose sight of the fact that the film is two-dimensional. Films usually happen on a flat screen. A character that in the story has three dimensions is only an illusion of light and actually has only two dimensions. It is only a two-dimensional shape on the screen and a three-dimensional form in our minds. This is why we often talk about a character's silhouette. If you fill a character's image in with a solid black, you will see only its shape, its silhouette. We should design our character, its pose, and its placement within the composition considering its two-dimensional interpretation.

Light and Patterns

Light patterns provide a way for an artist to break through the object contours and arrange the best shapes for telling a story. Any picture can be thought of as a puzzle pattern of two-dimensional shapes. There are dark, light and various colored shapes. The shapes of negative space between objects also form part of the puzzle. Sometimes the shapes of the darks and lights do not reveal an object's contours but cut across the contours and background to create different shapes and new design possibilities. A strong light may place the shaded side of a character's face into black shadow, if the background is also black then the head will merge with the background and some of the outside edge will be lost. The outer contour of the character's head will be less apparent than the light pattern on the face. Light and shadow patterns can create varied shapes regardless of the original contours of the objects. Filmmakers, photographers, and artists of all kinds have realized that lighting can redesign your world and create many compositional choices and dramatic possibilities.

Frame-in-Frame Composition by Gary Schumer

Contrast

Visual contrast means that one thing in the image looks different from everything else. It may be the one window light that is on in a big house with many windows, a small red fish swimming in a school of blue and gray fish. It may be the one person who gets up and leaves in an auditorium of seated, stationary people. Our eyes are drawn to things that stand out against the sameness of their surroundings. You can direct the viewer's eye by making something stand out visually. It is always important to consider where you want your audience to be focused in any shot. Don't give the audience too many things to focus on or it may not see what you need it to see. Upstaging is a term used to suggest that the wrong thing is stealing the attention away from where it is supposed to be. Don't let the wrong thing "upstage" your main area of focus. There should be one idea per storyboard and one main thing to focus the audience's attention on in each shot.

Directing the Eye with Contrast

CAMERA FOCUS

The depth of field in a camera can be used to "blur out" the background while the foreground is in focus, and then to reverse the effect and let the foreground become out of focus, while the background becomes clear. This is called *rack focus* and represents a way that the live-action cameraman keeps the audience looking at the right thing.

CONTRAST OF SCALE

One way to think about scale is the distance of the main subject from the viewer. The distance of the subject is determined by the distance of the camera from the subject or the way the zoom is set on the lens. The standard categories are close-up, mid shot and long shot. There are also extreme close-up, medium long shot, etc. to describe intermediate variations. Of course, close-up shots are more intimate and can show the audience subtleties of facial expression or beads of sweat on someone's upper lip. Distance shots can make the character look small and vulnerable in their environment.

Rack Focus

Close-up

Medium Shot

Long Shot, Storyboards by Steve Gordon

Many beginners tend to keep their camera at the same distance from the subject throughout a scene. You should use a range of shots to give your film visual variety and to take advantage of the emotional or psychological message that each type of shot can convey. You may want to avoid a medium-to-medium shot unless you change camera angle. It is often better to use a medium to close-up shot if the angle stays the same. Another aspect of scale relates to the comparative size of one shape or area of the screen to another shape or area. Since we are attracted to visual contrast, we tend to notice the shape that is biggest. In a cowboy movie gunfight, the camera may be behind one cowboy's holstered gun as his hand twitches in anticipation. This silhouette may fill 80% of the screen making his opponent look small and distant. This kind of shot is surely more dynamic then simply filming the entire gunfight in profile with the camera the same distance from each cowboy. Compose your shots with consideration to a variety of shape sizes. The visual richness that shape size variation brings to your shots can translate into a more powerful telling of your story.

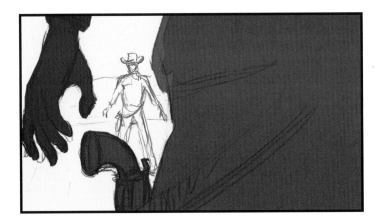

PICTORIAL SPACE

There is a great scene in the live-action film *The Abyss* (1989, 20th Century Fox). The screen is shown as if we are looking through the side of an aquarium. The aquarium is filling with water and our human character is drowning. The camera keeps moving closer, the water keeps rising and the ceiling keeps dropping until there is only a narrow strip of air space. Our character struggles to push her mouth into the narrow airspace to stay alive. The audience is watching, often with their necks fully extended and their chins pushing up, as they feel the space filling up and the anguished character fighting for her last breath. This is a great example of how the director makes the audience feel and on some levels experience the anguish of drowning through the manipulation of pictorial space.

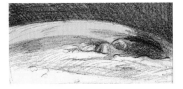

Drowning Scene from the Film, *Abyss*

The way we use the real space of the screen and the illusion of space that the character moves in are important elements of staging. A character may be staged to look open and free or trapped and claustrophobic. A feeling of submission or dominance can be attained if one character is up looking down at another character who is down looking up. A tracking shot could have the camera follow a character walking to the right but the character is on the right side of the screen. This draws attention to the space behind him and may suggest he is being followed. If this same scene has the character on the left, we may feel that he has a comfortable amount of space for the character to move forward into, so we may simply feel that he is moving merrily along his way. There are many ways to change the staging and as a result, change the story.

Character has Space to Move Into

Character is Possibly Being Followed

Nose Room

If a character looks to the right and speaks to someone, you may want to put the character on the left third of the composition so he has some room to look and speak into on the screen. When you show who he is speaking to, you may want to put that person on the right third for the same reason. You can keep the space feeling fluid and dynamic by considering the attraction of the empty space around the subject.

Shallow, Flat, Deep, and Ambiguous Space

A scene that takes place in a small room could be considered shallow space if the back wall is parallel to the screen shots will be considered in a flat space. The camera may follow a character down a long hallway and then the flatness will be lost and a deeper space results. A film that runs for 30 minutes in a shallow space could suddenly transport the viewer to the top of a mountain looking out over a vast panoramic landscape. This contrast may cause a very strong emotional reaction in the viewer. We can use the range of restrictions of shallow space to the illusion of nearly infinite space to affect our story ideas in different ways. Your story may require the depiction of a world from a bug's point of view or through the eyes of an eagle. Sometimes the story requires that the audience be kept uncomfortable or unsure about the space. Dreams and memories may be more effective if we are not entirely grounded in a familiar space. Other kinds of poetic solutions may require a more surreal departure from common experience of space. A film can make the audience feel the sensation of a type of space and the psychological associations that come with that experience.

Good staging will require a careful consideration of the type of space a shot is using in order to put the audience in the right emotional state.

RESEARCH

There is one sure way to learn and explore staging possibilities, and that is to study the choices of other filmmakers. Watch a film and notice the filmmaker's staging decisions. Watch for the lighting and placement of important information and ask yourself, "How did the filmmaker get me to see what I needed to see?" Think about how the filmmaker may have considered the emotional aspects of the story when making staging decisions. Most importantly, make drawings of what you see. Simple thumbnails showing placement and tonal distribution can help you understand how grandeur and intimacy or pathos and comedy can be presented to an audience in the best way. Learn how the masters achieve that magical experience we all recognize when we are truly moved by a great film.

Studies of Staging for Akira Kurosawa's *Ran* by Storyboard Artist Paul Briggs

STORYBOARDING CHECKLIST

How do you know if your storyboards are doing everything they need to do to captivate and inform your audience? We are often trying to consider many issues at once when planning a film. This checklist may prevent you from missing important choices.

- What is the important storytelling information in this frame? What exactly needs to be seen?

- Does the image convey the emotion of story as well as the specific data of the narrative?

- Does the image tell what is happening clearly? Is my craftsmanship effective? Is there any chance someone could be confused or unsure about what they are seeing?

- Are there "gaps" in my storyboard? Do I need more panels to make the story complete and to keep the flow of action and ideas working?

- Will the viewer look where I want them to look? Have I chosen the best camera angle? Do I need lighting or color to direct the audience's eye?

- Is this panel too predictable? Do I need to spice things up? What are some other options?

- Should I consider putting foreground elements between the camera and the main subject of my shot? Should I use "frame-in-frame" for this composition?

- Do the drawings flow visually and stylistically from the panels before and after?

- Should I move the camera to change this shot from the shot before and after; where and why?

- Have I put the audience "in the action" by using POV and other more intimate shots or have I kept the audience observing at a distance? Which is more appropriate at this point in the story?

- Will the storyboards that I am doing now require that I go back and re-evaluate, and then redraw some of my earlier story panels?

- Have I captured the most telling pose, gesture, action or facial expression? Does the body language convey what my character is thinking, feeling or doing? Do I need more reference, research?

- Does the character appear to be moving, in action, when action is required or does it look like a frozen pose? Do I need speed lines, arrows, or multiple images? Can I represent the essence or totality of this action in one drawing, or will I need to break it down into several panels?

- Is the light and atmosphere an important part of telling my story, setting its mood or emotional climate?

- What kind of space is right for this scene: flat, shallow, deep, ambiguous? Which best reinforces this aspect of the story? Is it important that my audience know of the season, time of day or weather conditions?

- Have I shown my boards to other people for a fresh perspective?

Summary

- Staging refers to the way you show us things in a film.
- The design of the shot can direct the viewer to see what you want them to see.
- The frame shape is your first design element.
- Some subdivisions of the frame are more effective.
- You can re-design the composition with lighting and framing devices.
- Contrast of movement, color, tonal value, scale and texture can direct the eye.
- Illusionistic space in a shot and the two-dimensional space of the screen can both be manipulated for emotional effect.
- The empty space around things helps to tell the story.
- Learn good staging by studying good filmmakers.

Recommended Reading

1. Marcie Begleiter, *From Word to Image Storyboarding and the Filmmaking Process*

2. Nancy Beiman, *Prepare to Board*

3. Bruce Block, *The Visual Story*

4. Mark T. Byrne, *Animation: The Art of Layout and Storyboarding*

5. Jeremy Vineyard, *Setting Up Your Shots*

On Staging: An Interview and Shot Analysis with Steve Hickner, DreamWorks Animation Studios

Steve Hickner has worked in animation for over 30 years. He started in TV animation, working on shows like *Fat Albert* and *He-Man*, then went to Disney for five years and worked on *The Black Cauldron*, *The Little Mermaid* and *Who Framed Roger Rabbit?* Since 1994 he has been with DreamWorks in their art department, directing *The Prince of Egypt* and *Bee Movie*.

Q: Take me through your process of directing.

Steve: Usually the script will be interpreted through storyboard artists. Occasionally, I will board something myself. I guard that tremendously because I'm not Orson Welles, who can do it all. I like the addition of other people's ideas.

Animation is incredibly iterative. You do it again and again. So the first stab at a blank sequence is something I guard tremendously because you never get that chance again. After the first storyboard pass, everyone will have seen something already. So you really want to give other people enough direction to give them the idea of what you're thinking of for the movie, but not too much so that you stifle them or you'll never find out what other ideas they might have. I want to give less direction at the start; I'm going to have plenty of bites of the apple throughout the process of making the film. So at the very beginning, I'll talk about the objective of the sequence, not how to do it. I never tell them shots.

When you put your trust in others, the process of making a movie for everybody else is much more fun.

Q: Can you give us an example?

Steve: Let's say you were going to do this scene in the movie. I wouldn't talk in terms of how to shoot that sequence because then the story artist is just "a wrist." You reduce your artist to a pair of hands and that is the absolute worst thing you can do because people will mentally check out and won't want to work on the picture anymore. So instead, I would ask, "What is this scene about? What is the character feeling? And what do you hope to achieve from them?" You talk about the emotional underpinnings just like you would to an actor in a live action film. And then you let them go and see what they come up with.

Q: Based on that, when you look at the storyboards, are you looking to see if the drawings communicate the note of the scene? And then also if the sequences/shots together describe the essence of the movie?

Steve: They should. You know, it's all "wheels and wheels" as they say. Everybody and everything should be servicing the one big idea. You want to ask, "What is the objective of this? That's what we're all going to be working on." It's a common goal and it's how each person brings their craft to it that makes it a rich, great movie.

Q: These are the type of things that make the difference between a good film and a great film. Why do so many films not get this?

Steve: Because it's damn hard. People ask me, "Why aren't there any good movies?"

I tell them, "Go make one." It's really, really hard. It's why I try not to ever bash another filmmaker because I've been there and I know how hard it is. Everybody's trying to make a good movie.

Sometimes you get it, sometimes you don't. Even some of the great people—Billy Wilder, Hitchcock, John Ford—everyone has a bad movie. Except Pixar.

Q: In storyboards, what are the most important things to think about?

Steve: Think about reactions. There is power in the reaction shot. Hal Roach, when working with Laurel and Hardy, would always get three or four laughs from one joke. When Ollie goes up the ladder with a bucket of paint, the audience is laughing in the anticipation of what is going to happen. Then it falls on Ollie and it gets a laugh. Then when he wipes the paint off his face and looks up they get a laugh. Then Stanley reacts to Ollie and you get a fourth laugh. It wasn't just the joke but the three or four laughs you get from the reaction shots.

Q: When you're looking at your film how do you know which parts are necessary and which should be cut?

Steve: When I put together a story reel I first do it the way that I want it. I then tell the editor to save it, and then I say, "Now let's break it." Let's do an aggressive cut. Once I see the aggressive cut, the other one feels so slow. Sometimes I'll make two versions, other times I just have the editor make the aggressive cut. I don't fall in love with anything that I have done. I like a lean movie—especially if I'm trying to be funny.

The thing I learned is that every sequence/shot should have a purpose, if it doesn't it shouldn't be in there. If there isn't a reason for it, get rid of it.

Q: How do you approach a sequence from a storyboarding point of view?

Steve: I want to get through it as fast as I can, almost as if I'm watching it. When you pitch a sequence it should be about the length of the time that ends up on screen when it's finished. So when I thumbnail, I work on them very fast. Sometimes I'll write ideas when I'm reading the script.

Steve Hickner: Storyboards and Analysis

Steve agreed to storyboard a portion of the script for *A Good Deed, Indeed!* which is one of the case studies on the web.

In this story, a pirate has been buried to the neck in the sand by his mutinous crew and left to die. Wrongly believing that the pirate is a squid, two crabs try to help him. We enter the story after the crabs have found him, determined that he is still alive and are trying to pull him by his beard (tentacles) back toward the water.

Shot 1: Evelyn has been trying to push the creature toward the sea as Herschel pulls. Evelyn scampers onto the top of the pirate's head and addresses Herschel: "It's not working! What do we do?!"

Evelyn: "It's not working..."   "...What do we do?"

"It's not working!"   **"What do we do?"**

Steve: Since this is the first shot of the series, I am establishing the geography between all the characters, and the environment. Note the hint of ocean in the bottom left corner.

Because Evelyn, the female crab, has dialogue, I have decided to favor her by shooting over the shoulder of Herschel, the male crab.

Shot 2: Herschel listens to Evelyn and thinks about the problem.

Once again, I am shooting wide to made sure the audience understands the geographical relationship between all the characters—and the ocean; which will become an essential part of the later story.

By choosing a downshot that is over Evelyn and the pirate, I allow the audience to be "close camera" to Herschel. (By "close camera", I mean that the character is more frontal to the face of the audience.)

Shot 3: Herschel begins to pull a tentacle around the head with all his might.

Steve: This is the third shot in a row that I have chosen to go with a wide shot, and that is because, up to now, the dialogue has been more expositional and not intimately personal to the character speaking. Therefore, I do not need to be too tight on any of the characters.

This shot is designed to be side-on so that the audience can easily see the faces of all the characters simultaneously. You will notice that as Herschel tugs on the beard into camera, the characters turn to follow him.

Shot 4: Herschel is determined.

Steve: In this shot, I am cutting on the action from Shot 3. Shot 3 leads the character from left to right, and Shot 4 is the reverse and deliberately creates a "counter dolly" by having Herschel move right to left—this will create a seamless cut and a strong dynamic of action in the scene montage.

Shot 5: Evelyn gasps! She has seen the trench that is forming under Herschel's feet and has an idea. "Gasp! Herschel!"

Evelyn: "Gasp!"   **"Herschel!"**

Steve: Once again, I am using a counter dolly to accentuate the action. The start of the shot has Evelyn looking left but framed to the right. As she begins to look right, the counter dolly moves her to screen left.

In both Shots 4 and 5, I have now moved in closer so the audience can better experience what the character is thinking and feeling. (By withholding my closer shots until this point, they will have more impact.)

Shot 6: Herschel looks at the trench.

Steve: Again, I am tighter on Herschel because he will have important acting to do in this shot. This is the shot where Herschel will begin to understand Evelyn's plan.

You will notice that at the most important point in the shot, where Herschel looks at the groove he has created in the sand, and then sees the ocean, he is very "close camera." By being close camera on Herschel, I allow the audience to connect better with him—as a person would if they were looking directly at their companion in conversation.

Shot 7: Herschel looks toward the goal (the water).

Steve: Even though this shot represents Herschel's Point-of-View, I have elected to include the character in the shot—which, of course, is impossible. In classical cinema, the way to shoot this shot would be to eliminate the character from the shot and just show what he is seeing.

Filmmaking in the past three decades has become more aggressive, and there is less of a tendency for today's moviemakers to conform to classical styles of cinema. Because I want to re-establish the geographical relationship between the crab and the ocean, I am including Herschel in his own point of view shot.

Sometimes you will see a hybrid of these two techniques. The shot will start classical-looking, with a point of view shot that does not include the character, only to have the filmmaker allow the character enter into his own point of view later in the shot.

Shot 8: Herschel understands, "Oh yeah! I gotcha!"

Herschel: "Oh yeah. I gotcha!"

Steve: This shot will serve two purposes: it will be a "cut back" to the character we have been following, and then to become a slam truck-back which will become the widest geographical shot for the whole scene of action.

By combining both of these ideas into one shot, I am reducing my shots so that the scene does not become too cut heavy, and—more importantly—I am allowing the audience to discover Evelyn's plan at the same time that Herschel does on screen. Having the audience come to a realization at the same time as the character does allows the audience to live vicariously through the on-screen personas.

Shot 9: The pirate believes the irritating crabs are finally going away. "Good riddance, you scurvy little sand rats . . . "

| **Pirate: "Good riddance . . ."** | **" . . . you scurvy little sand rats . . ."** | **" . . . you scurvy little sand rats . . ."** |

Steve: This story has an inherently unique staging situation. For most films, if you want to show a close-up of the lead character, you have to move in with the camera, and usually that means sacrificing being able to see other characters. But because we are only seeing the head of the lead character for this story, and the other characters are small in size, I can stage this shot as if it were a close-up of the pirate's face and still get all the characters in the same frame.

By staging the shot as I have, I can get close in on the pirate's expressions, and still include the geography of the two crabs.

Shot 10: Evelyn and Herschel meet and begin to dig the trench.

 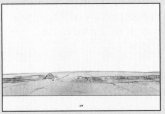

Steve: Another unusual aspect of the way I have staged this film so far is that I haven't yet shown a classic close-up of two of the three characters—the crabs. Because the crabs are so small, and their faces are built into their bodies, they work best in a wider, full-figure shot. Even though I am framing the shot wider than is standard for a closer dialogue shot, we still have no trouble seeing the acting performances from the crabs, and we can also see clearly that they are grabbing the pirate's beard "tentacles."

Shot 11: Pirate realizes they are digging a trench. "Aye! They is diggin' me out!"

Pirate: "Aye! They is digging me out!"

Pirate: "Aye! They is digging me out!"

Steve: For this action, I have chosen to cover it from the side so that I can see the pirate's face as he delivers his dialogue as well as show the female crab pulling on his beard and digging a trench as she moves.

Shot 12: Pirate is talking as crabs are digging. "Holy Jehoshaphat! Keep on going! Yeah! Yeah!"

Pirate: "Holy Jehoshaphat! . . ."

". . . Keep on going . . . ."

". . . Yeah. Yeah. Yeah."

" . . . Yeah. Yeah. Yeah."

Steve: We've had a few lower angle shots in a row, but now I need to reveal the fact that the crabs are digging a trench around the pirate's head. In order to show the action from the best angle, I raise the camera almost directly upwards—so that there is very little perspective on the ground plane. I want this action to be seen almost as it would if you were drawing a diagram on a piece of paper.

Shot 13: The crabs find a way to bring the water to the trench.

Steve: Now, I need to introduce the ocean and the starfish in the shot—but still allow the audience to watch the pirate's face as the events start to take a turn for the worse. By placing the camera just above the sand, in front of the pirate, I can get all the key story elements in the shot together.

Note: There is nothing in the script that specifically says how the crabs get the water to the trench. This is where the creativity of the board artist comes in.

Shot 14: Crabs are using the starfish to help dig a path from the water to the trench.

Pirate: "Hey! What are you doing?"

Pirate: "Hey! What are you doing?"　　**Pirate: "Hey! What are you doing?"**

Steve: You may have noticed that previously when I created a downshot, I placed the water at the bottom of the frame, and that allowed me to better see the pirate's face and the action of the crab.

For this shot, I need to show the action of the sea water moving towards the pirate, and for this reason, I need as much horizontal space in the film frame as possible.

By placing the pirate at the right of the frame, and the ocean at the left, I also get a very clear "read" of the crabs pulling the starfish along the sand, creating a trough for the sea water to follow.

Shot 15: The starfish reaches the trench.

Pirate: "Keep digging me out!..."   Pirate: "Keep digging me out!..."   "..Noooooool..."

**Pirate: "Keep digging me out!
. . ."**   **Pirate: "Keep digging me out!
. . ."**   **Pirate: "Noooooooo! . . ."**

Steve: I dropped the camera low to the sand here because I want the pirate to be "close camera" as he sees the crabs pulling the starfish towards him, creating a trough full of water. This way I can tell two story points in the same shot: the crabs digging the trough and the pirate reacting to the impending jeopardy. As a note, I am starting the shot with the starfish filling most of the frame, so I can make a dramatic reveal of the pirate's horror when the crabs raise the starfish out of shot.

Shot 16: The water begins to fill in around the pirate.

Steve: Once again I want to be high above the pirate so that I can show the complete action of the sea water filling in the trough and heading toward the pirate. By placing the water source at the bottom of the frame, the pirate is facing towards camera, and we can easily see his expression while, at the same time, we can see the water.

Shot 17: The crabs climb on top of the pirate's head as the water engulfs him.

Steve: This shot is all about seeing the water level rising, as the pirate begins to drown. By raising the camera slightly off the ground, we can see the ground level and all the characters in the same shot.

Shot 18: Herschel and Evelyn are checking on the condition of the pirate. Herschel: "How's he doing?" Evelyn (patting the top of the pirate's head): "Good. He's going to be fine now."

Herschel: "How's he doing?"   **Evelyn: "Good. He's going to be fine now."**

Steve: I am deliberately coming in tight on the crabs because I don't want to show what is happening with the pirate. Since the crabs are oblivious to the danger they have foisted onto the pirate, I want the audience to be following the story through their eyes.

Shot 19: Herschel: "Oh, he looks much happier under the water."

Steve: This is the visual payoff of the joke of the crabs thinking that all is well when, in fact, the pirate is drowning. In order to emphasize the comedy, I have chosen to shoot this action under water where I can show a fish looking at the action as the crabs speak nonchalantly above the waterline. Since this is a visual gag, I don't need to show the characters speaking. Consequently, the fact that the crabs are distorted from the water ripples is fine.

Herschel: (O.S.) "Oh, he looks much happier under the water."

Shot 20: Evelyn: "He sure does." Herschel: "Building that trench was such a good idea."

Evelyn: "He sure does."   **Herschel: "Digging that trench was such a good idea."**

Steve: The story is wrapping up now, so I want to show one last image of the whole disaster. In order to show the entire tableau, I am pulling back with the camera and shooting it wide and as a slight downshot. The camera here is an objective one, just recording the events for the audience as they happen.

Shot 21: Herschel: "You're a genius." Evelyn: "We did a good thing."

Herschel: "You're a genius."   **Evelyn: "We did a good thing."**

Steve: I wanted this to be a beauty shot, so I have chosen to shoot into the setting sun. I want to contrast the serenity of the crab's situation with the ironic fate of the drowned pirate.

Additional Resources: www.ideasfortheanimatedshort.com

See a complete preproduction case study of this piece:

- Final script
- Alternate scripts
- Production notes
- Character and Environment designs
- Animatic and additional shot analysis by storyboard artist, Nilah Magruder.

Chapter 10

Developing a Short Animated Film with Aubry Mintz

I have found a system for developing animated films after 13 years working with professional and student filmmakers to create short, one- to five-minute ideas that they are able to produce within a year. I also apply this system to my own work, and will use my current film *Countin' on Sheep* as a case study to show how to take a short film from idea to production. I hope you enjoy this chapter, and if you decide to make a film, I trust this can be of some use to you.

COUNTIN' ON SHEEP SYNOPSIS

This film takes place in Arkansas at the end of the 1930s Dustbowl and involves Zee, a six-year-old boy who has lost his lower bunk bed to his visiting grandmother. He has no choice but to climb all the way up to the top bunk. But Zee has an extreme fear of heights so he resorts to sleeping on a chair. Unable to get comfortable, he begins counting sheep, but there is one sheep that is also afraid of heights and won't jump the fence.

This animated short film is about overcoming fears by successfully confronting obstacles that stand in the way of our goals.

Images from *Countin' on Sheep*, Rough Drawings Aubry Mintz, Clean Drawings Dori Littell-Herrick, Color Frank Lima. Copyright Aubry Mintz, all rights reserved.

KNOW WHAT YOU ARE GOING TO WRITE ABOUT

Films take time. Films actually take longer than that; they take an enormous amount of time. Since you are going to live with this film for at least a year or two, it is important to do something you enjoy and believe in. You don't want to be a year or so into a project and realize you don't want to do it anymore. So, it is a good approach to develop several ideas when you begin this process to help you find the best one for you.

Beware of choosing an idea too quickly. I recommend that you carry a small notebook as you start to come up with film ideas. Carry this notebook with you everywhere. This will allow your brain to come up with new ideas constantly. Much like a computer, your brain will also process in the background while you are doing other things like eating or sleeping. I also recommend placing this notebook by your bedside; this way, you might inspire dreams that you can jot down as soon as you wake up.

This first stage is not about latching on to the perfect film idea, it is more about allowing your brain to start generating as many thoughts as possible. So don't hold back. Have some fun!

FINDING YOUR IDEA

At some point you can read through your notebook of ideas. You may find that the first ideas that come out of your head are the most typical or cliché ideas. I actually encourage students to go for the cliché at the start to get it out of their systems. This will allow you to develop ideas that already have preconceptions built in.

I call these types of ideas "universal knowledge." They are ideas that don't require too much set up (i.e., two naked people in the forest looking at an apple like Adam and Eve). However it is important to remember that when writing stories we have read before, you will need to unfold it in a new way to keep the audience engaged. The challenge is how to tell a story in a fresh and interesting way.

At some point you might start expanding on a new take of an old idea or it might even evolve to a unique idea. Allow the idea process to occur naturally without forcing it. This will let you come up with something that truly represents you.

I have heard many times that "no idea is original." It is how we individually choose to twist and turn it that makes it our own. As Bill Kroyer says: "At the end of the day you want to try and make something that's wholly your statement. If you do that it will be unique and hopefully it will be something that people respond to."

Finding Your Seed Idea

Once your brain is set in motion, it will most likely produce several quick "seed ideas." (For *Sheep* the seed idea was "a counting sheep that would not jump over the fence.") Jot down these seed ideas into your notebook.

Once you have several "seed ideas," start sharing them with someone. Writing your ideas down is one thing, but they take on a different meaning when speaking them aloud.

When I am listening to ideas, I find that the good ones spark the imagination. If I find myself wanting to know "what happens next," then it is probably an idea worth developing. That's what you should be listening for.

Brainstorming in Groups

Brainstorming is an ideal way to get a bunch of creative people together and hash out story ideas. They do it all the time in the studio system, why shouldn't we? You never know where an idea will come from. The group discussion should help unfold and refine your idea. You will have many different opinions, some will naysay parts that don't fit, and others will add scenes or gags that may work perfectly. A brainstorming session is a great way to unpeel the layers and uncover the story that begs to be told.

Although it is your idea, I would suggest allowing other people to speak. This is a good time for you to sit back and let the group-mind brainstorm. If the conversation slows down, you can help pick it back up, but otherwise, get out your notebook and write down what the group is saying. In the end, it's your film. You need to choose only the notes that you want to incorporate. So, no pressure; let them have at it!

Countin' On Sheep: Case Study #1

I came up with the idea for *Sheep* in a dream, or more like the lack of a dream. My goal was to make a simple film that would take less than a year to finish. Sounds easy enough, right?

I found it so difficult to write such "a simple film" that I couldn't sleep. I became exhausted from days of racking my brain. I lay in bed at night, fully awake, as ideas came in and out of my head with no substance, none worth jotting down. I was tired, but restless, and I needed something to get my brain to calm down. So, believe it or not I started counting sheep.

1 . . . 2 . . . 3 . . . 4 . . . Then, all of a sudden, the fifth one wasn't jumping. He was just standing there, staring at me. No matter how I tried to get him to move, he would disregard my imaginative direction and do everything but jump. He was smelling the flowers, sleeping, reading, but not jumping.

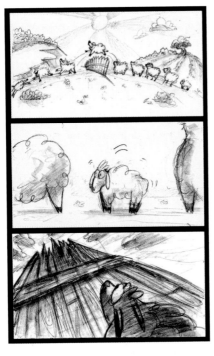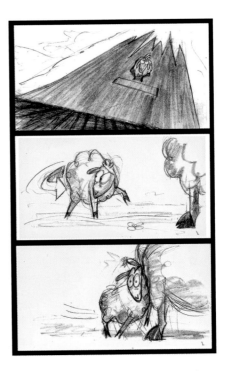

Images of *Countin' on Sheep* seed idea. Copyright Aubry Mintz, all rights reserved.

I couldn't sleep. My mind was going completely haywire. Or was it? Then, lightning struck.

My eyes popped open. I bolted out of bed and headed straight for my drawing board. I spent the next 12 hours storyboarding an idea for a short film about a counting sheep that would not jump over the fence. This became my seed idea.

Research Grows the Seed Idea

Once I find a seed idea I will then spend time researching the theme. The more research I do, the more I can put myself into the story, time period, character's mind, etc. My hope is that the story will have an authenticity to it, given that I have worked so hard getting to know my characters and their environment.

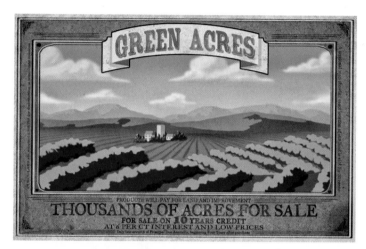

Images for *Countin' on Sheep* based on research of 1930s poster designs, Digital Paintings Jarvis Taylor, Art Direction Doug Post. Copyright Aubry Mintz, all rights reserved.

For *Sheep*, I knew I wanted the film to take place in a rural, farm area. Through research, I learned more about the Dustbowl of the 1930s and was blown away by the imagery and stories from this devastating decade.

I am very fortunate to work at California State University Long Beach that has an excellent research staff at the library. The librarians thought of things I would never have. The stacks of research materials were abundant, such as, interesting advertisements in periodicals from the time period, fruit crate labels from farms of the era, Dorothea Lange prints, Woody Guthrie songs and much more. I spent the better part of two weeks inspiring and informing my ideas with a richer understanding of the Dustbowl era.

In the stacks of books, there was one that really struck a chord. It was a compilation of poems written by children from that era. I remember one poem about a child who was given 30 cents to buy groceries to feed her family for a week. But when she got to the store, all she could think about was the candy she could get for the money in her pocket.

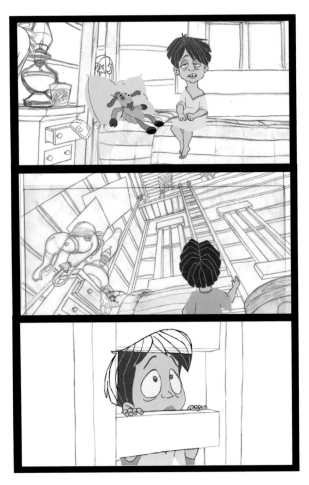

Images from *Countin' on Sheep*, Rough Drawings Aubry Mintz, Layout Lennie Graves and George Fleming, Clean Drawings Dori Littell-Herrick and David Coyne, Color Frank Lima, Lynn Barzola. Jesse McClurg, Whitney Brown, Jamie Ludovise. Copyright Aubry Mintz, all rights reserved.

This dramatically changed the way I thought about Zee, the boy in my film, and the decisions he makes. This poem helped me realize that the main character in my film (a six-year-old boy) would not be as concerned with the Dustbowl as he would be with regular child issues. Zee was more worried about Gramma taking over his bottom bunk and leaving him to climb to the top bunk.

While the Dustbowl is a very important element of my film, I did not want it to overshadow the main story. Instead, it became a layer of storytelling that I utilized to help portray the mood and era in which the story takes place.

For me, the library continues to be a great source and gives me more options than Google. I find Google's selections are sometimes limited and repetitive.

Once you have a strong seed idea, you can begin selecting books that call out to you. Explore these books page by page.

Don't rush this stage, as it will allow you to react to images and words that attract you. You do not need a particular intention. Just allow your brain and eyes to soak it all up. Flip through pages and get inspired!

PREPRODUCTION

Once you have what you feel is a solid idea, spend some time in preproduction to visualize your story.

Start with a few passes at a thumbnail storyboard (small rough quick sketches). This will help you produce a quick visual idea of what takes place in your story. If you focus on the main beats of the story and stage it in a straightforward manner (rather than worrying about a variety of angles or complex camera moves) this will allow you to narrow in on the story you are trying to tell.

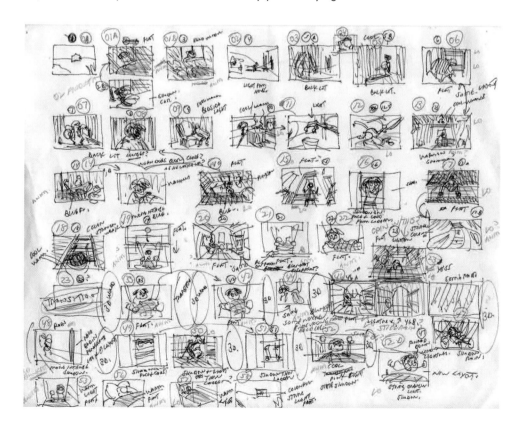

Images from *Countin' on Sheep*, Art Direction Notes Doug Post and Lennie Graves. Copyright Aubry Mintz, all rights reserved.

Often, film productions will hire visual development artists to inspire the directors while the script is developing. It is a good idea to create a few concept art pieces to set a tone for what your film might look like.

When I am at this stage, for inspiration, I will surround myself with reference materials of the time period (clothing, environment, photos from the era, etc.). I print the images and paste them on boards and literally surround my peripheral with visual reference. This allows my eyes to search the boards until I see an object, person or environment that inspires me to draw. Sometimes I'll focus on something as small as a rock or a character's boot, at other times it's an entire scene. I am not trying to make any final decisions; rather, I am searching to figure out what this film might look like. Basically, I am brainstorming with artwork.

Images from *Countin' on Sheep*, Rough Drawings Aubry Mintz, Drawings of Truck Cuyler Smith, Gramma Design Dori Littell-Herrick, Color Doug Post. Copyright Aubry Mintz, all rights reserved.

FINDING A PREMISE

At the point when you have enough images, references, rough storyboards and designs, you are now ready to really focus on what your movie is about. You could spend countless hours, days or even months developing story ideas that end up being rearranged from one story to another but seem to continually change. This can happen when you don't know the story you really want to tell.

The best way to combat this is to find the premise of your story. Author Lajos Egri writes an excellent chapter on premise in his book *The Art of Dramatic Writing*. I recommend this as a must to all of you searching to tell a story.

The important thing is to try and refine your story down to a sentence or two. The premise statement should have these three elements: character, conflict and resolution.

For my film, *Sheep*, the premise might be:

1. Taking the first step (character) leads to (conflict) overcoming your fears (resolution).

2. Not taking a chance leads to stagnancy.

3. Fears can't be overcome until you face them.

4. An acrophobic sheep must finally face his fears and jump over the fence or he will be stuck.

All of these might work, but I settled on the following for now: You can only overcome your fears (character) by facing them (conflict) on your own. No one can jump the fence or climb for you (resolution).

You want to try and define your film in the simplest way possible. A few sentences sound easy to write, but this is actually difficult. Take your time and try to whittle your idea down to a clear premise.

Once you find your premise, it is a good idea to step back and think about your statement and make sure that this really is the story you wish to tell. Lock it down and you are ready to move on.

Using Your Premise

Once I have my premise statement, I am then able to go through my images and decide what works best to tell this particular story. There may be some killer images that I fell in love with, but if they were not supporting my story then I would need to save them for another film. You need to focus on the premise. Here are some examples of images that did not make the cut into my film idea.

Images from *Countin' on Sheep*, Digital Painting Kristen Houser, Layout Lennie Graves, Art Direction Doug Post. Copyright Aubry Mintz, all rights reserved.

Images from *Countin' on Sheep*, Concept Art Ryan Richards. Copyright Aubry Mintz, all rights reserved.

If I'm clear about the story I am trying to tell, all of the shots must have a purpose. With this in mind, I review my storyboard and take out the scenes that don't push the story forward.

Sometimes you see films that have shots or camera moves that look really neat yet don't necessarily help tell the story. In Francois Truffaut's interview with famous film director Alfred Hitchcock (p. 47, *Hitchcock*, Simon & Schuster, 1983) they discuss a film where the camera shot is from inside a refrigerator and question the relevance of this. Hitchcock goes on to say:

> I am against virtuosity for its own sake. Technique should enrich the action. One doesn't set the camera at a certain angle just because the cameraman happens to be enthusiastic about that spot. The only thing that matters is whether the installation of the camera at a given angle is going to give the scene its maximum impact. The beauty of image and movement, the rhythm and the effects —everything must be subordinated to the purpose.

Hitchcock places importance on getting the right emotion out of the scene rather than choosing camera angles that just look interesting.

One of my professors from college and co-author of this book, Ellen Besen, once told me that everything in a film is "information" and that you want to try and do your best not to have any "misinformation" on any frame of your film. What she meant by that was to be clear about everything you are communicating to your audience. Every frame of your film counts and it is very important that all of the elements in your film are there for a reason.

Once you have the overall arc of your story, with a clear premise and have worked out your main story beats, you can then break down the beats into sequences. At this point, ideas gel and scattered fragments fall into place.

Based on the overall arc of the story, think about where you are in each sequence. Are you setting up a character? Building to the climax? And how are you communicating this? Can you say it stronger with a different camera angle? How about the lighting, color, sound, dialogue, etc.?

Images from *Countin' on Sheep*, Storyboards Aubry Mintz, Lighting Lennie Graves, Erik Caines and Cuyler Smith. Copyright Aubry Mintz, all rights reserved.

Every stage of animation or film production allows us to add another deeper level of storytelling into our films. If we know the story we are telling and plan it well enough we can make a strong impact on the audience.

The next example shows how using each of these elements strengthens the power of the scene.

Countin' on Sheep: Case Study #2

To help illustrate, in this sequence, Zee is stuck in his chair. He is exhausted from lack of sleep and his fear will not allow him to climb to the top of his bunk bed.

To strengthen this idea I played with Zee's posing and drew him as sinking deep into the chair, almost as if he was stuck.

There are strong shadows across his arms and legs appearing to hold him down.

Image from *Countin' on Sheep*, Digital Painting Jarvis Taylor, Layout Lennie Graves, Character Aubry Mintz, Art Direction Doug Post. Copyright Aubry Mintz, all rights reserved.

Image from *Countin' on Sheep*, Storyboard Aubry Mintz. Copyright Aubry Mintz, all rights reserved.

I added special effects of rain and lightning outside the window to create flashes of light with loud claps of thunder.

The color will be cold and dark, making it even harder to imagine getting up.

In terms of the layout, I placed Zee and the bed at opposite sides of the room showing how far he would have to walk. I also exaggerated the size of the bed illustrating how high he would have to climb to the top.

Image from *Countin' on Sheep*, **Layout Lennie Graves, Character Aubry Mintz, Digital Painting Kristen Houser, Art Direction Doug Post. Copyright Aubry Mintz, all rights reserved.**

The music that was once light and bouncy has held on the last chord and fades into silence, giving Zee nothing but himself to listen to and forcing him to make a decision.

When Zee finally does move, I show Zee slightly out of focus. As he walks toward us, I bring him more in focus. I show his growing confidence as he gains clarity concerning what he has to do.

It is these kinds of decisions that can strengthen the scene and give the audience more contexts to understand what the character is going through emotionally. You probably don't want to do this in every sequence of your film so that you can build the dramatic effect toward the climax. And as I mentioned, these sequences should evolve out of the story rather than utilize them only for dramatic effect. When it all works together you have the opportunity to really make an impact, and everything is working to strengthen the story.

FINDING THE MOTIVATION FOR YOUR CHARACTER

Until you understand your character's motivation in the story you cannot make your character move. Every aspect of the character should be motivated by what the character wants and is thinking.

In order to understand your character better, a good exercise is to write a few pages about who your character is. In Zach Schwartz's book *And Then What Happened*, he discusses finding the three dimensions of your character to help with this. They are:

1. Physiology: What do they look like (short, tall, heavy, skinny, skin color etc.)?

2. Sociology: Where does your character come from (neighborhood they grew up in, how they were treated by their parents, etc.)?

3. Psychology: How does your character think (are they positive and laugh a lot? Do they have a hot temper? etc.)?

I recommend writing at least a page on each category. You do not have to create an entire novella for a back-story, but it is good to concentrate on your character, as it will help you understand the decisions he/she/it will be making. You can then use the back-story to help feed into the character's design. For example, I knew that Zee in *Sheep* was a six-year-old boy living on a farm during the Depression who had a fear of heights. So, I drew him with messy hair, dressed in an old T-shirt probably that once belonged to his father, and created poses that showed his insecurity.

**Zee Poses
Scene 14**

Images from *Countin' on Sheep*, Character Design Aubry Mintz, Cleanup Dori Littell-Herrick and George Fleming. Copyright Aubry Mintz, all rights reserved.

With *Sheep*, I did not originally have a motivation for my sheep character. All I had was a seed idea about a counting sheep that would not jump over the fence. I felt this was a solid idea that most people would understand. The challenge for me was to tell this story in a fresh way. After pitching the initial storyboard it was clear that the idea needed more of a conflict rather than not being able to jump over the fence. I needed something more specific.

I was lucky that I had a small crew to work with so we started to brainstorm and came up with a solid idea that worked perfectly. We decided to make the sheep acrophobic (afraid of heights). We thought it would be a great conflict to show a sheep whose job it was to jump, but was incapable of lifting off the ground.

Now that we had the sheep character's motivation, we were then able to explore his design. Instead of creating a generic counting sheep, I thought we should go back to my research. I knew that my story took place at night in a six-year-old boy's room in a farmhouse during the Depression era. How could the sheep complement the boy and relate to the story?

This then gave me an "*aha* moment" as I tied it all together. What if the sheep was Zee's doll? And what if Gramma threw the sheep doll up on the top bunk? Not only was Zee unable to climb to the top bunk because of his fear of heights, now he was alone and without his sheep doll. I had a structure for my story.

Once we had a solid structure, we were then able to start creating the sheep character design. This led us into the fantastic world of Depression-era toys and fabrics. We discovered that a farm boy, at this time, would not have a doll that was store bought but rather a doll that was made up of scraps of fabric. Therefore we made the sheep a patchwork doll. And it all started to fit together into a world that felt right.

Images from *Countin' on Sheep*, Character Design Aubry Mintz. Copyright Aubry Mintz, all rights reserved.

The research led us to more ideas about other handmade toys that could be in Zee's bedroom. All of the concept artists took their turn reimaging different toy ideas for the boy's room. The magic of collaboration (see images on p. 235).

FINDING AN ENDING

Now that I have the story structure and the character's motivation I could just plop on a beginning, middle and end. Right? I only wish it was that easy.

Finding a fresh ending is probably one of the hardest things I find about storytelling. It's not just about finding a conclusion that no one has seen before, but one that logically grows out of the story you are telling. There is nothing more frustrating than becoming totally involved in a film and the character's journey, only to be sent off in a different direction with the main character making decisions that are completely out of character.

When I was searching for an ending for my film, I tried out several versions, and you should, too.

In one version, the other counting sheep help the hero sheep off the fence but that didn't work because the premise of my film is about the hero sheep taking his first step to overcoming his fear. Having the other sheep help meant that he was just a participant and the other sheep solved the problem for him.

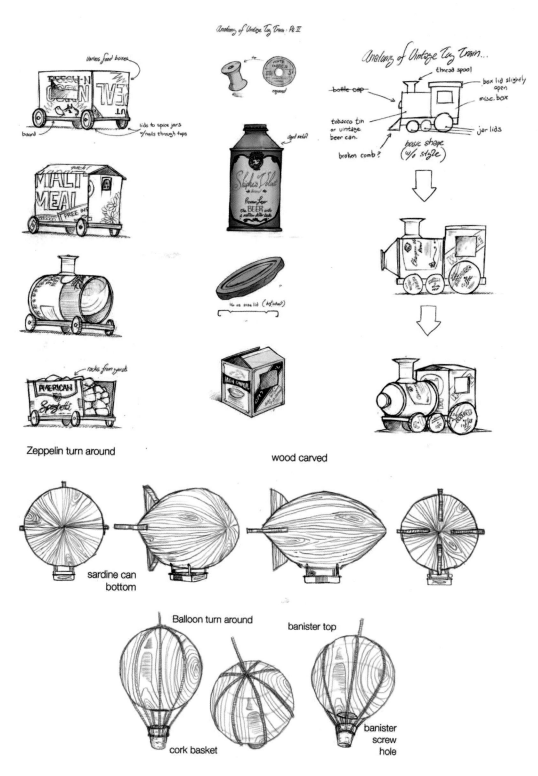

Images from *Countin' on Sheep*, Train Design Kevin White, Blimp and Air Balloon Design Cuyler Smith. Copyright Aubry Mintz, all rights reserved.

In another version, the sheep was knocked off the fence by a conveniently timed bird flying by. This did not work because, once again, it wasn't the sheep's conscious choice to jump; rather, it was an outside force that pushed him over.

I did not have my true ending until I was able to spend some time with master animator and director Eric Goldberg. He watched my film, thought for a moment, then gave me a new version with a clear, simple ending. It flowed so naturally that this idea really was the only idea that could have happened in this situation. Goldberg has years of experience and it shows with how quickly he was able to solve this problem.

What he came up with was this: The sheep appears to give up. He is assisted off the fence and walks away. This leaves Zee by himself, thus forcing him to work up the courage to finally climb the ladder. Back to the sheep, we see he was actually just gaining distance in order to make a running jump. With courage and conviction, both rise to the occasion and land in each other's arms.

In this ending, the sheep and boy reach their goal by their own volition rather than relying on an external force.

Images from *Countin' on Sheep*, Animation Aubry Mintz, Cleanup Mona Kozlowski, Color Cindy Cheng. Copyright Aubry Mintz, all rights reserved.

You'll know when you have the right finale because it is such a clear "aha" moment. I have also seen this happen many times with my students' films; once the right ending is found all of the pieces fall into place. Quite often, it is usually pretty straightforward, not obvious or predictable, but something that the characters would naturally do, based on the story that is being told. It is one of the hardest things to do, but once you have it, you know you have it and you are done.

Countin' on Sheep: Case Study #3

Doug Post, the film's art director, talks about the visual choices we made and how they supported our story.

We started with two overriding ideas that drove the visual process. First, this story needed to be told in two worlds: the boy's "real" world and the one he imagines. Second, the Dustbowl, Depression-era setting brought particular and interesting qualities with it.

The boy's world is a more impoverished, confined place where Zee feels trapped and afraid for most of the film. We assigned this world a traditional, hand-drawn animation process. Literally a flatter medium, we pushed this further by also giving it a palette with less value contrast and less intense colors.

The sheep's world of Zee's imagination needed to be more playful and open as it reflects the boy's desire to break out of his fear. It was decided that these scenes would be produced with a stop-motion animation process. The tangible three-dimensional quality of stop motion gives these scenes actual breathing space. Unlike the boy's world this one has much richer, more saturated colors. Additionally where most of Zee's scenes take place indoors, the world of his imagination, while made up of things from his room, suggests a vast landscape (see images on p. 239).

The Depression-era inspired us to give the things in this film a handmade, patched together, even layered look. There are obvious patch quilts throughout the story, but we also we gave the boy's world a lot of subtle textural layers taken from sources

Image from *Countin' on Sheep*, Stop Motion Set

like corrugated metal and newspapers of the day. We were going for a worn, dusty and gritty feeling. In the dream world because of the stop-motion process things are actually handmade for the film and the occasional fingerprint only adds to the intent.

Once the rules of the film were established we could visually weave the two worlds (and techniques) together as the boy and sheep work through, and eventually overcome their fears together.

By the end of the film Zee's traditionally animated world is a place where he can breathe again—the rain has washed the dust away and the morning has brought a more colorful, more "three-dimensional," and more hopeful environment.

**Image from *Countin' on Sheep*,
Sheep Maquette Dallas Worthy**

MAKING MUSIC

Music can absolutely strengthen or weaken your film. It is very important to work with your composer to make sure the music complements the film. As Perry La Marca states in his interview, "The greatest contribution music can make is to help enhance the emotional experience for the viewer."

For *Sheep*, I imagined the boy living on a farm, perhaps in an earlier time. I was very attracted to old time country music by the likes of Bob Willis and the Texas Playboys. Specifically the song "Time Changes Everything" rang in my head and I placed it as a temp-track on one of the first animatics. I decided that music was going to play an integral role in my film.

So in 2007 and 2008 I was fortunate to meet the members of the Arkansas band Harmony and songwriter Charley Sandage. Charley and I worked together to develop the music for the story. With Charley's guitar and my drawing paper, we sketched and played for three days until we found our song. We decided that the music would narrate the film.

Images from *Countin' on Sheep*, Concept Art Melissa Devine, Aubry Mintz, Robin Richesson, Jennifer Cotterill. Copyright Aubry Mintz, all rights reserved.

Musical Band Harmony, from left to right: Robert and Mary Gillihan, Charley Sandage and Dave Smith.

Charley Sandage, the film's composer talks about how he developed the music for *Sheep*:

> This was my first attempt to write music/songs for an animation project, and I was struck by what I found to be the degree of control the producer has in this medium. This may be only a layman's misperception, but it seems to me that the animator can make deeper and subtler decisions about look, feel, interpretation, staging—every element of a production—than can the producer of any live-action film, live theater production, or documentary piece.
>
> All of this underlines, in my view, the importance of Aubry's wish to work so closely and collaboratively with me at such an early stage of the project. This was something of a leap of faith on both our parts, since we hadn't met in person until the day when we sat down to start work. For good or ill, the process of shaping the music became inseparable from the process of shaping the overall project. Even when we were finally recording, Aubry and his art director were there, guiding and trimming.
>
> Since I'm a songwriter who usually starts with a lyric and then hears the music, this project came with some easy hooks for me. The essentials of the narrative focus on "sheep" and "sleep." Those words happen to rhyme. Zee's sheep counting led easily to the "counting on sheep" title. Repetition in the refrain works because the narrative unfolds in stages. The verses just tell the story. The feel of the piece calls for simple, ruralness-evoking, acoustic sounds such as banjo, autoharp and mandolin in a moderate tempo.
>
> Harmony, the trio, are gifted musical storytellers and traditional music stylists. When we took it to the little Mountain View, Ark., studio of Joe Jewell, who is also an Ozark musician, the elements flowed together. When it happens that way a writer is grateful.

In April of 2008, animation artist Lenny Graves and I took a trip to Mountain View, Ark., where we stayed four days to record the score with Charley Sandage and the band Harmony. Our research trip to Arkansas gave us more than just a great film score; it actually altered a pivotal plot point for the story.

Surrounding ourselves in the environment heightened our awareness of a small farm town in Arkansas. We breathed the same air that Zee breathed. This gave us further insight into how he might think. Reading about your research is one thing; actually experiencing it gives you a whole different appreciation.

The trip inspired us so much that we modeled the environment on the town. In fact, the design of Zee's home is directly based on the home of the guitarist of the band. You never know where your inspiration will come from.

SC#01   04/4LH036

Image from *Countin' on Sheep*, Photo of Arkansas House, Drawing of Zee's House Lennie Graves, Clean Up George Fleming and Kevin White. Copyright Aubry Mintz, all rights reserved.

We happened to visit Arkansas in late March. Charley Sandage, the film's music composer, constantly talked about the start of spring with the blooming of a tree called "the red bud." He talked about it with such passion; but I was unsure as to why. When I looked in the forest all I could see were leafless branches with little red bud dots scattered throughout. Charley kept talking about a dramatic change that would soon happen and told us to "just wait and see."

Then to my surprise, at the end of our trip, the red bud began to bloom. Overnight, the hillsides of the Ozark Mountains completely transformed and were covered in magnificent pink red bud bloom. What a sight to see!

The crew and I started thinking about how weather and the environment could play a part in this film. So we decided to use the weather as a storytelling element.

As it takes place in the Dustbowl, at the start of the film the land is covered in dirt. Then, as the climax builds, there is a thunderstorm. This creates supportive storytelling moments inside the farmhouse with shadows from lightning and loud claps of thunder.

In the end, the rain ceases which adds another layer of storytelling. Not only does Zee's decision to climb the ladder make his fear go away, but also the rain actually signifies the ending of the drought that has affected the land for almost a decade.

So when we see the exterior of the farm again we can paint it in a new light with the freshness you would see after a rainfall. I also added the blooms of the red bud throughout to signify new growth and renewal of the land.

Images from *Countin' on Sheep*, Concept Art Alina Chau. Copyright Aubry Mintz, all rights reserved.

I hope that this comes across subtly, yet emotionally, in the film. I was happy with uncovering the layers of this story and surprised that it all started with learning about a tree in Arkansas.

MANAGING IT

Dori Littell-Herrick, the film's co-producer talks about how to manage your film and keep yourself on schedule:

> Once you have a locked animatic, the best thing you can do is create a working production schedule. To do this you need to know three things: your deadline, your pipeline, and the size of your crew. Someone else, like your school or the freelance client, will likely set the deadline. You can adjust your project to meet the deadline by simplifying the look for an easier pipeline. Knowing how long you have to finish all of the tasks will tell you if you need help.

> I find my students are often unaware of how much time it takes to complete something. I suggest they write down what they do for seven days straight, Monday through Sunday. This includes when they wake up, have meals, go to classes, do homework, have social time, and finally when they sleep.

> Then I ask them to count the hours left between all of their daily/weekly stuff. This is often the "aha moment" when they realize how little spare time they have. Making a film can be a full-time job! Do not make the mistake of saying, "Oh, I'll get it done" and blindly starting a film. It is hard work; do not underestimate it.

> The more you can plan ahead of time, the more you can be realistic about what type of film you can make. If you have less than 20 hours a week and want to finish this film in a year, chances are you will be making a simpler film with fewer layouts and

Scene	Footage	Description	Layout	BG Painting	2D Animation	Clean-up	Photoshop	Scan	Ink and Paint	Compositing	SFX	Editing	Sound	Score master
SC 00	19.5	TITLE												
SC 01	7.625	Ext. Farm – Truck enters	LG/KW/GF											
SC 01a	5.5	Int. Bedroom - CU Z asleep	LG											
SC 01b	4	MS Z gets out of bed truck out to LS			AM	DH/GF/WB					blanket			
SC 02	5.5	Ext. Farm – Truck pulls up to Farm GRAMMA walks out	Kevin White		AM	DH/GF/RG			JB		blanket			
SC 03	6.75	Front porch Z and MOTHER – GRAMMA enters	LG/KW/GF		AM	JM								
SC 04	7	CU GRAMMA pinches Z's cheek and gives Z Bag	LG/KW/GF		AM									
SC 05	4	LS Z left alone on porch	LG/KW/GF		AM/DH									
SC 06	4.5	Z POV enters his bedroom			AM	DH/SB		SB	PD					
SC 07	3.375	MLS Z enters room			AM	GF		GF	PD		door			
SC 08	1.5	CU Z looks up			Aubry Mintz	DH/3C/HV		HV	FL					
SC 09	3	Gramma Shuffles chair			AM	DH/GF		GF	FL					
SC 11	5.125	PAN to GRAMMA's hands dropping dentures			AM									
SC 12	1.75	SHEEP TOY lifted off bed			AM	RG								
SC 13	1.625	LS GRAMMA throws SHEEP TOY onto top bunk			AM	DH/VL		JB	JB					
SC 14	16.25	LS Z runs up to GRAMMA sleeping,												
SC 14a	2	VERT PAN to top of bunk and rotate to down shot of Z looking up			Aubry Mintz	DH/GF/AM/SB/ISF		KA		Gramma	Blanket			
SC 15	3.25	upsot Z looking up at top bunk			AM	MK	JM	MK						
SC 16	3	CU Z at ladder			AM	OC	LB	OC	LB					
SC 17	4	POV Z vertigo			AM	DH/AU/AM/AU		AU						
SC 18	5.5	Z releases ladder			4									
SC 19	10	pan from clock to Z sitting on chair			AM	AM/OC		OC						
SC 20	5.125	LS Z sitting in chair in bedroom		JT	Held Cel AM	DLH/KA/DH		KA						
SC 21	9.5	MLS Z tireless in chair and falls off		KH	AM	DLH/KA/DH/GF		KA						
SC 22	4.25	CU Z tired looks up at HOWARD			RG									
SC 23	8.5	Elemets of bed transition to stop motion			5					3				

Scene	Footage	Description	Previs	3D Animation	Textures	Lighting	SFX	Rendering	Compositing	Editing	Sound	Score master
SC 24	11	ELS SHEEP jumping over fence										
SC 25	2.5	HOWARD hopping towards fence										
SC 26	6.5	HOWARD stops at fence			Bruce							
SC 27	2.25	POV HOWARD looking up at fence			sarah							
SC 28	2.25	downshot HOWARD looking up										
SC 29	2.5	MS HOWARD looks back										
SC 30	3.625	POV HOWARD looks at SHEEP										
SC 31	13.5	HOWARD ducks under SHEEP's legs										
SC 32	3.875	HOWARD hopping away										

Scene	Footage	Description	Layout	BG Painting	2D Animation	Clean-up	Effects	Scan	Ink and Paint	Compositing	Editing	Sound	Score master
SC 33	4	Z flicks blanket			4								

Scene	Footage	Description	Previs	3D Animation		Lighting	SFX	Rendering	Compositing	Editing	Sound	Score master
SC 34	4.25	PAN to HOWARD										
SC 35	2.5	ELS HOWARD is whipped up to top of fence										
SC 36	5	HOWARD lands on fence CU										
		TRUCK OUT to LS										
SC 37	1.75	MCU HOWARD looks down behind him										

Image from *Countin' on Sheep*, Production Schedule Dori Littell-Herrick. Copyright Aubry Mintz, all rights reserved.

stylized or limited animation. If you have more than 40 to 60 hours in your week then you can plan for a more complex, fully animated film. In the advertising world it is said that every project has three categories; time, money and quality but you can only choose two, you can never have all three. It is rare to have all of the money and time you need, which means you may have to compromise on quality. Don't let that stop you from making a good film; limits lead to creative solutions.

Unless you have a dedicated production manager, you are responsible for constant emails and phone calls to the crew to help people do good work and stay on schedule. This can take away from your creative time. You may have to fill shoes you are not prepared to fill in order to move the project forward. You have to be OK with making the wrong decisions sometimes and living with it for the sake of moving forward.

SHOW ME THE MONEY

Raising funds for a film is a challenging task. I have worked with producers, like my brother Billie Mintz, who are excellent at finding money. Whether he is grasping for grants or finding philanthropists, Billie is excellent at motivating donors to support projects he believes in.

Unfortunately, I do not possess this skill. I can bore people to death with why I made certain artistic decisions on the film; however, donors do not necessarily want to hear this. They want to know why they should get behind it financially. If you are going to approach people to fund your film you need to be a very charismatic person that has 100% conviction that your film will succeed.

Grants are an excellent way to keep your film going. This takes time. Usually I need to stop production for a week or so to organize images, write descriptions and collect CVs etc. to submit to each grant. Grants can come from all over, like regional arts councils and network grants to help finish films. You can go to your local nonprofit partnerships or research them online. They are out there.

You may also need to submit a budget for your film. This could be a spreadsheet with "line items" of all of the tasks in your film and how much you think they are going to cost. The more specific you can get the better. Try and be realistic so that you know what it would take if it was fully funded.

To help you do this, you can go through each scene of your storyboard and plan how many elements are needed and create an assets list (backgrounds, characters, props, effects, etc.). It is a great practice as it allows you to simplify the production down to nuts and bolts.

It is in this scheduling that you will also find places to create shortcuts and cut costs (i.e. reuse backgrounds and possibly animation). Taking the time to really think through each scene economically will allow you to plan each step of your film in an organized way.

Working with Minimal or No Budget

One of the most difficult things for me about working on independent films is not having a budget to hire people. However, even if you have little or no money you can get work done. Since it is rare that I am paying regular rates, it is difficult to demand that any task to be finished in a certain time; yet that is sometimes the exact thing that draws other artists to working on a short film. It is the ability to work on something with a creative outlet without a demanding schedule. This frees people up creatively to develop work for their portfolio.

When you hand off work to others you have to understand that this is a team effort. This means that sometimes you have to hand over some of your creative vision. Although you are the director, know that other artists can, and should be able to, bring their creativity to your project. In fact, this is often the reason that artists want to work on low or no budget projects. If the crew feels that you trust their creative decisions they are apt to produce their best work. So be open to interpretation of your idea.

When you are working on a project for a long time it is important to find ways to keep it moving. Even if this means that on some days you produce only one drawing or send a few emails. A project like this is like a large steam engine; all of the pieces working together make it move at a steady pace, even if it's moving slowly. But once stopped, it is much more difficult to start it up again.

IN CONCLUSION

With all of my preproduction complete, I now launch into production with renewed energy. At the same time, I am very aware that there will be obstacles ahead.

Due to my career, I am not able to work on this film full time. I depend on my winter and summer breaks.

Using the first steps, as outlined in this chapter, to develop and nail down my story with a clear premise and development art to support it, I have a structure that I can rely on. With my stop-and-start schedule, I can feel confident that I am creating animation that is hinged on a working story and will lead me to a film that I am happy with.

For anyone out there thinking of starting an animated short, making a film takes bravery. To set out on this path, you will need both sides of your brain (artistic and productive) to solve complicated problems. It will take a calm demeanor and a positive attitude to work with and, sometimes, coach others. Always try to keep yourself and crew motivated during every long, arduous step of the way. Sometimes the end of the film can seem so far away that it feels like it will take you years to complete. You have to find ways to challenge yourself and the team to keep going. Whether you finish one small prop design, or complete the animation for a scene, it is important to celebrate small successes.

Ultimately you have to believe that your film will one day get done. Believe it in your heart and know that each drawing, each email, is taking you one step closer to finishing.

Filmmaking to me is a process. Through time, I have learned to try and sit back and enjoy the ride. Far too many people have labored over this film; therefore, it would be a shame if time were not taken to show my appreciation. I have worked with some excellent designers, artists, animators, story artists, sound designers, musicians, actors and art directors in the industry and in the university and I would like to thank them all for their contributions and support.

All hail animated filmmaking.

Stay tooned!

Image from *Countin' on Sheep*, Animation Drawing, Aubry Mintz, Clean Up Dori Littell-Herrick, Color Jennifer But. Copyright Aubry Mintz, all rights reserved.

Additional Resources: www.ideasfortheanimatedshort.com

- Case Studies:

  ○ See more about *Countin' on Sheep* including animatics and production clips.
  ○ *The Fantastic Flying Books of Mr. Morris Lessmore,* including a "making of" film, film clips and notes from Brandon Oldenburg and Adam Volker.
  ○ *A Good Deed, Indeed* including animatics, staging notes, and production notes.

- Designing for a Skill Set. Notes, examples and interviews with shorts producers on traditional animation, stop motion animation, computer animation, modeling, lighting and collaborative projects.

Pitching Stories: Sande Scoredos, Sony Pictures Imageworks

Sande Scoredos was the executive director of training and artist development at Sony Pictures Imageworks. She was committed to working with academia, serving on school advisory boards, guiding curriculum, participating on industry panels, and lecturing at school programs. She was instrumental in founding the Imageworks Professional Academic Excellence (IPAX) program in 2004. Sande chaired the SIGGRAPH 2001 Computer Animation Festival and was the curator chair for the SIGGRAPH 2008 Computer Animation Festival.

Sande produced *Early Bloomer*, a short film that was theatrically released. Her other credits include: *Stuart Little, Hollow Man, Spider-Man, Stuart Little 2, I Spy, Spider-Man 2, Full Spectrum Warrior, The Polar Express, Open Season, Spider-Man 3, Surf's Up, Beowulf, I Am Legend,* and *Cloudy with a Chance of Meatballs.*

Before the Pitch: Register Your Work

Before you pitch your idea to anyone, your family, friends, your uncle Joe that works at a studio, or even random strangers, protect everyone—and your idea—by finding out who owns the rights to your idea. Do not talk about your idea until you have gone through the registration process or have an agent. You never know who is listening at Starbucks. If you are pitching for a school project you may find that your school already owns the rights. Likewise, if you work in the entertainment industry, your company may own the rights to anything resembling intellectual property. Ask your career services advisor or legal department about ownership rights and be sure to read your deal memo and contract agreement.

Most studios will only take pitch meetings through an agent. That is to protect you and them against copyright claims. For information on copyright filings, check the United States Copyright Office website, http://www.copyright.gov/. Read the guidelines carefully and follow the procedures.

Know Who Will Hear Your Pitch

Now, prepare for that pitch.

Successful pitches are carefully designed and orchestrated. Many brilliant ideas have fallen by the wayside due to poor pitching skills.

Whether you are pitching a 30-second short to your animation professor or an epic to a studio executive, *find out who is going to hear your pitch.*

You have just a few seconds to grab their attention and convince everyone in the room that your story is worth telling. How you describe it, visualize it, sell it, and sell yourself will all work for you or against you.

First, be honest and decide if you are the best person to make the pitch. If you get flustered speaking to a group, then let someone else do the talking. Not everyone needs to be part of the formal presentation so play to your strengths.

Talk to the "gatekeeper," the key contact who is setting up the meeting, and ask him or her to tell you who might attend. If you can, find out their titles and what influence they have on the process. Then do your homework.

The World Wide Web is a wealth of information. Check out the backgrounds of each person who may be in the meeting.

- Try to get a recent picture of each person.
- What types of projects do they like?
- What projects have they worked on?
- Where did they grow up?
- What college did they attend?
- What projects are in their catalog? Do they already have an animated film about two talking zebras? Oops, your project is about two zebras so think about how your project fits into their plans.
- Get your facts straight and then double check them. Just because it is on the web or IMDB does not make it true.

Why is this important? If you can find a relevant personal connection, then you can tap into that with a casual chat, discover mutual acquaintances or interests. But be careful. You want to stand out just a little more from the other pitches and be remembered in a good way. Your pitch should always be short and to the point, not too deep or detailed or it can get boring. You want a balance of well-rehearsed but not memorized, engaging and delivered with enthusiasm but not clownish, and delivered with confidence and passion for the project.

This business is all about relationships so you want to connect with the people in the room.

Preparing for the Pitch

Make sure you know your story. Research your idea and know what else is out there that remotely resembles it—is there a character, city, situation, movie or game that is similar to yours? You can bet that someone at the pitch will say this sounds like *XYZ*, the classic film from 1932 directed by some obscure foreign director. Assume that anyone in the pitch session has seen it and heard it all. Nothing is worse than the silence you hear that follows the comment, "What else have you got?" A potentially embarrassing moment can turn in your favor if you can intelligently discuss the other work, and its relationship to yours. You will look good if you not only know of this piece but can intelligently discuss this reference.

You also want to make sure you have the rights to the properties and characters. Say your story centers around a landmark building in downtown New York. Believe it or not, you may not be able to obtain or afford the rights to use that building. Same goes for characters and music. If your story cannot be made without that specific Beatles song, consider the reality and cost of acquiring the rights.

If your project requires getting the rights, be prepared to discuss the status of your negotiations in the meeting. If you do not have an original concept and cannot afford to obtain rights for existing properties, check out the properties in the public domain.

Read the industry trade publications to see what types of projects are going into production. If there is something similar to your proposal, then you should be able to address any concerns about copyright infringement upfront and explain what makes your idea better. Let the people hearing the pitch initiate talk about what actors or other talent would be good for the project.

Pitch the Entertainment Value

You can show you are looking at the whole package by suggesting the entertainment value, genre, audience age and appeal of your project. Describe the concept giving a general sense of the visuals for the characters, environments and style. Use sketches, color drawings, color palettes, reference material, special lighting, video clips—anything that will get the visuals across. Sometimes you can get into the room early to stage the pitch. This is another benefit to knowing the "gatekeeper." Remember, you are pitching to people who hear dozens of ideas and you want them to remember your project. If you can entertain them, they will see you can entertain audiences too.

Be ready to answer questions about finances and marketability since there may be financial people at the pitch.

At the Pitch

Remember that your pitch starts the minute you arrive—in the parking lot or in the elevator—you never know who you might run into so be nice to everyone. Once in the room, have a friendly handshake, thank them all for meeting with you and tell them you admire their work. Show them by your posture, body language and demeanor that you are enthusiastic and excited. Don't be overly intense. Get everyone's name in the room and try to identify the leader, but don't forget to make eye contact with each of them.

You need to conquer the whole room. Dress appropriately and watch your language. Listen to all the ideas and suggestions with openness and encourage suggestions. Show them how you work with others.

After the Pitch

Have a closing prepared. Never end your pitch with "Well, that's it." or "So, what do you think?" End with a positive note and thank them again emphasizing how much you want to work with them. Ask them if they have any suggestions and show your willingness to make adjustments.

It helps to have some sort of "leave behind" object, something more creative than a business card or demo reel. For a story about dogs, maybe a small stuffed animal with a creative dog tag containing your contact information and the name of the project.

Within a week, follow up with the "gatekeeper" and see if you can get a pulse on interest in your project.

Hand-written thank you notes are welcome but emails are usually not. Keep track of everyone you pitch to with a journal tracking names, dates, titles, and contact information. Selling your idea is really about relationships and at the end of the pitch, you want everyone in the room wanting to work with you and confident your project is their next winner.

Appendix

What's on the Web (www.ideasfortheanimatedshort.com)

1. **Case Studies**

   a. *The Fantastic Flying Books of Mr. Morris Lessmore*, Moonbot Studios

      i. Movie Trailer
      ii. The Full Interview with Brandon Oldenburg and Adam Volker
      iii. The "Making of" Video

   b. *Countin' on Sheep*

      i. Work in Progress Animatic

   c. *A Good Deed, Indeed*

      i. Script
      ii. Preproduction Notes
      iii. Animatic and Shot Analysis

2. **Designing for a Skill Set**

   a. Introduction

   b. The Traditional Animator

      i. The Traditional Animation Skill Set
      ii. *Flight of Fancy* Animatic
      iii. *Flight of Fancy*: An Interview with Casey Robin Neal

   c. The Stop Motion Animator

      i. The Stop Motion Skill Set
      ii. *The Bottle:* Animation and Animatic
      iii. *The Bottle:* An Interview with Kristen Lepore
      iv. The Making of *Bottle*

   d. The 3D CG Modeler

      i. The Modeling Skill Set
      ii. *Treasure:* The Animation and Animatic
      iii. *Treasure:* An Interview with Chelsea Bartlett

   e. The Computer Animator

   i. The Computer Animation Skill Set
   ii. *Beware of Monster* Animation and Animatic
   iii. *Beware of Monster*: An Interview with Meghan Stockham

  f. The 3D CG Lighting Artist

   i. The Lighting Skill Set
   ii. *Origin* Animation and Animatic
   iii. *Origin*: An Interview with Robert Showalter
   iv. Telling a Story with Light: An Interview with Bert Poole, DreamWorks Animation Studios

  g. Working in Collaboration

   i. Introduction: Working in Collaboration
   ii. *Defective Detective* Animation and Animatic
   iii. *Defective Detective*: An Interview with Avner Geller and Stevie Lewis
   iv. The Disney Summer Associates Program: An Interview with Terry Moews
   v. *The Animator and the Composer: A Case Study in Collaboration*

3. The Acting Process

  a. Overview: The Method

   i. The Actor's Toolbox: Building Block 1: Using Images
   ii. The Actor's Toolbox: Building Block 2: Exploring Physicality
   iii. The Actor's Toolbox: Building Block 3: Developing Intentions and Tactics

4. More Industry Interviews

  a. Ideas

   i. The Ideas Behind *Gopher Broke*: An Interview with Jeff Fowler, Blur Studios

  b. The Importance of Play

   i. The Importance of Play: An Interview with Jason O'Connell, Actor, Writer and Comic

  c. Humor

   i. Story and Humor: An Interview with Chris Renaud and Mike Thurmeier, Blue Sky Animation Studios

  d. Storyboarding

   i. Barry Cook, former Effects Animator and Story Development Artist, Walt Disney Feature Animation and other Studios
   ii. Frank Gladstone, Professional Animation, Director, Writer and Teacher, President of Gladstone Film, Inc.
   iii. Jim Story, former Disney Feature Animation Story Artist, Instructor of Story at University of Central Florida
   iv. Paul Briggs, Walt Disney Feature Animation, and former Story Artist, Warner Brothers Television Animation
   v. Steve Gordon, Animator, Director and Storyboard Artist at various studios including Disney Feature Animation and DreamWorks Animation

5. More Films

  a. *A Great Big Robot from Outer Space Ate My Homework*, Mark Shirra
  b. *Beware of Monster*, Meghan Stockham
  c. *Bottle*, Kirsten Lepore
  d. *Caps*, Moritz Mayerhofer and Jan Locher
  e. *Catch*, Chris Perry

f. *Das Floss*, Jan Thuring, Film Akademie Baden-Wuerttemberg
g. *Defective Detective*, Avner Geller and Stevie Lewis
h. *Early Bloomer*, Sande Scoredos, Sony Pictures Imageworks
i. *Eureka*, Parris Ley
j. *Fantasia Taurina*, Alejandra Perez Gonzalez
k. *Flight of Fancy* Animatic, Casey Robin Neal
l. *Fox Promo*, Kevin Passmore
m. *Gopher Broke*, Jeff Fowler and Blur Studios
n. *Noggin*, Alex Cannon
o. *Origins*, Robert Showalter
p. *Our Special Day*, Fernanda Santiago
q. *Poor Bogo*, Thelvin Cabezas
r. *Respire, Mon Ami*, Chris Nabholz
s. *Ritterschlag*, Sven Martin
t. *Sarasota Film Festival*, Nicole Gutzman
u. *Sarasota Film Festival*, Yahira Milagros Hernandez Vazquez and Javier Aparicio Lorente
v. Storyboards, Maria Clapis
w. *Technological Threat*, Bill Kroyer
x. *Teddy* Animatic, Nilah Magruder
y. *The Animator and the Seat*, Eric Drobile
z. *The ChubbChubbs*, Eric Armstrong, Sony Pictures Imageworks
aa. *The Dancing Thief*, Meng Vue
bb. *The Kite*, Gwenn Olson-Wheeler
cc. *Treasure*, Chelsea Bartlett

Index